# Poly-Olbion by Michael Drayton

## PART I (of II) - The First Song to The Eighteenth Song (1612)

Michael Drayton was born in 1563 at Hartshill, near Nuneaton, Warwickshire, England. The facts of his early life remain unknown.

Drayton first published, in 1590, a volume of spiritual poems; The Harmony of the Church. Ironically the Archbishop of Canterbury seized almost the entire edition and had it destroyed.

In 1593 he published Idea: The Shepherd's Garland, 9 pastorals celebrating his own love-sorrows under the poetic name of Rowland. This was later expanded to a 64 sonnet cycle.

With the publication of The Legend of Piers Gaveston, Matilda and Mortimeriados, later enlarged and re-published, in 1603, under the title of The Barons' Wars. His career began to gather interest and attention.

In 1596, The Legend of Robert, Duke of Normandy, another historical poem was published, followed in 1597 by England's Heroical Epistles, a series of historical studies, in imitation of those of Ovid. Written in the heroic couplet, they contain some of his finest writing.

Like other poets of his era, Drayton wrote for the theatre; but unlike Shakespeare, Jonson, or Samuel Daniel, he invested little of his art in the genre. Between 1597 and 1602, Drayton was a member of the stable of playwrights who worked for Philip Henslowe. Henslowe's Diary links Drayton's name with 23 plays from that period, and, for all but one unfinished work, in collaboration with others such as Thomas Dekker, Anthony Munday, and Henry Chettle. Only one play has survived; Part 1 of Sir John Oldcastle, which Drayton wrote with Munday, Robert Wilson, and Richard Hathwaye but little of Drayton can be seen in its pages.

By this time, as a poet, Drayton was well received and admired at the Court of Elizabeth 1st. If he hoped to continue that admiration with the accession of James 1st he thought wrong. In 1603, he addressed a poem of compliment to James I, but it was ridiculed, and his services rudely rejected.

In 1605 Drayton reprinted his most important works; the historical poems and the Idea. Also published was a fantastic satire called The Man in the Moon and, for the for the first time the famous Ballad of Agincourt.

Since 1598 he had worked on Poly-Olbion, a work to celebrate all the points of topographical or antiquarian interest in Great Britain. Eighteen books in total, the first were published in 1614 and the last in 1622.

In 1627 he published another of his miscellaneous volumes. In it Drayton printed The Battle of Agincourt (an historical poem but not to be confused with his ballad on the same subject), The Miseries of Queen Margaret, and the acclaimed Nimphidia, the Court of Faery, as well as several other important pieces.

Drayton last published in 1630 with The Muses' Elizium.

Michael Drayton died in London on December 23rd, 1631. He was buried in Westminster Abbey, in Poets' Corner. A monument was placed there with memorial lines attributed to Ben Jonson.

## Index of Contents
The First Song
The Second Song
The Third Song
The Fourth Song
The Fifth Song
The Sixth Song
The Seventh Song
The Eighth Song
The Ninth Song
The Tenth Song
The Eleventh Song
The Twelfth Song
The Thirteenth Song
The Fourteenth Song
The Fifteenth Song
The Sixteenth Song
The Seventeenth Song
The Eighteenth Song
Michael Drayton – A Short Biography by Cyril Brett
A Chronology of Michael Drayton's Life and Works
Michael Drayton – A Concise Bibliography. The Major Works


THE FIRST SONG

THE ARGUMENT

The sprightly Muse her wing displaies,
And the French Ilands first survaies,
Beares-up with Neptune, and in glory
Transcends proud Cornwalls Promontorie;
There crownes Mount-Michaell, and discries
How all those Riverets fall and rise;
Then takes in Tamer, as shee bounds
The Cornish and Devonian grounds.
And whilst the Devonshire-Nymphes relate
Their loves, their fortunes, and estate,
Dert undertaketh to revive
Our Brute, and sings his first arrive:

Then North-ward to the verge shee bends,
And her first Song at Ax shee ends.

Of Albions glorious Ile the Wonders whilst I write,
The sundry varying soyles, the pleasures infinite
(Where heate kills not the cold, nor cold expells the heat,
The calmes too mildly small, nor winds too roughly great,
Nor night doth hinder day, nor day the night doth wrong,
The Summer not too short, the Winter not too long)
What helpe shall I invoke to ayde my Muse the while?
Thou Genius of the place (this most renowned Ile)
Which livedst long before the All-earth-drowning Flood,
Whilst yet the world did swarme with her Gigantick brood;
Goe thou before me still thy circling shores about,
And in this wandring Maze helpe to conduct me out:
Direct my course so right, as with thy hand to showe
Which way thy Forrests range, which way thy Rivers flowe;
Wise Genius, by thy helpe that so I may discry
How thy faire Mountaines stand, and how thy Vallyes lie;
From those cleere pearlie Cleeves which see the Mornings pride,
And check the surlie Impes of Neptune when they chide,
Unto the big-swolne waves in the Iberian streame,
Where Titan still unyokes his fiery-hoofed Teame,
And oft his flaming locks in lushious Nectar steepes,
When from Olympus top he plungeth in the Deepes:
That from th' Armorick sands, on surging Neptunes leas
Through the Hibernick Gulfe (those rough Vergivian seas)
My verse with wings of skill may flie a loftie gate,
As Amphitrite clips this Iland Fortunate,
Till through the sleepy Maine to Thuly I have gone,
And seene the frozen Iles, the cold d Ducalidon,
Amongst whose Iron rockes grym Saturne yet remaines,
Bound in those gloomie Caves with Adamantine chaines.

Yee sacred Bards, that to your Harps melodious strings
Sung th'ancient Heroës deeds (the monuments of Kings)
And in your dreadfull verse ingrav'd the prophecies,
The aged worlds descents, and Genealogies;
If, as those Druides taught, which kept the British rites,
And dwelt in darksome Groves, there counsailing with sprites
(But their opinions faild, by error led awry,
As since cleere truth hath shew'd to their posteritie)
When these our soules by death our bodies doe forsake,
They instantlie againe doe other bodies take;
I could have wisht your spirits redoubled in my breast,
To give my verse applause, to times eternall rest.

Thus scarcelie said the Muse, but hovering while she hung

Upon the Celtick wastes, the Sea-Nymphes loudlie sung:
O ever-happie Iles, your heads so high that beare,
By Nature stronglie fenc't, which never need to feare
On Neptunes watry Realmes when Eolus raiseth warres,
And every billow bounds, as though to quench the starres:
Faire Jersey first of these heere scattred in the Deepe,
Peculiarlie that boast'st thy double-horned sheepe:
Inferior nor to thee, thou Jernsey, bravelie crown'd
With rough-imbatteld rocks, whose venom-hating ground
The hardned Emerill hath, which thou abroad doost send:
Thou Ligon, her belov'd, and Serk, that doost attend
Her pleasure everie howre; as Jethow, them at need,
With Phesants, fallow Deere, and Conies that doost feed:
Yee seaven small sister Iles, and Sorlings, which to see
The halfe-sunk sea-man joyes, or whatsoe're you be,
From fruitfull Aurney, neere the ancient Celtick shore,
To Ushant and the Seames, whereas those Nunnes of yore
Gave answers from their Caves, and tooke what shapes they please:
Ye happie Ilands set within the British Seas,
With shrill and jocund shouts, th'unmeasur'd deepes awake,
And let the Gods of Sea their secret Bowres forsake,
Whilst our industrious Muse great Britaine forth shall bring,
Crown'd with those glorious wreathes that beautifie the Spring;
And whilst greene Thetis Nymphes, with many an amorous lay
Sing our Invention safe unto her long-wisht Bay.
Upon the utmost end of Cornwalls furrowing beake,
Where a Bresan from the Land the tilting waves doth breake;
The shore let her transcend, the Promont to discry,
And viewe about the Point th'unnumbred Fowle that fly.
Some, rising like a storme from off the troubled sand,
Seeme in their hovering flight to shadow all the land;
Some, sitting on the beach to prune their painted breasts,
As if both earth and aire they onelie did possesse.
Whence, climing to the Cleeves, her selfe she firmlie sets
The Bourns, the Brooks, the Becks, the Rills, the Rivilets,
Exactlie to derive; receiving in her way
That straightned tongue of Land, where, at Mount-Michaells Bay,
Rude Neptune cutting in, a cantle forth doth take;
And, on the other side, Hayles vaster mouth doth make
Chersonese thereof, the corner clipping in:
Where to th' industrious Muse the Mount doth thus begin;

Before thou further passe, and leave this setting shore,
Whose Townes unto the Saints that lived heere of yore
(Their fasting, works, & pray'rs, remaining to our shames)
Were rear'd, and justly call'd by their peculiar names,
The builders honour still; this due and let them have,
As deigne to drop a teare upon each holie Grave;

Whose charitie and zeale, in steed of knowledge stood:
For, surely in themselves they were right simply good.
If, credulous too much, thereby th'offended heaven
In their devout intents, yet be their sinnes forgiven.
Then from his rugged top the teares downe trickling fell;
And in his passion stirr'd, againe began to tell
Strange things, that in his daies times course had brought to pass,
That fortie miles now Sea, sometimes firme fore-land was;
And that a Forrest then, which now with him is Flood,
Whereof he first was call'd the Hoare-Rock in the Wood;
Relating then how long this soile had laine forlorne,
As that her Genius now had almost her forsworne,
And of their ancient love did utterly repent,
Sith to destroy her selfe that fatall toole she lent
By which th' insatiate slave her intrailes out doth draw,
That thrusts his gripple hand into her golden mawe;
And for his part doth wish, that it were in his power
To let the Ocean in, her wholly to devoure.
Which, Hayle doth over-heare, and much doth blame his rage,
And told him (to his teeth) hee doated with his age.
For Hayle (a lustie Nymph, bent all to amorous play,
And having quicke recourse into the Severne Sea
With Neptunes Pages oft disporting in the Deepe;
One never touch't with care; but how her selfe to keepe
In excellent estate) doth thus againe intreate;
Muse, leave the wayward Mount to his distempred heate,
Who nothing can produce but what doth taste of spight:
Ile shew thee things of ours most worthy thy delight.
Behold our Diamonds heere, as in the quarr's they stand,
By Nature neatly cut, as by a skilfull hand,
Who varieth them in formes, both curiouslie and oft;
Which for shee (wanting power) produceth them too soft,
That vertue which she could not liberallie impart,
Shee striveth to amend by her owne proper Art.
Besides, the Seaholme heere, that spreadeth all our shore,
The sick consuming man so powerfull to restore:
Whose roote th' Eringo is, the reines that doth inflame
So stronglie to performe the Cytheræan game,
That generally approov'd, both farre and neere is sought.
And our Main-Amber heere, and Burien Trophy, thought
Much wrongd, not yet preferd for wonders with the rest.

But, the laborious Muse, upon her journey prest,
Thus uttereth to her selfe; To guide my course aright,
What Mound or steddie Mere is offered to my sight
Upon this out-stretcht Arme, whilst sayling heere at ease,
Betwixt the Southern waste, and the Sabrinian seas,
I view those wanton Brookes, that waxing, still doe wane;

That scarcelie can conceive, but brought to bed againe;
Scarce rising from the Spring (that is their naturall Mother)
To growe into a streame, but buried in another.
When Chore doth call her on, that wholly doth betake
Her selfe unto the Loo; transform'd into a Lake,
Through that impatient love shee had to entertaine
The lustfull Neptune oft; whom when his wracks restraine,
Impatient of the wrong, impetuouslie hee raves:
And in his ragefull flowe, the furious King of waves,
Breaks foming o're the Beach, whom nothing seemes to coole,
Till he have wrought his will on that capacious Poole
Where Menedge, by his Brookes, a Chersonese is cast,
Widening the slender shore to ease it in the wast;
A Promont jutting out into the dropping South,
That with his threatning cleeves in horrid Neptunes mouth,
Derides him and his power: nor cares how him he greets.
Next, Roseland (as his friend, the mightier Menedge) meets
Great Neptune when he swells, and rageth at the Rocks
(Set out into those seas) inforcing through his shocks
Those armes of Sea, that thrust into the tinny strand,
By their Meandred creeks indenting of that Land
Whose fame by everie tongue is for her Myneralls hurld,
Neere from the mid-daies point, throughout the Westerne world.
Heere Vale, a livelie flood, her nobler name that gives
To Flamouth; and by whom, it famous ever lives,
Whose entrance is from sea so intricatelie wound,
Her haven angled so about her harbrous sound,
That in her quiet Bay a hundred ships may ride,
Yet not the tallest mast, be of the tall'st descri'd;
Her braverie to this Nymph when neighbouring rivers told,
Her mind to them againe shee brieflie doth unfold;

Let Camell, of her course, and curious windings boast,
In that her Greatness raignes sole Mistress of that coast
Twixt Tamer and that Bay, where Hayle poures forth her pride:
And let us (nobler Nymphs) upon the mid-daie side,
Be frolick with the best. Thou Foy, before us all,
By thine owne named Towne made famous in thy fall,
As Low, amongst us heere; a most delicious Brooke,
With all our sister Nymphes, that to the noone-sted looke,
Which glyding from the hills; upon the tinny ore,
Betwixt your high-rear'd banks, resort to this our shore:
Lov'd streames, let us exult, and thinke our selves no lesse
Then those upon their side, the Setting that possesse.

Which, Camell over-heard: but what doth she respect
Their taunts, her proper course that loosely doth neglect?
As frantick, ever since her British Arthurs blood,

By Mordreds murtherous hand was mingled with her flood.
For, as that River, best might boast that Conquerours breath,
So sadlie shee bemoanes his too untimelie death;
Who, after twelve proud fields against the Saxon fought,
Yet back unto her banks by fate was lastly brought:
As though no other place on Britaines spacious earth,
Were worthie of his end, but where he had his birth:
And carelesse ever since how shee her course doe steere,
This muttreth to her selfe, in wandring here and there;
Even in the agedst face, where beautie once did dwell,
And nature (in the least) but seemed to excell,
Time cannot make such waste, but something wil appeare,
To shewe some little tract of delicacie there.
Or some religious worke, in building manie a day,
That this penurious age hath suffred to decay,
Some lim or modell, dragd out of the ruinous mass,
The richness will declare in glorie whilst it was:
But time upon my waste committed hath such theft,
That it of Arthur heere scarce memorie hath left:

The Nine-ston'd Trophie thus whilst shee doth entertaine,
Proude Tamer swoopes along, with such a lustie traine
As fits so brave a flood two Countries that divides:
So, to increase her strength, shee from her equall sides
Receives their severall rills; and of the Cornish kind,
First, taketh Atre in: and her not much behind
Comes Kensey: after whom, cleere Enian in doth make,
In Tamers roomthier bankes, their rest that scarcelie take.
Then Lyner, though the while aloofe shee seem'd to keepe,
Her Soveraigne when shee sees t'approach the surgefull deepe,
To beautifie her fall her plentious tribute brings.
This honours Tamer much: that shee whose plentious springs,
Those proud aspyring hills, Bromwelly and his frend
High Rowter, from their tops impartiallie commend,
And is by Carewes Muse, the river most renound,
Associate should her grace to the Devonian ground.
Which in those other Brookes doth Emulation breed.
Of which, first Car comes crown'd, with oziar, segs and reed:
Then Lid creeps on along, and taking Thrushel, throwes
Her selfe amongst the rocks; and so incavern'd goes,
That of the blessed light (from other floods) debarr'd,
To bellowe under earth, she onelie can be heard,
As those that view her tract, seemes strangelie to affright:
So, Toovy straineth in; and Plym, that claimes by right
The christning of that Bay, which beares her nobler name.
Upon the British coast, what ship yet ever came
That not of Plymouth heares, where those brave Navies lie,
From Canons thundring throats, that all the world defie?

Which, to invasive spoile, when th'English list to draw,
Have checkt Iberias pride, and held her oft in awe:
Oft furnishing our Dames, with Indias rar'st devices,
And lent us gold, and pearle, rich silks, and daintie spices.
But Tamer takes the place, and all attend her here,
A faithfull bound to both; and two that be so neare
For likeliness of soile, and quantitie they hold,
Before the Roman came; whose people were of old
Knowne by one generall name, upon this point that dwell,
All other of this Ile in wrastling that excell:
With collars be they yokt, to prove the arme at length,
Like Bulls set head to head, with meere delyver strength:
Or by the girdles graspt, they practise with the hip,
The forward, backward, falx, the mare, the turne, the trip,
When stript into their shirts, each other they invade
Within a spacious ring, by the beholders made,
According to the law. Or when the Ball to throw,
And drive it to the Gole, in squadrons forth they goe:
And to avoid the troupes (their forces that fore-lay)
Through dikes and rivers make, in this robustious play;
By which, the toiles of warre most livelie are exprest.

But Muse, may I demaund, Why these of all the rest
(As mightie Albyons eld'st) most active are and strong?
From Corin came it first, or from the use so long?
Or that this fore-land lies furth'st out into his sight,
Which spreads his vigorous flames on everie lesser light?
With th'vertue of his beames, this place that doth inspire:
Whose pregnant wombe prepar'd by his all-powerful fire,
Being purelie hot and moist, projects that fruitfull seed,
Which stronglie doth beget, and doth as stronglie breed:
The weldisposed heaven heere prooving to the earth,
A Husband furthering fruite; a Midwife helping birth.

But whilst th'industrious Muse thus labours to relate
Those rillets that attend proud Tamer and her state,
A neighbourer of this Nymphes, as high in Fortunes grace,
And whence calme Tamer trippes, cleere Towridge in that place
Is poured from her spring; and seemes at first to flowe
That way which Tamer straines: but as she great doth growe
Remembreth to fore-see, what Rivalls she should find
To interrupt her course: whose so unsettled mind
Ock comming in perceives, & thus doth her perswade;

Now Neptune shield (bright Nymph) thy beautie should be made
The object of her scorne, which (for thou canst not be
Upon the Southern side so absolute as shee)
Will awe thee in thy course. Wherefore, faire flood recoile:

And where thou maist alone be soveraigne of the soile,
There exercise thy power, thy braveries and displaie:
Turne Towridge, let us back to the Sabrinian sea;
Where Thetis handmaids still in that recoursefull deepe
With those rough Gods of Sea, continuall revells keepe;
There maist thou live admir'd, the mistress of the Lake.

Wise Ock shee doth obey, returning, and doth take
The Tawe: which from her fount forc't on with amorous gales,
And easely ambling downe through the Devonian dales,
Brings with her Moule and Bray, her banks that gentlie bathe;
Which on her daintie breast, in many a silver swathe
Shee beares unto that Bay, where Barstable beholds,
How her beloved Tawe cleere Towridge there enfolds.

The confluence of these Brooks divulg'd in Dertmoore, bred
Distrust in her sad breast, that shee, so largelie spred,
And in this spacious Shire the neer'st the Center set
Of anie place of note; that these should bravelie get
The praise, from those that sprung out of her pearlie lap;
Which, nourisht and bred up at her most plentious pap,
No sooner taught to dade, but from their Mother trip,
And in their speedie course, strive others to out-strip.
The Yalme, the Awne, the Aume, by spacious Dertmoore fed,
And in the Southern Sea, b'ing likewise brought to bed;
That these were not of power to publish her desert,
Much griev'd the ancient Moore: which understood by Dert
(From all the other floods that onely takes her name,
And as her eld'st (in right) the heire of all her fame)
To shew her nobler spirit it greatlie doth behove.

Deare Mother, from your breast this feare (quoth she) remove:
Defie their utmost force: ther's not the proudest flood,
That falls betwixt the Mount and Exmore, shall make good
Her royaltie with mine, with me nor can compare:
I challenge any one, to answere me that dare;
That was, before them all, predestinate to meet
My Britaine-founding Brute, when with his puissant fleet
At Totnesse first he toucht: which shall renowne my streame
(Which now the envious world doth slander for a dreame.)
Whose fatall flight from Greece, his fortunate arrive
In happy Albyon heere whilst stronglie I revive,
Deare Harburne at thy hands this credit let me win,
Quoth she, that as thou hast my faithfull hand-maid bin:
So now (my onelie Brooke) assist me with thy spring,
Whilst of the God-like Brute the storie thus I sing.

When long-renowned Troy lay spent in hostile fire,

And aged Priams pompe did with her flames expire,
Aeneas (taking thence Ascanius, his young sonne,
And his most reverent Sire, the grave Anchises, wonne
From sholes of slaughtering Greeks) set out from Simois shores;
And through the Tirrhene Sea, by strength of toyling ores,
Raught Italie at last: where, King Latinus lent
Safe harbor for his ships, with wrackfull tempests rent:
When, in the Latine Court, Lavinia young and faire
(Her Fathers onely child, and kingdoms onely heire)
Upon the Trojan Lord her liking stronglie plac't,
And languisht in the fiers that her faire breast imbrac't:
But, Turnus (at that time) the proud Rutulian King,
A suter to the maid, Aeneas malicing,
By force of Armes attempts, his rivall to extrude:
But, by the Teucrian power courageouslie subdu'd,
Bright Cythereas sonne the Latine crowne obtain'd;
And dying, in his stead his sonne Ascanius raign'd.
Next, Silvius him succeeds, begetting Brute againe:
Who in his Mothers wombe whilst yet he did remaine,
The Oracles gave out, that next borne Brute should bee
His Parents onelie death: which soone they liv'd to see.
For, in his painfull birth his Mother did depart;
And ere his fifteenth yeere, in hunting of a Hart,
He with a lucklesse shaft his haplesse Father slew:
For which, out of his throne, their King the Latines threw.

Who, wandring in the world, to Greece at last doth get.
Where, whilst he liv'd unknowne, and oft with want beset,
He of the race of Troy a remnant hapt to find,
There by the Grecians held; which (having still in mind
Their tedious tenne yeeres warre, and famous Heroës slaine)
In slaverie with them still those Trojans did detaine:
Which Pyrrhus thither brought (and did with hate pursue,
To wreake Achilles death, at Troy whom Paris slew)
There, by Pandrasus kept, in sad and servile awe.
Who, when they knew young Brute, & that brave shape they saw,
They humbly him desire, that he a meane would bee,
From those imperious Greeks, his countrymen to free.

Hee, finding out a rare and sprightly Youth, to fit
His humour every way, for courage, power, and wit,
Assaracus (who, though that by his Sire he were
A Prince amongst the Greeks, yet held the Trojans deere;
Descended of their stock upon the Mothers side:
For which, he by the Greeks his birth-right was deni'd)
Impatient of his wrongs, with him brave Brute arose,
And of the Trojan youth courageous Captaines chose,
Raysd Earth-quakes with their Drummes, the ruffling Ensignes reare;

And, gathering young and old that rightlie Trojan were,
Up to the Mountaines march, through straits and forrests strong:
Where, taking-in the Townes, pretended to belong
Unto that Grecian Lord, some forces there they put:
Within whose safer walls their wives and children shut,
Into the fields they drew, for libertie to stand.

Which when Pandrasus heard, he sent his strict command
To levie all the power he presentlie could make:
So, to their strengths of warre the Trojans them betake.

But whilst the Grecian Guides (not knowing how or where
The Teucrians were entrencht, or what their forces were)
In foule disordred troupes yet straggled, as secure,
This loosness to their spoyle the Trojans did allure,
Who fiercely them assail'd: where stanchlesse furie rap't
The Grecians in so fast, that scarcely one escap't:
Yea, proud Pandrasus flight, himselfe could hardlie free.
Who, when he saw his force thus frustrated to bee,
And by his present losse, his passed error found
(As by a later warre to cure a former wound)
Doth reinforce his power to make a second fight.
When they whose better wits had over-matcht his might,
Loth what they got to lose, as politiquelie cast
His Armies to intrap, in getting to them fast
Antigonus as friend, and Anaclet his pheere
(Surpriz'd in the last fight) by gifts who hired were
Into the Grecian Campe th'insuing night to goe
And faine they were stolne forth, to their Allies to show
How they might have the spoile of all the Trojan pride;
And gaining them beleefe, the credulous Grecians guide
Into th'ambushment neere, that secretlie was laid:
So to the Trojans hands the Grecians were betraid;
Pandrasus selfe surpriz'd; his Crown who to redeeme
(Which scarcely worth their wrong the Trojan race esteeme)
Their slaverie long sustain'd did willinglie release:
And (for a lasting league of amitie and peace)
Bright Innogen, his child, for wife to Brutus gave,
And furnisht them a fleete, with all things they could crave
To set them out to Sea. Who lanching, at the last
They on Lergecia light, an Ile; and, ere they past,
Unto a Temple built to great Diana there,
The noble Brutus went; wise Trivia to enquire,
To shew them where the stock of ancient Troy to place.

The Goddesse, that both knew and lov'd the Trojan race,
Reveal'd to him in dreames, that furthest to the West,
He should discrie the Ile of Albion, highlie blest;

With Giants latelie stor'd; their numbers now decaid:
By vanquishing the rest, his hopes should there be staid:
Where, from the stock of Troy, those puissant Kings should rise,
Whose conquests from the West, the world should scant suffice.

Thus answer'd; great with hope, to sea they put againe,
And safelie under saile, the howres doe entertaine
With sights of sundrie shores, which they from farre discrie:
And viewing with delight th'Azarian Mountaines hie,
One walking on the deck, unto his friend would say
(As I have heard some tell) So goodly Ida lay.

Thus talking mongst themselves, they sun-burnt Africk keepe
Upon the lee-ward still, and (sulking up the deepe)
For Mauritania make: where putting-in, they find
A remnant (yet reserv'd) of th'ancient Dardan kind,
By brave Antenor brought from out the Greekish spoiles
(O long-renowned Troy! Of thee, and of thy toyles,
What Country had not heard?) which, to their Generall, then
Great Corineus had, the strong'st of mortall men:
To whom (with joyfull harts) Dianas will they show.

Who easlie beeing wonne along with them to goe,
They altogether put into the watry Plaine:
Oft-times with Pyrats, oft with Monsters of the Maine
Distressed in their way; whom hope forbids to feare.
Those pillars first they passe which Joves great sonne did reare.
And cuffing those sterne waves which like huge Mountaines roule
(Full joy in every part possessing every soule)
In Aquitane at last the Ilion race arrive.
Whom strongly to repulse when as those recreants strive,
They (anchoring there at first but to refresh their fleet,
Yet saw those savage men so rudely them to greet)
Unshipt their warlike youth, advauncing to the shore.
The Dwellers, which perceiv'd such danger at the dore,
Their King Groffarius get to raise his powerfull force:
Who, mustring up an host of mingled foote and horse,
Upon the Trojans set; when suddainly began
A fierce and dangerous fight: where Corineus ran
With slaughter through the thick-set squadrons of the foes;
And with his armed Axe laid on such deadlie blowes,
That heapes of livelesse trunks each passage stopt up quite.
Groffarius having lost the honour of the fight,
Repaires his ruin'd powers; not so to give them breath:
When they, which must be free'd by conquest or by death,
And, conquering them before, hop't now to doe no lesse
(The like in courage still) stand for the like successe.
Then sterne and deadlie Warre put-on his horridst shape;

And wounds appear'd so wide, as if the Grave did gape
To swallow both at once; which strove as both should fall,
When they with slaughter seem'd to be encircled all:
Where Turon (of the rest) Brutes Sisters valiant sonne
(By whose approved deeds that day was chiefly wonne)
Sixe hundred slue out-right through his peculiar strength:
By multitudes of men yet over-prest at length.
His nobler Uncle there, to his immortall name,
The Citie Turon built, and well endow'd the same.

For Albion sayling then, th'arrived quicklie heere
(O! never in this world men halfe so joyful were
With shoutes heard up to heaven, when they beheld the Land)
And in this verie place where Totnesse now doth stand,
First set their Gods of Troy, kissing the blessed shore;
Then, forraging this Ile, long promisd them before,
Amongst the ragged Cleeves those monstrous Giants sought:
Who (of their dreadfull kind) t'appall the Trojans, brought
Great Gogmagog, an Oake that by the roots could teare:
So mightie were (that time) the men who lived there:
But, for the use of Armes he did not understand
(Except some rock or tree, that comming next to hand
Hee raz'd out of the earth to execute his rage)
Hee challenge makes for strength, and offereth there his gage.
Which, Corin taketh up, to answer by and by,
Upon this sonne of Earth his utmost power to try.

All, doubtful to which part the victorie would goe,
Upon that loftie place at Plimmouth call'd the Hoe,
Those mightie Wrastlers met; with many an irefull looke
Who threatned, as the one hold of the other tooke:
But, grapled, glowing fire shines in their sparkling eyes.
And, whilst at length of arme one from the other lyes,
Their lusty sinewes swell like cables, as they strive:
Their feet such trampling make, as though they forc't to drive
A thunder out of earth; which stagger'd with the weight:
Thus, eithers utmost force urg'd to the greatest height.
Whilst one upon his hip the other seekes to lift,
And th'adverse (by a turne) doth from his cunning shift,
Their short-fetcht troubled breath a hollow noise doth make,
Like bellowes of a Forge. Then Corin up doth take
The Giant twixt the grayns; and, voyding of his hould
(Before his combrous feet he well recover could)
Pitcht head-long from the hill; as when a man doth throw
An Axtree, that with sleight deliverd from the toe
Rootes up the yeelding earth: so that his violent fall,
Strooke Neptune with such strength, as shouldred him withall;
That where the monstrous waves like Mountaines late did stand,

They leap't out of the place, and left the bared sand
To gaze upon wide heaven: so great a blowe it gave.
For which, the conquering Brute, on Corineus brave
This horne of land bestow'd, and markt it with his name;
Of Corin, Cornwall call'd, to his immortall fame.

Cleere Dert delivering thus the famous Brutes arrive,
Inflam'd with her report, the stragling rivelets strive
So highlie her to raise, that Ting (whose banks were blest
By her beloved Nymph deere Leman) which addrest
And fullie with her selfe determined before
To sing the Danish spoyles committed on her shore,
When hither from the East they came in mightie swarmes,
Nor could their native earth containe their numerous Armes,
Their surcrease grew so great, as forced them at last
To seeke another soyle (as Bees doe when they cast)
And by their impious pride how hard she was bested,
When all the Country swam with blood of Saxons shed:
This River (as I said) which had determin'd long
The Deluge of the Danes exactlie to have song,
It utterlie neglects; and studying how to doe
The Dert those high respects belonging her unto,
Inviteth goodlie Ex, who from her ful-fed spring
Her little Barlee hath, and Dunsbrook her to bring
From Exmore: when she yet hath scarcely found her course,
Then Creddy commeth in, and Forto, which inforce
Her faster to her fall; as Ken her closelie clips,
And on her Easterne side sweet Leman gentlie slips
Into her widened banks, her Soveraigne to assist;
As Columb winnes for Ex, cleere Wever and the Clist,
Contributing their streames their Mistress fame to raise.
As all assist the Ex, so Ex consumeth these;
Like some unthriftie youth, depending on the Court,
To winne an idle name, that keepts a needless port;
And raising his old rent, exacts his Farmers store
The Land-lord to enrich, the Tenants wondrous poore:
Who having sent him theirs, he then consumes his owne,
That with most vaine expense upon the Prince is throwne:
So these, the lesser Brooks unto the greater pay;
The greater, they againe spend all upon the Sea:
As, Otrey (that her name doth of the Otters take,
Abounding in her banks) and Ax, their utmost make
To ayde stout Dert, that dar'd Brutes storie to revive.
For, when the Saxon first the Britans forth did drive,
Some up into the hills themselves o're Severne shut:
Upon this point of land, for refuge others put,
To that brave race of Brute still fortunate. For where
Great Brute first disembarqu't his wandring Trojans, there

His ofspring (after long expulst the Inner land,
When they the Saxon power no longer could withstand)
Found refuge in their flight; where Ax and Otrey first
Gave these poore soules to drinke, opprest with grievous thirst.
Heere I'le unyoke awhile, and turne my steeds to meat:
The land growes large and wide: my Teame begins to sweat.


THE SECOND SONG

THE ARGUMENT

The Muse from Marshwood way commands,
Along the shore through Chesills sands:
Where, overtoyld, her heate to coole,
Shee bathes her in the pleasant Poole:
Thence, over-land againe doth scowre,
To fetch in Froome, and bring downe Stowre;
Falls with New-forrest, as she sings
The wanton Wood-Nymphes revellings.
Whilst Itchin in her loftie layes,
Chaunts Bevis of South-hamptons praise,
Shee Southward with her active flight
Is wafted to the Ile of Wight,
To see the rutte the Sea-gods keepe:
There swaggering in the Solent deepe.
Thence Hampshire–ward her way shee bends;
And visiting her Forrest friends,
Neere Salsbury her rest doth take:
Which shee her second pause doth make.

March strongly forth my Muse, whilst yet the temperat aire
Invites us, easely on to hasten our repaire.
Thou powerfull God of flames (in verse divinely great)
Touch my invention so with thy true genuine heate,
That high and noble things I slightly may not tell,
Nor light and idle toyes my lines may vainly swell;
But as my subject serves, so hie or lowe to straine,
And to the varying earth so sute my varying vaine,
That Nature in my worke thou maist thy power avow:
That as thou first found'st Art, and didst her rules allow;
So I, to thine owne selfe that gladlie neere would bee,
May herein doe the best, in imitating thee:
As thou hast heere a hill, a vale there, there a flood,
A mead here, there a heath, and now and then a wood,
These things so in my Song I naturally may showe;
Now, as the Mountaine hie; then, as the Valley lowe:

Heere, fruitfull as the Mead, there as the Heath be bare;
Then, as the gloomie wood, I may be rough; though rare.

Through the Dorsetian fields that lie in open view,
My progresse I againe must seriouslie pursue,
From Marshwoods fruitfull Vale my journey on to make:
(As Phoebus getting up out of the Easterne lake,
Refresht with ease and sleepe, is to his labour prest;
Even so the labouring Muse, heere baited with this rest.)
Whereas the little Lim along doth easelie creepe,
And Car, that comming downe unto the troubled Deepe,
Brings on the neighbouring Bert, whose batning mellowed banke,
From all the British soyles, for Hempe most hugely ranke
Doth beare away the best; to Bert-port which hath gain'd
That praise from every place, and worthilie obtain'd
Our cordage from her store, and cables should be made,
Of any in that kind most fit for Marine trade:
Not sever'd from the shore, aloft where Chesill lifts
Her ridged snake-like sands, in wrecks and smouldring drifts,
Which by the South-wind raysd, are heav'd on little hills:
Whose valleys with his flowes when foming Neptune fills,
Upon a thousand Swannes the naked Sea-Nymphes ride
Within the ouzie Pooles, replenisht every Tide:
Which running on, the Ile of Portland pointeth out;
Upon whose moisted skirt with sea-weed fring'd about,
The bastard Corall breeds, that drawne out of the brack,
A brittle stalke becomes, from greenish turn'd to black:
Which th'Ancients, for the love that they to Isis bare
(Their Goddesse most ador'd) have sacred for her haire.
Of which the Naïdes, and the blew a Nereïdes make
Them Taudries for their necks: when sporting in the Lake,
They to their secrete Bowres the Sea-gods entertaine.
Where Portland from her top doth over-peere the Maine;
Her rugged front empal'd (on every part) with rocks,
Though indigent of wood, yet fraught with woolly flocks:
Most famous for her folke, excelling with the sling,
Of any other heere this Land inhabiting;
That there-with they in warre offensivelie might wound,
If yet the use of shot Invention had not found.
Where, from the neighbouring hills her passage Wey doth path:
Whose haven, not our least that watch the mid-day, hath
The glories that belong unto a complete Port;
Though Wey the least of all the Naïdes that resort
To the Dorsetian sands, from off the higher shore.
Then Frome (a nobler flood) the Muses doth implore
Her mother Blackmores state they sadly would bewaile;
Whose bigge and lordlie Oakes once bore as brave a saile
As they themselves that thought the largest shades to spred:

But mans devouring hand, with all the earth not fed,
Hath hew'd her Timber downe. Which wounded, when it fell,
By the great noise it made, the workmen seem'd to tell
The losse that to the Land would shortlie come thereby,
Where no man ever plants to our posteritie:
That when sharp Winter shoots her sleet and hardned haile,
Or suddaine gusts from Sea, the harmlesse Deere assaile,
The shrubs are not of power to sheeld them from the wind.

Deere Mother, quoth the Froome, too late (alas) we find
The softness of thy sward continued through thy soile,
To be the onely cause of unrecover'd spoile:
When scarce the British ground a finer grasse doth beare;
And wish I could, quoth shee, (if wishes helpfull were)
Thou never by that name of White-hart hadst been known,
But stiled Blackmore still, which rightly was thine owne.
For why, that change foretold the ruine of thy state:
Lo, thus the world may see what tis to innovate.

By this, her owne nam'd Towne the wandring Froome had past:
And quitting in her course old Dorcester at last,
Approaching neere the Poole, at Warham on her way,
As easelie shee doth fall into the peacefull Bay,
Upon her nobler side, and to the South-ward neere,
Faire Purbeck shee beholds, which no where hath her peere:
So pleasantlie in-Il'd on mightie Neptunes marge,
A Forest-Nymph, and one of chaste Dianas charge,
Imploy'd in Woods and Launds her Deere to feed and kill:
On whom the watrie God would oft have had his will,
And often her hath woo'd, which never would be wonne;
But, Purbeck (as profest a Huntresse and a Nunne)
The wide and wealthy Sea, nor all his power respects:
Her Marble-minded breast, impregnable, rejects
The a uglie Orks, that for their Lord the Ocean wooe.

Whilst Froome was troubled thus where nought shee hath to doe,
The Piddle, that this while bestird her nimble feet,
In falling to the Poole her sister Froome to meet,
And having in her traine two little slender rills
(Besides her proper Spring) where-with her banks shee fills,
To whom since first the world this later name her lent,
Who ancientlie was knowne to be instiled b Trent,
Her small assistant Brookes her second name have gain'd.
Whilst Piddle and the Froome each other entertain'd,
Oft praysing lovely Poole, their best-beloved Bay,
Thus Piddle her bespake, to passe the time away;
When Poole (quoth shee) was young, a lustie Sea-borne Lass,
Great Albyon to this Nymph an earnest suter was;

And bare himselfe so well, and so in favour came,
That he in little time, upon this lovelie Dame
Begot three mayden Iles, his darlings and delight:
The eldest, Brunksey call'd; the second, Fursey hight;
The youngest and the last, and lesser then the other,
Saint Hellens name doth beare, the dilling of her Mother.
And, for the goodlie Poole was one of Thetis traine,
Who scorn'd a Nymph of hers, her Virgin-band should staine,
Great Albyon (that fore-thought, the angrie Goddesse would
Both on the Dam and brats take what revenge shee could)
I'th bosome of the Poole his little children plac't:
First, Brunksey; Fursey next; and little Hellen last;
Then, with his mightie armes doth clip the Poole about,
To keepe the angrie Queene, fierce Amphitrite out.
Against whose lordlie might shee musters up her waves;
And strongly thence repulst (with madness) scoulds and raves.

When now, from Poole, the Muse (up to her pitch to get)
Her selfe in such a place from sight doth almost set,
As by the active power of her commanding wings,
She (Falcon-like) from farre doth fetch those plentious Springs.
Where Stour receives her strength from sixe cleere Fountaines fed;
Which gathering to one streame from every severall head,
Her new-beginning banke her water scarcely weelds;
And fairelie entreth first on the Dorsetian feelds:
Where Gillingham with gifts that for a God were meet
(Enameld paths, rich wreaths, and every soveraine sweet
The earth and ayre can yeeld, with many a pleasure mixt)
Receives her. Whilst there past great kindness them betwixt,
The Forrest her bespoke; How happie floods are yee,
From our predestin'd plagues that priviledged bee;
Which onelie with the fish which in your banks doe breed,
And dailie there increase, mans gurmandize can feed?
But had this wretched Age such uses to imploy
Your waters, as the woods we latelie did enjoy,
Your chanels they would leave as barren by their spoile,
As they of all our trees have lastlie left our soile.
Insatiable Time thus all things doth devour:
What ever saw the sunne, that is not in Times power?
Yee fleeting Streames last long, out-living manie a day:
But, on more stedfast things Time makes the strongest pray.

Now tow'rds the Solent sea as Stour her way doth ply,
On Shaftsbury (by chance) shee cast her crystall eye,
From whose foundation first, such strange reports arise
As brought into her mind the Eagles prophecies;
Of that so dreadfull plague, which all great Britaine swept,
From that which highest flew, to that which lowest crept,

Before the Saxon thence the Britaine should expell,
And all that there-upon successively befell.

How then the bloodie Dane subdu'd the Saxon race;
And, next, the Norman tooke possession of the place:
Those ages, once expir'd, the Fates to bring about,
The British Line restor'd; the Norman linage out.
Then, those prodigious signes to ponder shee began,
Which afterward againe the Britans wrack fore-ran;
How here the Owle at noone in publique streets was seene,
As though the peopled Townes had way-less Deserts been.
And whilst the loathly Toad out of his hole doth crall,
And makes his fulsome stoole amid the Princes hall,
The crystall fountaine turn'd into a gory wound,
And bloodie issues brake (like ulcers) from the ground;
The Seas against their course with double Tides returne,
And oft were seene by night like boyling pitch to burne.

Thus thinking, livelie Stour bestirres her tow'rds the Maine;
Which Lidden leadeth out: then Dulas beares her traine
From Blackmore, that at once their watry tribute bring:
When, like some childish wench, shee looselie wantoning,
With tricks and giddie turnes seemes to in-Ile the shore.
Betwixt her fishfull banks, then forward shee doth scowre,
Untill shee lastlie reach cleere Alen in her race:
Which calmlie commeth downe from her deere mother Chase,
Of Cranburn that is call'd; who greatly joyes to see
A Riveret borne of her, for Stours should reckned bee,
Of that renowned flood, a favourite highlie grac't.

Whilst Cranburn, for her child so fortunatelie plac't,
With Ecchoes everie way applauds her Alens state,
A suddaine noise from d Holt seems to congratulate
With Cranburn for her Brooke so happily bestow'd:
Where, to her neighboring Chase, the curteous Forrest show'd
So just conceived joy, that from each rising a hurst,
Where many a goodlie Oake had carefullie been nurst,
The Sylvans in their songs their mirthfull meeting tell;
And Satyres, that in slades and gloomy dimbles dwell,
Runne whooting to the hills to clappe their ruder hands.

As Holt had done before, so Canfords goodlie Launds
(Which leane upon the Poole) enricht with Coppras vaines,
Rejoyce to see them joyn'd. When downe from Sarum Plaines
Cleere Avon comming in her sister Stour doth call,
And at New-forrests foote into the Sea doe fall,
Which every day bewaile that deed so full of dred
Whereby shee (now so proud) became first Forrested:

Shee now who for her site even boundless seem'd to lie,
Her beeing that receiv'd by Williams tyrannie;
Providing Lawes to keepe those Beasts heere planted then,
Whose lawless will from hence before had driven men;
That where the harth was warm'd with Winters feasting fiers,
The melancholie Hare is form'd in brakes and briers:
The aged ranpick trunk where Plow-men cast their seed,
And Churches over-whelm'd with nettles, ferne and weed,
By Conquering William first cut off from every trade,
That heere the Norman still might enter to invade;
That on this vacant place, and unfrequented shore,
New forces still might land, to ayde those heere before.
But shee, as by a King and Conqueror made so great,
By whom shee was allow'd and limited her seat,
Into her owne-selfe praise most insolently brake,
And her lesse fellow Nymphs, New-forrest, thus bespake:

Thou Buckholt, bow to mee, so let thy sister Bere;
Chute, kneele thou at my name on this side of the Shiere:
Where, for their Goddesse, mee the b Driads shall adore,
With Waltham, and the Bere, that on the Sea-worne shore
See at the Southerne Iles the Tides at tilt to runne;
And Woolmer, placed hence upon the rising sunne,
With Ashholt thine Allie (my Wood-Nymphs) and with you,
Proud Pamber tow'rds the North, ascribe me worship due.
Before my Princelie State let your poore greatness fall:
And vaile your tops to mee, the Soveraigne of you all.

Amongst the Rivers, so, great discontent there fell.
Th'efficient cause thereof (as loud report doth tell)
Was, that the sprightly Test arising up in Chute,
To Itchin, her Allie, great weakeness should impute,
That shee, to her owne wrong, and every others griefe,
Would needs be telling things exceeding all beliefe:
For, she had given it out South-hampton should not loose
Her famous Bevis so, wer't in her power to choose;
And, for great Arthurs seat, her Winchester preferres,
Whose old Round-table, yet she vaunteth to be hers:
And swore, th'inglorious time should not bereave her right;
But what it could obscure, she would reduce to light.
For, from that wondrous Pond, whence shee derives her head,
And places by the way, by which shee's honored
(Old Winchester, that stands neere in her middle way,
And Hampton, at her fall into the Solent Sea)
Shee thinks in all the Ile not any such as shee,
And for a Demy-god she would related bee.

Sweet sister mine (quoth Test) advise you what you doe;

Thinke this; For each of us, the Forests heere are two:
Who, if you speake a thing whereof they hold can take,
Bee't little, or bee't much, they double will it make:
Whom Hamble helpeth out; a handsome proper flood,
In curtesie well skild, and one that knew her good.
Consider, quoth this Nymph, the times be curious now,
And nothing of that kind will any way allow.
Besides, the Muse hath, next, the British cause in hand,
About things later done that now shee cannot stand.

The more they her perswade, the more shee doth persist;
Let them say what they will, shee will doe what shee list.
Shee stiles her selfe their Chiefe, and sweares shee will command;
And, what-so-ere shee saith, for Oracles must stand.
Which when the Rivers heard, they further speech forbare.
And shee (to please her selfe that onely seem'd to care)
To sing th'atchievement great of Bevis thus began;

Redoubted Knight (quoth shee) ô most renowned man!
Who, when thou wert but young, thy Mother durst reprove
(Most wickedly seduc't by the unlawfull love
Of Mordure, at that time the Almain Emperors sonne)
That shee thy Sire to death disloyally had done:
Each circumstance whereof shee largelie did relate;
Then, in her song pursu'd his Mothers deadlie hate;
And how (by Sabers hand) when shee suppos'd him dead,
Where long upon the Downes a Shepheards life hee led;
Till by the great recourse, he came at length to knowe
The Country there-about could hardly hold the showe
His Mothers mariage feast to faire South-hampton drue,
Be'ing wedded to that Lord who late her husband slue:
Into his noble breast which pierc't so wondrous deepe,
That (in the poore attire he us'd to tend the sheepe,
And in his hand his hooke) unto the Towne hee went;
As having in his heart a resolute intent
Or manfullie to die, or to revenge his wrong:
Where pressing at the gate the multitude among,
The Porter to that place his entrance that forbad
(Supposing him some swaine, some boystrous Country-lad)
Upon the head hee lent so violent a stroke,
That the poore emptie skull, like some thin potsheard broke,
The braines and mingled blood, were spertled on the wall
Then hasting on he came into the upper Hall,
Where murderous Mordure sate imbraced by his Bride:
Who (guiltie in himselfe) had hee not Bevis spide,
His boanes had with a blowe been shattred: but, by chance
(He shifting from the place, whilst Bevis did advance
His hand, with greater strength his deadly foe to hit,

And missing him) his chaire hee all to shivers split:
Which strooke his Mothers breast with strange and sundry feares,
That Bevis beeing then but of so tender yeares
Durst yet attempt a thing so full of death and doubt.
And, once before deceiv'd, shee newlie cast about
To rid him out of sight; and, with a mighty wage,
Wonne such, themselves by oath as deeplie durst ingage,
To execute her will: who shipping him away
(And making forth their course into the Mid-land sea)
As they had got before, so now againe for gold
To an Armenian there that young Alcides sold:
Of all his gotten prize, who (as the worthiest thing,
And fittest where-withall to gratifie his King)
Presented that brave youth; the splendor of whose eye
A wondrous mixture shew'd of grace and majestie:
Whose more then man-like shape, and matchlesse stature, tooke
The King; that often us'd with great delight to looke
Upon that English Earle. But though the love he bore
To Bevis might be much, his daughter tenne times more
Admir'd the god-like man: who, from the howre that first
His beautie shee beheld, felt her soft bosome pierst
With Cupids deadliest shaft; that Josian, to her guest,
Alreadie had resign'd possession of her breast.

Then sang shee, in the fields how as hee went to sport,
And those damn'd Panims heard, who in despightfull sort
Derided Christ the Lord; for his Redeemers sake
He on those heathen hounds did there such slaughter make,
That whilst in their black mouthes their blasphemies they drue,
They headlong went to hell. As also how hee slue
That cruell Boare, whose tusks turn'd up whole fields of graine
(And, wrooting, raised hills upon the levell Plaine;
Digd Caverns in the earth, so darke and wondrous deepe
As that, into whose mouth the desperate Roman leepe):
And cutting off his head, a Trophy thence to beare;
The Forresters that came to intercept it there,
How he their scalps and trunks in chips and peeces cleft,
And in the fields (like beasts) their mangled bodies left.
As to his further praise, how for that dangerous fight
The great Armenian King made noble Bevis Knight:
And having raised power, Damascus to invade,
The Generall of his force this English Heroë made.
Then, how faire Josian gave him Arundell his steed,
And Morglay his good sword, in many a valiant deed
Which manfully he tri'd. Next, in a Buskind straine,
Sung how himselfe he bore upon Damascus Plaine
(That dreadful battell) where, with Bradamond he fought;
And with his sword and steed such earthlie wonders wrought,

As even amongst his foes him admiration won;
Incountring in the throng with mightie Radison;
And lopping off his armes, th'imperiall standard tooke.
At whose prodigious fall, the conquered Foe forsooke
The Field; where, in one day so many Peeres they lost,
So brave Commaunders, and so absolute an host,
As to the humbled earth tooke proud Damascus downe,
Then tributarie made to the Armenian Crowne.
And how at his returne, the King (for service done,
The honor to his raigne, and to Armenia won)
In mariage to this Earle the Princess Josian gave;

As into what distresse him Fortune after drave,
To great Damascus sent Ambassador againe;
When, in revenge of theirs, before by Bevis slaine
(And now, at his returne, for that he so despis'd
Those Idols unto whom they dailie sacrifiz'd:
Which he to peeces hew'd and scattred in the dust)
They, rising, him by strength into a Dungeon thrust;
In whose blacke bottom, long two Serpents had remain'd
(Bred in the common sewre that all the Cittie drain'd)
Empoysning with their smell; which seiz'd him for their pray:
With whom in strugling long (besmeard with blood and clay)
He rent their squallid chaps, and from the prison scap't.

As how adultrous Joure, the King of Mambrant, rap't
Faire Josian his deere Love, his noble sword and steed:
Which afterward by craft, he in a Palmers weed
Recoverd, and with him from Mambrant bare away.

And with two Lions how hee held a desperat fray,
Assayling him at once, that fiercelie on him flew:
Which first he tam'd with wounds, then by the necks them drew,
And gainst the hardned earth their jawes and shoulders burst;
And that (Golia-like) great Ascupart inforc't
To serve him for a slave, and by his horse to runne.

At Colein as againe the glorie that he wonne
On that huge Dragon, like the Country to destroy;
Whose sting strooke like a Lance: whose venom did destroy
As doth a generall plague: his scales like shields of brass;
His bodie, when hee moov'd, like some unweeldie mass,
Even brus'd the solid Earth. Which boldlie having song,
With all the sundry turnes that might thereto belong,
Whilst yet shee shapes her course how he came back to show
What powers he got abroad, how them he did bestow;
In England heere againe, how he by dint of sword
Unto his ancient lands and titles was restor'd,

New-forrest cry'd enough: and Waltham with the Bere,
Both bad her hold her peace; for they no more would heare.
And for shee was a flood, her fellowes nought would say;
But slipping to their banks, slid silentlie away.

When as the pliant Muse, with faire and even flight,
Betwixt her silver wings is wafted to the Wight:
That Ile, which jutting out into the Sea so farre,
Her ofspring traineth up in exercise of warre;
Those Pyrats to put backe that oft purloine her trade,
Or Spaniards, or the French attempting to invade.
Of all the Southerne Iles shee holds the highest place,
And evermore hath been the great'st in Britaines grace:
Not one of all her Nymphs her Soveraigne favoureth thus,
Imbraced in the armes of old Oceanus.
For none of her account, so neere her bosome stand,
Twixt Penwiths furthest point, and Goodwins queachy sand,
Both for her seat and soyle, that farre before the other,
Most justlie may account great Britaine for her Mother.
A finer fleece then hers not Lemsters selfe can boast,
Nor Newport for her Mart, o'r-matcht by any Coast.
To these, the gentle South, with kisses smooth and soft,
Doth in her bosome breathe, and seemes to court her oft.
Besides, her little Rills, her in-lands that doe feed,
Which with their lavish streames doe furnish everie need:
And Meads, that with their fine soft grassie towels stand
To wipe away the drops and moisture from her hand.
And to the North, betwixt the fore-land and the firme,
Shee hath that narrow Sea, which we the Solent tearme:
Where those rough irefull Tides, as in her Straits they meet,
With boystrous shocks and rores each other rudely greet:
Which fiercelie when they charge, and sadlie make retreat,
Upon the bulwarkt Forts of Hurst and Calsheot beat,
Then to South-hampton runne: which by her shores supplide
(As Portsmouth by her strength) doth vilifie their pride;

Both, Roads that with our best may boldlie hold their plea,
Nor Plimmouths selfe hath borne more braver ships then they;
That from their anchoring Bayes have travailed to finde
Large Chinas wealthie Realms, and view'd the either Inde,
The pearlie rich Peru; and with as prosperous fate,
Have borne their ful-spred sailes upon the streames of Plate:
Whose pleasant harbors oft the Sea-mans hope renue,
To rigge his late-craz'd Barke, to spred a wanton clue;
Where they with lustie Sack, and mirthfull Sailers songs,
Defie their passed stormes, and laugh at Neptunes wrongs:
The danger quite forgot wherein they were of late;
Who halfe so merrie now as Maister and his Mate?

And victualling againe, with brave and man-like minds
To Sea-ward cast their eyes, and pray for happie winds.
But, partlie by the floods sent thither from the shore,
And Ilands that are set the bordring coast before:
As one amongst the rest, a brave and lustie Dame
Call'd Portsey, whence that Bay of Portsmouth hath her name:
By her, two little Iles, her handmaids (which compar'd
With those within the Poole, for deftness not out-dar'd)
The greater Haling hight: and fairest though by much,
Yet Thorney verie well, but some-what rough in tuch.
Whose beauties farre and neere divulged by report,
And by the a Trytons told in mightie Neptunes Court,
Old b Proteus hath been knowne to leave his finny Heard,
And in their sight to spunge his foame-bespawled beard.
The Sea-gods, which about the watry kingdome keepe,
Have often for their sakes abandoned the Deepe;
That Thetis many a time to Neptune hath complaind,
How for those wanton Nymphes her Ladies were disdain'd:
And there arose such rut th'unrulie rout among,
That soone the noyse thereof through all the Ocean rong.

When Portsey, weighing well the ill to her might grow,
In that their mightie stirres might be her over-throw,
Shee stronglie straightneth-in the entrance to her Bay;
That, of their haunt debard, and shut out to the Sea
(Each small conceived wrong helps on distempred rage.)
No counsell could be heard their choler to aswage:
When every one suspects the next that is in place
To be the onely cause and meanes of his disgrace.
Some comming from the East, some from the setting Sunne,
The liquid Mountaines still together mainlie runne;
Wave woundeth wave againe; and billow, billow gores:
And topsie turvie so, flie tumbling to the shores.
From hence the Solent Sea, as some men thought, might stand
Amongst those things, which wee call Wonders of our Land.

When toghing up c that streame, so negligent of fame,
As till this verie day shee yet conceales her name;
By Bert and Waltham both, that's equally imbrac't,
And lastlie, at her fall, by Tichfield highlie grac't.
Whence, from old Windsor hill, and from the aged d Stone,
The Muse those Countries sees, which call her to be gone.
The Forests tooke their leave: Bere, Chute, and Buckholt, bid
Adieu; so Wolmer, and so Ashholt, kindly did.
And Pamber shooke her head, as grieved at the hart;
When farre upon her way, and ready to depart,
As now the wandring Muse so sadlie went along,
To her last Farewell, thus, the goodlie Forests song.

Deere Muse, to plead our right, whom time at last hath brought,
Which else forlorne had lyen, and banisht everie thought,
When thou ascend'st the hills, and from their rising shrouds
Our sisters shalt commaund, whose tops once toucht the clouds;
Old Arden when thou meet'st, or doost faire Sherwood see,
Tell them, that as they waste, so everie day doe wee:
Wish them, we of our griefes may be each others heirs;
Let them lament our fall, and we will mourne for theirs.

Then turning from the South which lies in publique view,
The Muse an oblique course doth seriously pursue:
And pointing to the Plaines, she thither takes her way;
For which, to gaine her breath shee makes a little stay.


THE THIRD SONG

THE ARGUMENT

In this third Song, great threatnings are,
And tending all to Nymphish warre.
Old Wansdike uttereth words of hate,
Depraving Stonendges estate.
Cleere Avon and faire Willy strive,
Each pleading her prerogative.
The Plaine the Forrests doth disdaine:
The Forrests raile upon the Plaine.
The Muse then seekes the Shires extreames,
To find the Fountaine of great Tames;
Falls downe with Avon, and discries
Both Bathes and Bristowes braveries:
Then viewes the Sommersetian soyle;
Through Marshes, Mines, and Mores doth toyle,
To Avalon to Arthurs Grave,
Sadlie bemoan'd of Ochy Cave.
Then with delight shee bravelie brings
The Princely Parret from her Springs:
Preparing for the learned Plea
(The next Song) in the Severne Sea.

Up with the jocund Larke (Too long we take our rest.)
Whilst yet the blushing Dawne out of the cheerfull East
Is ushering forth the Day to light the Muse along:
Whose most delightfull touch, and sweetnesse of her Song,
Shall force the lustie Swaines out of the Country-townes,
To lead the loving Girles in daunces to the Downes.

The Nymphs, in Selwoods shades and Bradens woods that bee,
Their Oaken wreathes, ô Muse, shall offer up to thee.
And when thou shap'st thy course tow'rds where the soile is rank,
The Sommersetian mayds, by swelling Sabryns bank
Shall strewe the waies with flowers (where thou art comming on)
Brought from the Marshie-grounds by aged Avalon.

From Sarum thus we set, remov'd from whence it stood
By Avon to reside, her deerest loved Flood:
Where her imperious a Fane her former seate disdaines,
And proudly over-tops the spacious neighboring Plaines.
What pleasures hath this Ile, of us esteem'd most deere,
In any place, but poore unto the plentie heere?
The chaulkie Chiltern fields, nor Kelmarsh selfe compares
With Everley for store and swiftnes of her Hares:
A horse of greater speed, nor yet a righter hound,
Not any where twixt Kent and d Calidon is found.
Nor yet the levell South can shewe a smoother Race,
Whereas the ballow Nag out-strips the winds in chase;
As famous in the West for matches yeerelie tride,
As e Garterley, possest of all the Northen pride:
And on his match, as much the Western horseman layes,
As the rank-riding Scots upon their Gallowayes.

And as the Westerne soyle as sound a Horse doth breed,
As doth the land that lies betwixt the Trent and Tweed:
No Hunter, so, but finds the breeding of the West,
The onely kind of Hounds, for mouth and nostrill best;
That cold doth sildome fret, nor heat doth over-haile;
As standing in the Flight, as pleasant on the Traile;
Free hunting, easely checkt, and loving every Chase;
Straight running, hard, and tough, of reasonable pase:
Not heavie, as that hound which Lancashire doth breed;
Nor as the Northerne kind, so light and hot of speed,
Upon the cleerer Chase, or on the foyled Traine,
Doth make the sweetest cry, in Wood-land, or on Plaine.

Where she, of all the Plaines of Britaine, that doth beare
The name to be the first (renowned everie where)
Hath worthily obtaind that Stonendge there should stand:
Shee, first of Plaines; and g that, first Wonder of the Land.
Shee Wansdike also winnes, by whom shee is imbrac't,
That in his aged armes doth gird her ampler wast:
Who (for a mightie Mound sith long he did remaine
Betwixt the Mercians rule, and the West-Saxons raigne,
And therefore of his place him selfe hee proudly bare)
Had very oft beene heard with Stonendge to compare;
Whom for a paltry Ditch, when Stonendge pleasd t'upbraid,

The old man taking heart, thus to that Trophy said;

Dull heape, that thus thy head above the rest doost reare,
Precisely yet not know'st who first did place thee there;
But Traytor basely turn'd to Merlins skill doost flie,
And with his Magiques doost thy Makers truth belie:
Conspirator with Time, now growen so meane and poore,
Comparing these his spirits with those that went before;
Yet rather art content thy Builders praise to lose,
Then passed greatnes should thy present wants disclose.
Ill did those mightie men to trust thee with their storie,
That hast forgot their names, who rear'd thee for their glorie:
For all their wondrous cost, thou that hast serv'd them so,
What tis to trust to Tombes, by thee we easely know.

In these invectives thus whilst Wansdick doth complaine,
He interrupted is by that imperious Plaine,
To hear two crystall Floods to court her, that apply
Themselves, which should be seene most gracious in her eye.

First, Willy boasts her selfe more worthy then the other,
And better farre deriv'd: as having to her mother
Faire a Selwood, and to bring up b Diver in her traine;
Which, when the envious soile would from her course restraine,
A mile creeps under earth, as flying all resort:
And how cleere Nader waits attendance in her Court;
And therefore claimes of right the Plaine should hold her deere,
Which gives that Towne the name; which likewise names the Shire.

The Easterne Avon vaunts, and doth upon her take
To be the onelie child of shadefull Savernake,
As Ambrayes ancient flood; her selfe and to enstile
The Stonendges best-lov'd, first wonder of the Ile;
And what (in her behoofe) might any want supply,
Shee vaunts the goodlie seat of famous Saliburie;
Where meeting prettie Bourne, with many a kind embrace,
Betwixt their crystall armes they clip that loved place.

Report, as lately rais'd, unto these Rivers came,
That Bathes cleere Avon (waxt imperious through her fame)
Their daliance should deride; and that by her disdaine,
Some other smaller Brooks, belonging to the Plaine,
A question seem'd to make, whereas the Shire sent forth
Two Avons, which should be the flood of greatest worth;
This streame, which to the South the d Celtick Sea doth get,
Or that which from the North saluteth Somerset.

This when these Rivers heard, that even but lately strove

Which best did love the Plaine, or had the Plaines best love,
They straight themselves combine: for Willy wiselie waide,
That should her Avon lose the day for want of aide,
If one so great and neere were overprest with power,
The Foe (shee beeing lesse) would quicklie her devour.
As two contentious Kings, that on each little jarre,
Defiances send forth, proclaiming open warre,
Untill some other Realme, that on their frontires lies,
Be hazarded againe by other enemies,
Doe then betwixt themselves to composition fall,
To countercheck that sword, else like to conquer all:
So falls it with these Floods, that deadlie hate doe beare.
And whilst on either part strong preparations were,
It greatly was suppos'd strange strife would there have been,
Had not the goodly Plaine (plac't equally betweene)
Fore-warn'd them to desist, and off their purpose brake:
When in behalfe of Plaines thus (gloriously) she spake;
 a Away yee barb'rous Woods; How ever yee be plac't
On Mountaines, or in Dales, or happily be grac't
With floods, or marshie fels, with pasture, or with earth
By nature made to till, that by the yeerely birth
The large-bay'd Barne doth fill, yea though the fruitfulst ground.
For, in respect of Plaines, what pleasure can be found
In darke and sleepie shades? where mists and rotten fogs
Hang in the gloomie thicks, and make unstedfast bogs,
By dropping from the boughs, the o're-growen trees among,
With Caterpillers kells, and duskie cobwebs hong.

The deadlie Screech-owle sits, in gloomie covert hid:
Whereas the smooth-brow'd Plaine, as liberallie doth bid
The Larke to leave her Bowre, and on her trembling wing
In climing up tow'rds heaven, her high-pitcht Hymnes to sing
Unto the springing Day; when gainst the Sunnes arise
The earlie Dawning strewes the goodly Easterne skies
With Roses every where: who scarcelie lifts his head
To view this upper world, but hee his beames doth spred
Upon the goodlie Plaines; yet at his Noonesteds hight,
Doth scarcelie pierce the Brake with his farre-shooting sight.

The gentle Shepheards heer survay their gentler sheepe:
Amongst the bushie woods luxurious Satyrs keepe.
To these brave sports of field, who with desire is wonne,
To see his Grey-hound course, his Horse (in diet) runne,
His deepe mouth'd Hound to hunt, his long-wingd Haulk to flie,
To these most noble sports his mind who doth apply,
Resorts unto the Plaines. And not a foughten Field,
Where Kingdoms rights have laine upon the speare and shield,
But Plaines have beene the place; and all those Trophies hie

That ancient times have rear'd to noble memorie:
As, Stonendge, that to tell the British Princes slaine
By those false Saxons fraud, here ever shall remaine.
It was upon the Plaine of Mamre (to the fame
Of mee and all our kind) whereas the Angels came
To Abraham in his Tent, and there with him did feed;
To Sara his deere wife then promising the seed
By whom all Nations should so highly honor'd bee,
In which the Sonne of God they in the flesh should see.
But Forests, to your plague there soone will come an Age,
In which all damned sinnes most vehemently shall rage.
An Age! what have I said! nay, Ages there shall rise,
So senselesse of the good of their posterities,
That of your greatest Groves they scarce shall leave a tree
(By which the harmelesse Deere may after sheltred bee)
Their luxurie and pride but onely to maintaine,
And for your long excesse shall turne ye all to paine.

Thus ending; though some hils themselves that doe applie
To please the goodly Plaine, still standing in her eie,
Did much applaud her speech (as Haradon, whose head
Old Ambry still doth awe, and Bagden from his sted,
Survaying of the Vies, whose likings do allure
Both Ouldbry and Saint Anne; and they againe procure
Mount Marting-sall: and he those hils that stand aloofe,
Those brothers Barbury, and Badbury, whose proofe
Addes much unto her praise) yet in most high disdaine,
The Forrests take her words, and sweare the prating Plaine
Growne old began to doate: and Savernake so much
Is galled with her taunts (whom they so nearely touch)
That she in spitefull tearmes defies her to her face;
And Aldburne with the rest, though being but a Chase,
At worse then nought her sets: but Bradon all afloate
When it was tolde to her, set open such a throate,
That all the countrey rang. She cals her barren Jade,
Base Queane, and riv'ld Witch, and wisht she could be made
But worthy of her hate (which most of all her grieves)
The basest beggers Baude, a harborer of theeves.
Then Peusham, and with her old Blackmore (not behinde)
Do wish that from the Seas some soultrie Southerne winde,
The foule infectious damps, and poisned aires would sweepe,
And poure them on the Plaine, to rot her and her Sheepe.

But whilst the sportive Muse delights her with these things,
She strangely taken is with those delicious Springs
Of Kenet rising here, and of the nobler Streame
Of Isis setting forth upon her way to Tame,
By Greeklade; whose great name yet vaunts that learned tong,

Where to great Britaine first the sacred Muses song;
Which first were seated here, at Isis bountious head,
As telling that her fame should through the world be spread;
And tempted by this flood, to Oxford after came,
There likewise to delight her bridegroome, lovely Tame:
Whose beautie when they saw, so much they did adore,
That Greeklade they forsooke, and would goe backe no more.

Then Bradon gently brings forth Avon from her source:
Which Southward making soone in her most quiet course,
Receives the gentle Calne: when on her rising side,
First Blackmoore crownes her banke, as Peusham with her pride
Sets out her murmuring sholes, till (turning to the West)
Her, Somerset receives, with all the bounties blest
That Nature can produce in that Bathonian Spring,
Which from the Sulphury Mines her med'cinall force doth bring;
As Physick hath found out by colour, taste, and smell,
Which taught the world at first the vertue of that Well;
What quickliest it could cure: which men of knowledge drew
From that first minerall cause: but some that little knew
(Yet felt the great effects continually it wrought)
Ascrib'd it to that skill, which Bladud hither brought,
As by that learned King the Bathes should be begunne;
Not from the quickned Mine, by the begetting Sunne
Giving that naturall power, which by the vig'rous sweate,
Doth lend the lively Springs their perdurable heate
In passing through the veines, where matter doth not need;
Which in that minerous earth insep'rably doth breed:
So nature hath purvai'd, that during all her raigne
The Bathes their native power for ever shall retaine:
Where Time that Citie built, which to her greater fame,
Preserving of that Spring, participates her name;
The Tutilage whereof (as those past worlds did please)
Some to Minerva gave, and some to Hercules:
Proud Phoebus loved Spring, in whose Diurnall course,
When on this point of earth he bends his greatest force,
By his so strong approach, provokes her to desire;
Stung with the kindly rage of loves impatient fire:
Which boiling in her wombe, projects (as to a birth)
Such matter as she takes from the grosse humorous earth;
Till purg'd of dregs and slime, and her complexion cleere,
She smileth on the light, and lookes with mirthfull cheere.

Then came the lustie Froome, the first of floods that met
Faire Avon entring in to fruitfull Somerset,
With her attending Brooks; and her to Bathe doth bring,
Much honoured by that place, Minerva's sacred Spring.
To noble Avon, next, cleere Chute as kindly came,

To Bristow her to beare, the fairest seat of Fame:
To entertaine this flood, as great a mind that hath,
And striving in that kind farre to excell the Bath.
As when some wealthy Lord, prepares to entertaine
A man of high account, and feast his gallant traine;
Of him that did the like, doth seriously enquire
His diet, his device, his service, his attire;
That varying every thing (exampled by his store)
He everie way may passe what th'other did before:
Even so this Citie doth; the prospect of which place
To her faire building addes an admirable grace;
Well fashioned as the best, and with a double wall,
As brave as any Towne; but yet excelling all
For casement, that to health is requisit and meete;
Her piled shores, to keepe her delicate and sweete:
Hereto, she hath her Tides; that when she is opprest
With heat or drought, still poure their floods upon her breast.
To Mendip then the Muse upon the South inclines,
Which is the onely store, and Coffer of her Mines:
Elsewhere the Fields and Meades their sundry traffiques suit:
The Forrests yeeld her wood, the Orchards give her fruit.
As in some rich mans house his severall charges lie,
There stands his Wardrobe, here remaines his Treasurie;
His large prouision there, of Fish, of Fowl, and Neat;
His Cellars for his Wines, his Larders for his meate;
There Banquet houses, Walkes for pleasure; here againe
Cribs, Graners, Stables, Barnes, the other to maintaine:
So this rich countrey hath, it selfe what may suffice;
Or that which through exchange a smaller want supplies:
Yet Ochyes dreadfull Hole still held her selfe disgrac't,
With th'wonders of this Ile that she should not be plac't:
But that which vext her most, was, that the aPeakish Caue
Before her darkesome selfe such dignitie should have;
And b th'Wyches for their Salts such state on them should take;
Or Cheshire should preferre her sad cDeath-boding-lake;
And Stonendge in the world should get so high respect,
Which imitating Arte but idly did erect:
And that amongst the rest, the vaine inconstant dDee,
By changing of his Foards, for one should reckond bee;
As of another sort, wood turn'd to e stone; among,
Th'anatomized f Fish, and Fowles from g planchers sprong:
And on the Cambrian side those strange and wondrous h Springs,
Our i beasts that seldome drinke; a thousand other things
Which Ochy inly vext, that they to fame should mount,
And greatly griev'd her friends for her so small account;
That there was scarcely Rock, or River, Marsh, or Meare
That held not Ochyes wrongs (for all held Ochy deare)
§ In great and high disdaine: and Froome for her disgrace

Since scarcely ever washt the Colesleck from her face;
But (melancholy growne) to Avon gets a path,
Through sickenesse forc't to seeke for cure unto the Bath:
And Chedder for meere griefe his teene he could not wreake,
Gusht forth so forcefull streames, that he was like to breake
The greater bankes of Ax, as from his mothers Caue,
He wandred towards the Sea; for madnesse who doth raue
At his drad mothers wrong: but who so wo begon
For Ochy, as the Ile of ancient Aualon?
Who having in her selfe, as inward cause of griefe,
Neglecteth yet her owne, to give her friend reliefe.
The other so againe for her doth sorrow make,
And in the Iles behalfe the dreadfull Cauerne spake;
O three times famous Ile, where is that place that might
Be with thy selfe compar'd for glorie and delight,
Whilst Glastenbury stood? exalted to that pride,
Whose Monasterie seem'd all other to deride?
O who thy ruine sees, whom wonder doth not fill
With our great fathers pompe, deuotion, and their skill?
Thou more then mortall power (this judgement rightly wai'd)
Then present to assist, at that foundation lai'd;
On whom for this sad waste, should Justice lay the crime?
Is there a power in Fate, or doth it yeeld to Time?
Or was their error such, that thou could'st not protect
Those buildings which thy hand did with their zeale erect?
To whom didst thou commit that monument, to keepe,
That suffreth with the dead their memory to sleepe?
When not great Arthurs Tombe, not holyalosephs Graue,
From sacriledge had power their sacred bones to saue;
He who that God in man to his sepulchre brought,
Or he which for the faith twelue famous battels fought.
What? Did so many Kings do honor to that place,
For Auarice at last so vilely to deface?
For reu'rence, to that seat which hath ascribed beene,
bTrees yet in winter bloome, and beare their Summers greene.
This said, she many a sigh from her full stomacke cast,
Which issued through her breast in many a boystrous blast;
And with such floods of teares her sorrowes doth condole,
As into rivers turne within that darkesome hole:
Like sorrow for her selfe, this goodly Ile doth trie;
Imbrac't by Selwoods sonne, her flood the lovely Bry,
On whom the Fates bestow'd (when he conceived was)
He should be much belou'd of many a daintie Lasse;
Who gives all leaue to like, yet of them liketh none:
But his affection sets on beautious Aualon;
Though many a plump-thigh'd moore, & ful-flanck't marsh do proue
To force his chaste desires, so dainty of his love.
First Sedgemore shewes this floud, her bosome all unbrac't,

And casts her wanton armes about his slender wast:
Her lover to obtaine, so amorous Audry seekes:
And Gedney softly steales sweet kisses from his cheekes.
One takes him by the hand, intreating him to stay:
Another pluckes him backe, when he would faine away:
But, having caught at, length, whom long he did pursue,
Is so intranc't with love, her goodly parts to view,
That altring quite his shape, to her he doth appeare,
And casts his crystall selfe into an ample Meare:
But for his greater growth when needs he must depart,
And forc't to leaue his Love (though with a heavie hart)
As hee his back doth turne, and is departing out,
The batning marshie Brent enuirons him about:
But lothing her imbrace, away in haste he flings,
And in the Severne Sea surrounds his plentious Springs.
But, dallying in this place so long why doost thou dwell,
So many sundry things here having yet to tell?
Occasion calls the Muse her pynions to prepare.
Which (striking with the wind the vast and open aire)
Now, in the finnie Heaths, then in the Champains roues;
Now, measures out this Plaine; and then survayes those groues;
The batfull pastures fenc't, and most with quickset mound,
The sundry sorts of soyle, diversitie of ground;
Where Plow-men cleanse the Earth of rubbish, weed, and filth,
And give the fallow lands their seasons and their tylth:
Where, best for breeding horse; where cattell fitst to keepe;
Which good for bearing Corne; which pasturing for sheepe:
The leane and hungry earth, the fat and marly mold,
Where sands be alwaies hot, and where the clayes be cold;
With plentie where they waste, some others toucht with want:
Heere set, and there they sowe; here proine, and there they plant.
As Wiltshire is a place best pleas'd with that resort
Which spend away the time continuallie in sport;
So Somerset, her selfe to profit doth apply,
As given all to gaine, and thriving huswifrie.
For, whereas in a Land one doth consume and wast,
Tis fit another be to gather in as fast:
This liketh moorie plots, delights in sedgie Bowres,
The grassy garlands loves, and oft attyr'd with flowres
Of ranke and mellow gleabe; a sward as soft as wooll,
With her complexion strong, a belly plumpe and full.
Thus whilst the active Muse straines out these various things,
Cleere Parret makes approach, with all those plentious Springs
Her fruitful banks that blesse; by whose Monarchall sway,
Shee fortifies her selfe against that mightie day
Wherein her utmost power she should be forc't to try.
For, from the Druides time there was a prophecie,
That there should come a day (which now was neere at hand

By all forerunning signes) that on the Easterne Strand,
If Parret stood not fast upon the English side,
They all should be supprest: and by the British pride
In cunning ouer-come; for why, impartiall Fate
(Yet constant alwaies to the Britains crazed state)
Forbad they yet should fall; by whom she meant to showe
How much the present Age, and after-times should owe
Unto the line of Brute. Cleere Parret therefore prest
Her tributarie Streames, and whollie her addrest
Against the ancient Foe: First, calling to her ayde
Two Rivers of one name; which seeme as though they stayd
Their Empresse as she went, her either hand that take.
The first upon the right, as from her source, doth make
Large Muchelney an Ile, and unto Ivell lends
Her hardlie-rendred name: That on her left, descends
From Neroch's neighboring woods; which, of that Forest borne,
Her rivalls proffered grace opprobriously doth scorne.
Shee by her wandring course doth Athelney in-Ile:
And for the greater state, herselfe she doth instile
The nearest neighbouring flood to Arthurs ancient seat,
Which made the Britaines name through all the world so great.
Like Camelot, what place, was ever yet renownd?
Where, as at Carlion, oft, hee kept the Table-round,
Most famous for the sports at Pentecost so long,
From whence all Knightlie deeds, and brave atchievements sprong.
As some soft-sliding Rill, which from a lesser head
(Yet in his going forth, by many a Fountaine fed)
Extends it selfe at length unto a goodly streame:
So, almost through the world his fame flew from this Realme;
That justlie I may charge those ancient Bards of wrong,
So idly to neglect his glorie in their Song.
For some aboundant braine, ô there had been a storie
Beyond the Blind-mans might to have inhanc't our glorie.
Tow'rds the Sabrinian Sea then Parret setting on,
To her attendance next comes in the beautious Tone,
Crown'd with embroidred banks, and gorgeously arraid
With all th'enamild flowers of manie a goodly Mead:
In Orchards richly clad; whose proud aspyring boughes
Euen of the tallest woods doe scorne a iote to loose,
Though Selwoods mighty selfe and Neroch standing by:
The sweetnes of her soyle through every Coast doth fly.
What eare so empty is, that hath not heard the sound
Of Tauntons fruitfull aDeane? not matcht by any ground;
By bAthelney ador'd, a neighbourer to her Land;
Whereas those higher hills to view faire Tone that stand,
Her coadiuting Springs with much content behold:
Where Sea-ward Quantock stands as Neptune he controld,
And Blackdown In-land borne, a Mountain and a Mound,

As though he stood to look about the Country round:
But Parret as a Prince, attended heere the while,
Inricht with every Moore, and every In-land Ile,
Upon her taketh State, well forward tow'rds her fall
Whom lastly yet to grace, and not the least of all,
Comes in the lively Carre, a Nymph, most lovely cleere,
From Somerton sent downe the Soueraigne of the Sheere;
Which makes our Parret proude. And wallowing in excesse,
Whilst like a Prince she vaunts amid the watry presse,
The breathlesse Muse awhile her wearied wings shall ease,
To get her strength to stem the rough Sabrinian Seas.


THE FOURTH SONG

THE ARGUMENT

England and Wales strive, in this Song,
To whether, Lundy doth belong:
When eithers Nymphs, to cleere the doubt,
By Musick meane to try it out.
Of mightie Neptune leaue they aske:
Each one betakes her to her taske;
The Britaines, with the Harpe and Crowd:
The English, both with still and loud.
The Britaines chaunt King Arthurs glory
The English sing their Saxons storie.
The Hills of Wales their weapons take,
And are an uprore like to make,
To keepe the English part in awe.
There's heaue, and shoue, and hold, and draw;
That Severne can them scarce divide,
Till Judgment may the Cause decide.

This while in Sabrin's Court strong factions strangely grew,
Since Cornwall for her owne, and as her proper due,
Claim'd Lundy, which was said to Cambria to belong,
Who oft had sought redresse for that her ancient wrong:
But her inveterate Foe, borne-out by Englands might,
O're-swaies her weaker power; that (now in eithers right)
As Severne finds no Flood so great, nor poorelie meane,
But that the naturall Spring (her force which doth maintaine)
aFrom this or that shee takes; so from this Faction free
(Begun about this Ile) not one was like to bee.
This Lundy is a Nymph to idle toyes inclin'd;
And, all on pleasure set, doth whollie give her mind
To see upon her shores her Fowle and Conies fed,

And wantonlie to hatch the Birds of Ganimed.
Of trafique or returne shee never taketh care:
Not prouident of pelfe, as many Ilands are:
A lustie black-brow'd Girle, with forehead broad and hie,
That often had bewitcht the Sea-gods with her eye.
Of all the In-laid Iles her Soueraigne Severne keepes,
That bathe their amorous breasts within her secret Deepes
(To love her Barry much and Silly though shee seeme,
The Flat Holme and the Steepe as likewise to esteeme)
This noblest British Nymph yet likes her Lundy best,
And to great Neptunes grace preferres before the rest.
Thus, Cambria to her right that would her selfe restore,
And rather then to losec Loëgria, lookes for more;
The Nymphs of either part, whom passion doth invade,
To triall straight will goe, though Neptune should disswade:
But of the weaker sex, the most part full of spleene,
And onely wanting strength to wreake their angry teene,
For skill their challenge make, which everie one profest,
And in the learned Arts (of knowledges the best,
And to th'heroïck spirit most pleasing under skie)
Sweet Musick, rightlie matcht with Heavenlie Poësie,
In which they all exceed: and in this kind alone
They Conquerers vow to be, or lastlie overthrowne.
Which when faire Sabrine saw (as shee is wondrous wise)
And that it were in vaine them better to advise,
Sith this contention sprang from Countries like alli'd,
That shee would not be found t'incline to either side,
To mightie Neptune sues to have his free consent
Due triall they might make: When he incontinent
His Trytons sendeth out the challenge to proclaime.
No sooner that divulg'd in his so dreadfull name,
But such a shout was sent from everie neighboring Spring,
That the report was heard through all his Court to ring:
And from the largest Streame unto the lesser Brooke,
Them to this wondrous taske they seriouslie betooke:
They curle their Ivory fronts, and not the smallest Beck
But with white Pebles makes her Tawdries for her neck;
Lay forth their amorous breasts unto the publique view,
Enamiling the white, with veines that were as blew;
Each Moore, each Marsh, each Mead, preparing rich array
To set their Rivers forth against this generall day.
Mongst Forrests, Hills, and Floods, was ne're such heaue and shoue
Sinced Albion weelded Armes against the sonne of loue.
When as the English part their courage to declare,
Them to th'appointed place immediatly prepare.
A troupe of stately Nymphs proud Avon with her brings
(As shee that hath the charge of wisee Mineruas Springs)
From Mendip tripping downe, about the tinny Mine.

And Ax, no lesse imploy'd about this great designe,
Leads forth a lustie Rout, when Bry, with all her throng
(With very madnes swolne that she had stai'd so long)
Comes from the boggie Mears and queachy fens below:
That Parret (highly pleas'd to see the gallant show)
Set out with such a traine as bone so great a sway,
The soyle but scarcely serues to give her hugenesse way.
Then the Deuonian Tawe, from Dertmore deckt with pearle,
Unto the conflict comes; with her that gallant Girle
Cleere Towridge, whom they fear'd would have estrang'd her fall:
Whose comming, lastlie, bred such courage in them all,
As drew downe many a Nymph from the Cornubian shore,
That paint their goodlie breasts with sundrie sorts of Ore.
The British, that this while had stood a view to take
What to her utmost power the publique Foe could make,
But slightlie weigh their strength: for, by her naturall kind,
As still the Britan heares a brave and noble mind;
So, trusting to their skill, and goodnes of their Cause,
For speedie Triall call, and for indifferent Lawes.
At length, by both allow'd, it to this issue grew;
To make a likely choise of some most expert crew,
Whose number comming neere unto the others dowre,
The English should not vrge they were o're-borne by powre.
Yet hardlie upon Powse they dare their hopes to lay,
For that shee hath commerce with England every day:
Nor Rosse; for that too much shee Aliens doth respect;
And following them, forgoes her ancient Dialect;
TheaVenedotian Floods, that ancient Britans were,
The Mountaines kept them backe, and shut them in the Reare:
But Brecknock, long time knowne a Country of much worth,
Unto this conflict brings her goodly Fountaines forth:
For almost not a Brooke of Morgany nor Gwent,
But from her fruitfull wombe doe fetch their hie descent.
For Brecan, was a Prince once fortunate and great
(Who dying, lent his name to that his nobler seat)
With twice twelve daughters blest, by one and onely wife:
Who for their beauties rare, and sanctive of life,
To Rivers ware transform'd; whose pureness doth declare
How excellent they were, by beeing what they are:
Who dying virgins all, and Rivers now by Fate,
To tell their former love to the unmaried state,
To Severne ships this course which now their forme doth beare;
Ere shee was made a flood, a virgin as they were.
And from the Irish seas with feare they still doe flie:
So much they yet delight in mayden companie.

Then most renowned Wales thou famous ancient place,
Which still hast been the Nurse of all the British race,

Since Nature thee denies that purple-cluster'd Vine,
Which others Temples chafes with fragrant sparkling Wine;
And being now in hand, to write thy glorious praise;
Fill me a bowle of Meath, my working spirit to raise:
And ere seuen Bookes have end, I'le strike so high a string,
Thy Bards shall stand amaz'd with wonder, whilst I sing;
That Taliessen, once which made the Rivers dance,
And in his rapture raiz'd the Mountaines from their trance,
Shall tremble at my Verse, rebounding from the skies;
Which like an earth-quake shakes the Tomb wherein he lies.
First our triumphing Muse of sprightly Uske shall tell,
And what to every Nymph attending her, befell:
Which Cray and Camlas first for Pages doth retenne;
With whom the next in place comes in the tripping Breane,
With Isker; and with her comes Hodny fine and cleere,
Of Brecknock best belov'd, the Soueraigne of the Sheere:
And Grony, at an inch, waits on her Mistress heeles.
But entring (at the last) the Monumethian fields,
Small Fidan, with Cledaugh, increase her goodly Menie,
Short Kebby, and the Brooke that christneth Abergeny.
With all her watry traine, when now at last she came
Unto that happie Towne which beares her onely name,
Bright Birthin, with her friend faire Olwy, kindly meet her;
Which for her present haste, have scarcely time to greet her:
But earnest on her way, she needsly will be gone;
So much she longs to see the ancient Carleon.
When Avon commeth in then which amongst them all
A finer is not found betwixt her head and fall.
Then Ebwith, and with her slides Snowy; which forelay
Her progresse; and for Uske keepe entrance to the Sea.
When Munno, all this while that (for her owne behoofe)
From this their great recourse had strangely stood aloofe,
Made proude by Monmouths name appointed her by Fate,
Of all the rest herein obserued speciall state.
For once the Bards foretold she should produce a a King,
Which everlasting praise to her great name should bring,
Who by his conquering sword should all the land surprise,
Which twixt the Penmenmaur and the Pyreni lies:
She therefore is allow'd her leasure; and by her
They winne the goodly Wye whome strongly she doth stirre
Her powerfull helpe to lend: which else she had denide,
Because her selfe so oft to England she allyed:
But b'ing by Munno made for Wales, away she goes.
Which when as Throggy sees her selfe she headlong throwes
Into the watry throng, with many another Rill,
Repairing to the Welch, their number up to fill.
That Remny when shee saw, those gallant Nymphes of Gwent
On this appointed match, were all so hotlie bent,

Where shee of ancient time had parted, as a Mound
The Monumethian fields, and Glamorganian ground,
Intreats the Taffe along, as gray as any glasse:
With whom cleere Cunno comes, a lustie Cambrian Lasse:
Then Elwy, and with her Ewenny holds her way,
And Ogmore, that would yet be there as soone as they,
By Avon called in: when nimbler Neath anon
(To all the neighbouring Nymphs for her rare beauties known;
Besides her double head, to helpe her streame that hath
Her handmaids, Melta sweet, cleere Hepsey, and Tragath)
From Brecknock forth doth breake then Dulas and Cledaugh,
By Morgany doe drive her through her watry a saugh;
With Tawt taking part t'assist the Cambrian power:
Then Lhu and Logar, given to strengthen them by Gower.
Mongst whom, some Bards there were, that in their sacred rage
Recorded the Descents, and acts of everie Age.
Some with their nimble joynts that strooke the warbling string;
In fingering some unskild, but onelie us'd to sing
Unto the others Harpe: of which you both might find
Great plentie, and of both excelling in their kind,
That at the Stethva oft obtain'd a Visitors praise,
Had wonne the Siluer Harpe, and worne Apollos Bayes:
Whose Verses they deduc't from those first golden times,
Of sundry sorts of Feet, and sundly sutes of Rimes.
In Englins some there were that on their subiect straine;
Some Makers that againe affect the loftier vaine,
Rehearse their high conceits in Cowiths: other-some
In Owdells theirs expresse as matter haps to come;
So varying still their Moods, obseruing yet in all
Their Quantities, their Rests, their Geasures metricall:
For to that sacred skill they most themselues apply:
Addicted from their births so much to Poësie,
That in the Mountaines those who scarce have seene a Booke,
Most skilfully will make, as though from Art they tooke.
And as Loëgria spares not any thing of worth
That any way might set her goodly Rivers forth,
As stones by nature out from the Cambrian Strond;
Her Dertmore sends them Pearle; Rock vincent, Diamond:
So Cambria, of her Nymphs especiall care will have.
For Conwy sends them Pearle to make them wondrous brave;
The sacred Virgins well, her mosse most sweet and rare,
Against infectious damps for Pomander to weare:
And Goldeliff of his Ore in plentious sort allowes,
To spangle their attyers, and deck their amorous browes
And lastlie, holie Dee (whose pray're were highly priz'd,
As one in Heavenlie things deuourlie exercis'd
Who, a changing of his Fourds, by divination had
Fore-told the neighboring folke of fortune good or bad)

In their intended course sith needs they will proceed,
His Benediction sends in way of happy speed.
And though there were such haste unto this long-lookt howre,
Yet let they not to call upon th'Eternall Power.
For, who will have his worke his wished end to winne,
Let him with hartie prayer religiouslie beginne.
Wherefore the English part, with full deuoutintent,
In meet and godlie sort to Glastenbury sent,
Beseeching of the Saints in Avalon that were,
There offring at their Tombes for everie one a teare,
And humblie to Saint George their Countries Patron pray,
To prosper their designe now in this mightie day.
The Britans, like deuout, their Messengers direct
To David, that he would their ancient right protect.
Mongst Hatterills loftie hills, that with the clowds are crown'd,
The Vally bEwias lies, immur'd so deep and round,
As they belowe that see the Mountaines rise so hie,
Might thinke the stragling Heards were grazing in the skie:
Which in it such a shape of solitude doth beare,
As Nature at the first appointed it for pray're
Where, in an aged Cell, with mosse and Ivie growne,
In which, not to this day the Sunne hath ever showne,
That reverent British Saint in zealous Ages past,
To contemplation liv'd, and did so trulie fast,
As he did onelie drinke what crystall Hodney yeelds,
And fed upon the Looks he gather'd in the fields.
In memorie of whom, in the reuoluing yeere
The Welch-men on his day that sacred herbe doe weare:
Where, of that holie man, as humblie they doe craue,
That in their just defence they might his furtherance have.
Thus either, well prepard the others power before,
Conuenientlie be'ing plac't upon their equall shore;
The Britans, to whose lot the Onset doth belong,
Give signall to the Foe for silene to their Song.
To tell each various Straine and turning of their Rimes,
How this in compasse falls, or that in sharpeness climes
(As where they rest and rise, how take it one from one,
As every severall Chord hath a peculiar Tone)
Euen Memorie her selfe, though striving, would come short:
But the materiall things Muse helpe me to report.
As first, t'affront the Foe, in th'ancient Britans right,
With Arthur they begin, their most renowned Knight;
The richness of the Armes their well-made a Worthie wore,
The temper of his sword the (try'd Escalaboure)
The bignes and the length of Rone, his noble Speare;
With Pridwin his great Shield, and what the proofe could beare;
His Baudrick how adorn'd with stones of wondrous price,
The sacred Virgins shape he bore for his deuice;

These monuments of worth, the ancient Britans song.
Now, doubting least these things might hold them but too long,
His warres they tooke to taske; the Land then ouer-layd
With those proud German powers: when, calling to his ayde
His kinsman Howell, brought from Britany the lesse,
Their Armies they unite, both swearing to suppresse
The Saxon, heer that sought through conquest all to gaine.
On whom he chanc't to light at Lincolne: where the Plaine
Each where from side to side lay scatter'd with the dead.
And when the conquer'd Foe, that from the conflict fled,
Betooke them to the woods, hee never left them there
Untill the British earth he forc't them to forsweare.
And as his actions rose, so raise they still their veine,
In words, whose weight best sute a sublimated straine.
They sung how he, him selfe at Badon bore that day,
When at the glorious Gole his British Scepter lay:
Two daies together how the battell stronglie stood:
bPendragons worthie sonne who waded there in blood,
Three hundred Saxons slew with his owne valiant hand.
And after (cald, the Pict, and Irish to withstand)
How he, by force of Armes Albania ouer-ran,
Pursuing of the Pict beyond Mount Calidon:
There strongly shut them up whom stoutly he subdu'd.
How Gillamore againe to Ireland he pursu'd
So oft as he presum'd the envious Pict to ayde:
And having slaine the King, the Country waste hee laid.
To Goth-land how againe this Conqueror maketh-forth
With his so prosp'rous powers into the farthest North:
Where, Island first he wonne, and Orkney after got.
To Norway sayling next with his deere Nephew Lot,
By deadlie dint of sword did Ricoll there defeat:
And having plac't the Prince on that Norwegian seat,
How this courageous King did Denmarke then controle:
That scarcelie there was found a Countrie to the Pole
That dreaded not his deeds, too long that were to tell.
And after these, in France th'adventures him befell
At Paris, in the Lists, where he with Flollio fought;
The Emperor Leons power to raise his Siege that brought.
Then bravelie set they sorth, in combat how these Knights
On horseback and on foote perform'd their severall fights:
As with what maruailous force each other they assaild,
How mighty Flollio first, how Arthur then prevail'd;
For best advantage how they trauersed their grounds,
The horrid blowes they lent, the world-amazing wounds,
Untill the Tribune, tyr'd, sanke under Arthurs sword.
Then sing they how hee first ordain'd the Circled-board,
The Knights whose martiall deeds farre fam'd that Table-round;
Which, truest in their loves; which, most in Armes renown'd:

The Lawes, which long up-held that Order, they report;
The Pentecosts prepar'd at Carleon in his Court,
That Tables ancient seate; her Temples and her Groues,
Her Palaces, her Walks, Baths, Theaters, and Stoues:
Her Academie, then, as likewise they prefer:
Of Camilot they sing, and then of Winchester.
The feasts that under-ground the Faërie did him make,
And there how he enjoyd the Lady of the Lake.
Then told they, how him selfe great Arthur did advance,
To meet (with his Allies) that puissant force in France,
By Lucius thither led; those Armies that while-ere
Affrighted all the world, by him strooke dead with feare:
Th'report of his great Acts that ouer Europe ran,
In that most famous Field he with the Emperor wan:
As how great Rython's selfe hee slew in his repaire,
Who ravisht Howells Neece, young Hellena the faire;
And for a Trophy brought the Giants coat away
Made of the beards of Kings. Then bravelie chanted they
The severall twelue pitcht Fields he with the Saxons fought:
The certaine day and place to memorie they brought;
Then by false Mordreds hand how last hee chanc't to fall,
The howre of his decease, his place of buriall.
When out the English cry'd, to interrupt their Song:
But they, which knew to this more matter must belong,
Not out at all for that, nor any whit dismay'd,
But to their well-tun'd Harps their fingers closelie laid:
Twixt every one of which they plac't their Countries Crowd,
And with courageous spirits thus boldly sang aloud;
How Merlin by his skill, and Magiques wondrous might,
From Ireland hither brought the Stonendge in a night:
And for Carmardens sake, would faine have brought to passe,
About it to have built a wall of solid Brasse:
And set his Fiends to work upon the mightie frame;
Some to the Anvile: some, that still inforc't the flame:
But whilst it was in hand, by louing of an Elfe
(For all his wondrous skill) was coosned by him selfe.
For, walking with his Fay, her to the Rocke hee brought,
In which hee oft before his Nigromancies wrought:
And going in thereat his Magiques to have showne,
Shee stopt the Cauerns mouth with an inchanted stone:
Whose cunning strongly crost, amaz'd whilst he did stand,
Shee captive him convay'd unto the Fairie Land.
Then, how the laboring spirits, to Rocks by fetters bound,
With bellowes rumbling groanes, and hammers thundring sound,
A fearefull horrid dinne still in the Earth doe keepe,
Their Master to awake, suppos'd by them to sleepe;
As at their work how still the grieved spirits repine,
Tormented in the Fire, and tyred at the Mine.

When now the British side scarce finished their Song,
But th'English that repyn'd to be delay'd so long,
All quicklie at the hint, as with one free consent,
Strooke up at once and sung each to the Instrument;
(Of sundry sorts that were, as the Musician likes)
On which the practic'd hand with perfect'st fingring strikes,
Whereby their height of skill might liveliest be exprest.
The trembling Lute some touch, some straine the Violl best
In sets which there were seene, the musick wondrous choice:
Some likewise there affect the Gamba with the voice,
To shew that England could varietie afford.
Some that delight to touch the sterner wyerie Chord,
The Cythron, the Pandore, and the Theorbo strike:
The Gittern and the Kit the wandring Fidlers like.
So were there some againe, in this their learned strife
Loud Instruments that lov'd; the Cornet and the Phife,
The Hoboy, Sagbut deepe, Recorder, and the Flute:
Euen from the shrillest Shaw me unto the Cornamute.
Some blowe the Bagpipe up, that plaies the Country-round:
The Taber and the Pipe, some take delight to sound.
Of Germanie they sung the long and ancient fame,
From whence their noble Sires the valiant Saxons came,
Who sought by Sea and Land Adventures farre and neere;
And seizing at the last upon the Britans heere,
Surpriz'd the spacious Ile, which still for theirs they hold:
As in that Countries praise how in those times of old,
Tuisco, Gomers sonne, from unbuilt Babell brought
His people to that place, with most high knowledge fraught,
And under wholsome Lawes establisht their aboad;
Whom his Tudeskt since have honor'd as a God:
Whose cleare creation made them absolute in all,
Retaining till this time their pure Originall.
And as they boast themselues the Nation most unmixt,
Their language as at first, their ancient customes fixt,
The people of the world most hardie, wise and strong;
So gloriously they show, that all the rest among
The Saxons of her sorts the very noblest were:
And of those crooked Skaines they us'd in warre to beare,
Which in their thundring tongue, the Germans, Handseax name,
They Saxons first were call'd: whose farre extended fame
For hardiness in warre, whom danger never fraid,
Allur'd the Britans here to call them to their ayde:
From whom they after reft Loëgria as their own,
Brutes ofspring then too weake to keepe it beeing grown.
This told: the Nymphs againe, in nimbler straines of wit,
Next neatly come about, the Englishmen to quit
Of that inglorious blot by Bastard William brought
Upon this conquered Ile: then which Fate never wrought

A fitter meane (say they) great Germany to grace;
To graft againe in one, two Remnants of her race:
Upon their severall waies, two severall times that went
To forrage for themselues. The first of which shee sent
To get their seat in Gaul: which on Nuestria light,
And (in a famous warre the Frenchmen put to flight)
Possest that fruitfull place, where onely from their name
Call'd North-men (from the North of Germanie that came,
Who thence expeld the Gaules, and did their roomes supply)
This, first Nuestria nam'd, was then call'd Normandy.
That by this meanes, the lesse (in conquering of the great)
Be'ing drawne from their late home unto this ampler seat,
Resyding heere, resign'd what they before had wonne;
That as the Conquerors blood, did to the conquered runne:
So kindlie beeing mixt, and up together growne,
As severed, they were here; united, stil her owne.

But these mysterious things desisting now to show
(The secret works of heaven) to long Descents they goe:
How Egelred (the Sire of Edward the last King
Of th'English Saxon Line) by nobly marying
With hardie Richards heire, the Norman Emma, bred
Alliance in their bloods. Like Brooks that from one head
Beare severall waies (as though to sundry Seas to hast)
But by the varying soyle, int'one againe are cast:
So chanced it in this the neernes of their blood.
For when as Englands right in question after stood,
Proud Harould, Goodwins heire, the Scepter having wonne
From Edgar Etheling young, the outlaw'd Edwards sonne;
The valiant Bastard this his onelie colour made,
With his brave Norman powers this kingdome to invade.
Which leaving, they proceed to Pedigrees againe,
Their after-Kings to fetch from that old Saxon straine;
From Margarit that was made the Scottish Malcoms Bride,
Who to her Grandsire had courageous Ironside:
Which out-law'd Edward left; whose wife to him did bring
This Margarit Queene of Scots, and Edgar Etheling:
That Margarit brought forth Maud; which gracious Macolme gaue
To Henry Beuclarks bed (so Fate it pleas'd to have)
Who him a daughter brought; which Heaven did strangely spare:
And for the speciall love he to the mother bare,
Her Maude againe he nam'd, to th'Almain Emperor wed:
Whose Dowager whilst shee liv'd (her puissant Caesar dead)
She th'Earle of Anjou next to husband doth prefer.
The second Henry then by him begot of her,
Into the Saxon Line the Scepter thus doth bring.

Then presently againe prepare themselues to sing

The sundry foraine Fields the English-men had fought.
Which when the Mountaines sawe (and not in vaine) they thought
That if they still went on as thus they had begon,
Then from the Cambrian Nymphs (sure) Lundy would be won.
And therefore from their first they challeng'd them to flie;
And (idly running on with vaine prolixitie)
A larger subiect tooke then it was fit they should.

But, whilst those would proceed, these threatning them to hold,
Black-Mountaine for the love he to his Country bare,
As to the beautious Uske, his joy and onely care
(In whose defence t'appeare more sterne and full of dread)
Put on a Helme of clowds upon his rugged head.
Mounchdeny doth the like for his beloved Tawe:
Which quicklie all the rest by their example drawe:
As Hatterell in the right of ancient Wales will stand.
To these three Mountaines, first of the Erekinnian Band,
The Monumethian Hills, like insolent and stout,
On lostie tip-toes then began to looke about;
That Skeridvaur at last (a Mountaine much in might,
In hunting that had set his absolute delight)
Caught up his Country Hooke; nor cares for future harmes,
But irefully enrag'd, would needs to open Armes:
Which quicklie put Penvayle in such outrageous heat,
That whilst for verie teene his hairelesse scalpe doth sweat,
The Blorench looketh bigge upon his bared crowne:
And tall Tomberlow seemes so terribly to frowne,
That where it was suppos'd with small adoe or none
Th'event of this debate would easely have been known,
Such strange tumultuous stirres upon this strife ensue,
As where all griefes should end, old sorrowes still renue:
That Severne thus forewarn'd to looke unto the worst
(And findes the latter ill more dangerous then the first)
The doome she should pronounce, yet for a while delay'd,
Till these rebellious routs by justice might be stay'd;
A period that doth put to my Discourse so long,
To finish this debate the next ensuing Song.


THE FIFTH SONG

THE ARGUMENT

In this Song, Severne gives the doome
What of her Lundy should become
And whilst the nimble Cambrian Rills
Daunce Hy-day-gies amongst the Hills,

The Muse them to Carmarden brings;
Where Merlins wondrous birth shee sings.
From thence to Penbrooke shee doth make,
To see how Milford state doth take:
The scattered Ilands there doth tell:
And, visiting Saint Davids Cell,
Doth sport her all the shores along,
Preparing the ensuing Song.

Now Sabrine, as a Queene, miraculouslie faire,
Is absolutelie plac't in her Emperiall Chaire
Of Crystall richlie wrought, that gloriously did shine,
Her Grace becomming well, a creature so Divine:
And as her God-like selfe, so glorious was her Throne,
In which himselfe to sit great Neptune had been known;
Whereon there were ingrau'd those Nymphs the God had woo'd,
And every severall shape wherein for love he su'd;
Each daughter, her estate and beautie, every sonne;
What Nations he had rul'd, what Countries he had wonne.
No Fish in this wide waste but with exceeding cost
Was there in Antique worke most curiously imbost.
Shee, in a watchet weed, with manie a curious waue,
Which as a princelie gift great Amphitrite gaue;
Whose skirts were to the knee, with Corall fring'd belowe
To grace her goodly steppes. And where she meant to goe,
The path was strew'd with Pearle: which though they Orient were,
Yet scarce knowne from her feet, they were so wondrous cleere:
To whom the Mermaids hold her Glasse, that she may see
Before all other Floods how farre her beauties bee:
Who was by Nereus taught, the most profoundly wise,
That learned her the skill of hidden Prophecies,
By Thetis speciall care; as aChiron earst had done
To that proud bane of Troy, her god-resembling sonne.
For her wise censure now, whilst everie listning Flood
(When reason some-what coold their late distempred mood)
Inclosed Severne in; before this mightie rout,
Shee sitting well prepar'd, with countenance graue and stout,
Like some great learned Judge, to end a waightie Cause,
Well furnisht with the force of Arguments and Lawes,
And everie speciall proofe that justlie may be brought;
Now with a constant brow, a firme and setled thought,
And at the point to give the last and finall doome:
The people crowding neere within the pestred roome,
A slowe, soft murmuring moues amongst the wondring throng,
As though with open eares they would deuoure his tongue:
So Severne bare her selfe, and silence so she wanne,
When to th'assembly thus shee seriouslie began;

My neere and loved Nymphs, good hap yee both betide:
Well Britans have yee sung; you English, well repli'd:
Which to succeeding times shall memorize your stories
To either Countries praise, as both your endlesse glories.
And from your listning eares, sith vaine it were to hold
What all-appointing Heaven will plainlie shall be told,
Both gladlie be you pleas'd: for thus the Powers reueale,
That when the Norman Line in strength shall lastlie faile
(Fate limiting the time) th'ancient Britan race
Shall come againe to sit upon the soueraigne place.
A branch sprung out of Brute, th'imperiall top shall get,
Which grafted in the stock of great Plantaginet,
The Stem shall strongly wax, as still the Trunk doth wither:
That power which bare it thence, againe shall bring it thither
By Tudor, with faire winds from little Britaine driven,
To whom the goodlie Bay of Milford shall be given;
As thy wise Prophets, Wales, fore-told his wisht arrive,
And how Lewellins Line in him should doubly thrive.
For from his issue sent to Albany before,
Where his neglected blood, his vertue did restore,
Hee first unto himselfe in faire succession gain'd
The Stewards nobler name; and afterward attain'd
The royall Scottish wreath, upholding it in state.
This Stem, to Tudors joyn'd (which thing all-powerfull Fate
So happily produc't out of that prosperous Bed,
Whose mariages conjoynd the White-rose and the Red)
Suppressing every Plant, shall spred it selfe so wide,
As in his armes shall clip the Ile on every side.
By whom three sever'd Realmes in one shall firmlie stand,
As Britain-founding Brute first Monarchiz'd the Land:
And Cornwall, for that thou no longer shalt contend,
But to old Cambria cleaue, as to thy ancient friend,
Acknowledge thou thy Brood, of Brutes high blood to bee;
And what hath hapt to her, the like t'have chanc't to thee;
The Britains to receive, when Heaven on them did lowre,
Loegria forc't to leaue; who from the Saxons powre
Themselues in Deserts, Creeks, and Mount'nous wasts bestow'd,
Or where the fruitlesse Rocks could promise them aboad:
Why strive yee then for that, in little time that shall
(As you are all made one) be one unto you all;
Then take my finall doome pronounced lastlie, this:
That Lundy like ally'd to Wales and England is.

Each part most highlie pleas'd, then up the Session brake:
When to the learned Maids againe Invention spake;
O yee Pegasian Nymphs, that hating viler things;
Delight in loftie Hills, and in delicious Springs,
That on Piërus borne, and named of the place,

The Thracian Pimpla love, and Pindus often grace;
In Aganippas Fount, and in Castalia's brims,
That often have been known to bathe your crystall lims,
Conduct me through these Brooks, and with a fastned clue,
Direct mee in my course, to take a perfect view
Of all the wandring Streames, in whose entransing gyres,
Wise Nature oft her selfe her workmanship admires
(So manifold they are, with such Meanders wound,
As may with wonder seeme invention to confound)
That to those British names, untaught the eare to please,
Such relish I may give in my delicious layes,
That all the armed Orks of Neptunes grislie Band,
With musick of my verse, amaz'd may listning stand;
As when his Trytons trumps doe them to battell call
Within his surging lists to combat with the Whale.

Thus, have we ouer-gone the Glamorganian Gowre,
Whose Promontorie (plac't to check the Oceans powre)
Kept Severne yet her selfe, till beeing growne too great,
Shee with extended armes unbounds her ancient seat:
And turning lastlie Sea, resignes unto the Maine
What soueraigntie her selfe but latelie did retaine.
Next, Loghor leads the way, who with a lustie crue
(Her wild and wandring steps that ceaseleslie pursue)
Still forward is inforc't: as, Amond thrusts her on,
And Morlas (as a mayd shee much relies upon)
Intreats her present speed assuring her withall,
Her best-beloved Ile, Bachannis, for her fall,
Stands specially prepar'd, of every thing suppli'd.

When Guendra with such grace deliberatly doth glide
As Tovy doth entice: who setteth out prepar'd
At all points like a Prince, attended with a Guard:
Of which, as by her name, the neer'st to her of kin
Is Toothy, tripping downe from Verwins rushie a Lin,
Through Rescob running out, with Pescouer to meet
Those Rills that Forest loves; and doth so kindly greet,
As to intreat their stay shee gladlie would preuaile.
Then Tranant nicelie treads upon the watry traile:
The livelie skipping Brane, along with Gwethrick goes;
In Tovies wandring banks themselues that scarcely lose,
But Mudny, with Gledaugh, and Sawthy, soone resort,
Which at Langaddock grace their Soueraignes watry Court.

As when the seruile world some gathering man espies,
Whose thriving fortune showes, he to much wealth may rise,
And through his Princes grace his followers may preferre,
Or by reuenew left by some dead Ancester;

All lowting lowe to him, him humbly they obserue,
And happy is that man his nod that may deserue:
To Tovy so they stoupe, to them upon the way
Which thus displaies the Spring within their view that lay.

Neere Denevoir the seat of the Demetian King
Whilst Cambria was herselfe, full, strong, and florishing,
There is a pleasant Spring, that constant doth abide
Hard-by these winding shores wherein wee nimblie slide;
Long of the Ocean lov'd, since his victorious hand
First proudlie did insult upon the conquer'd Land.
And though a hundred Nymphs in faire Demetia bee,
Whose features might allure the Sea-gods more then shee,
His fancie takes her forme, and her he onelie likes
(Who ere knew halfe the shafts where-with blind Cupid strikes?)
Which great and constant faith, shew'd by the God of Sea,
This cleere and lovelie Nymph so kindlie doth repay,
As suffring for his sake what love to Lover owes,
With him she sadlie ebbs, with him she proudlie flowes,
To him her secret vowes perpetually doth keepe,
Obseruing everie Lawe and custome of the Deepe.

Now Tovy towa'rd her fall (Langaddock ouer-gon)
Her Dulas forward drives: and Cothy comming on
The traine to ouer-take, the neerest way doth cast
Ere shee Carmarden get: where Gwilly, making hast,
Bright Tovy entertaines at that most famous Towne
Which her great Prophet bred who Wales doth so renowne:
And taking her a Harpe, and tuning well the strings,
To Princely Tovy thus shee of the Prophet sings;
Of Merlin and his skill what Region doth not heare?
The world shall still be full of Merlin everie where.
A thousand lingering yeeres his prophecies have runne,
And scarcely shall have end till Time it selfe be done:
Who of a British Nymph was gotten, whilst shee plaid
With a seducing Spirit, which wonne the goodlie maid;
(As all Demetia through, there was not found her peere)
Who, be'ing so much renown'd for beautie farre and neere,
Great Lords her liking sought, but still in vaine they prov'd:
That Spirit (to her unknowne) this Virgin onelie lov'd;
Which taking humane shape, of such perfection seemd,
As (all her Suters scorn'd) shee onelie him esteem'd.
Who, fayning for her sake that he was come from farre,
And richlie could endow (a lustie Batcheler)
On her that Prophet got, which from his Mothers wombe
Of things to come fore-told untill the generall Doome.

But, of his fayned birth in sporting idlie thus,

Suspect mee not, that I this dreamed Incubus
By strange opinions should licentiouslie subsist;
Or, selfe-conceited, play the humorous Platonist,
Which boldlie dares affirme, that Spirits, themselues supply
With bodies, to commix with fraile mortalitie,
And heere allow them place, beneath this lower Sphere
Of the unconstant Moone; to tempt us dailie here.
Some, earthly mixture take; as others, which aspire,
Them subt'ler shapes resume, of water, ayre, and fire,
Being those immortalls long before the Heaven, that fell,
Whose deprivation thence, determined their hell:
And loosing through their pride that place to them assign'd,
Predestined that was to mans regenerate kind,
They, for th'inveterate hate to his Election, still
Desist not him to tempt to every damned ill:
And to seduce the spirit, oft prompt the frailer blood,
Invegling it with tastes of counterfetted good,
And teach it all the sleights the Soule that may excite
To yeeld up all her power unto the appetite.
And to those curious wits if we our selues apply,
Which search the gloomie shades of deepe Philosophy,
They Reason so will clothe, as well the mind can show,
That contrarie effects, from contraries may grow;
And that the soule a shape so stronglie may conceat,
As to her selfe the-while may seeme it to creat;
By which th'abused Sense more easelie oft is led
To thinke that it enjoyes the thing imagined.

But, toyld in these darke tracts with sundrie doubts repleat,
Calme shades, and cooler streames must quench this furious heat:
Which seeking, soone we finde where Cowen in her course,
Tow'rds the Sabrinian shores, as sweeping from her sourse,
Takes Towa, calling then Karkenny by the waie,
Her through the waylesse woods of Cardisse to conuaie;
A Forrest, with her floods inuiron'd so about,
That hardly she restraines th'unruly watrie rout,
When swelling, they would seeme her Empire to inuade:
And oft the lustfull Fawnes and Satyres from her shade
Were by the streames entic't, abode with them to make.
Then Morlas meeting Taw, her kindly in doth take:
Cair comming with the rest, their watrie tracts that tread,
Increase the Cowen all; that as their generall head
Their largesse doth receive, to beare out his expence:
Who to vast Neptune leads this Courtly confluence.

To the Penbrokian parts the Muse her still doth keepe,
Upon that utmost point to the Iberian Deepe,
By Cowdra comming in: where cleere delightfull aire,

(That Forrests most affect) doth welcome her repaire;
The Heliconian Maids in pleasant groues delight:
(Floods cannot still content their wanton appetite)
And wandring in the woods, the neighbouring hils below,
With wise Apollo meet (who with his Ivory bowe
Once in the paler shades, the Serpent Python slew)
And hunting oft with him, the heartlesse Deere pursue;
Those beames then layde aside he us'd in Heaven to weare.
Another Forrest Nymph is Narber, standing neare;
That with her curled top her neighbor would astound,
Whose Groues once bravely grac't the faire Penbrokian ground,
When Albion here beheld on this extended land,
Amongst his wel-growne Woods, the shag-haird Satyrs stand
(The Syluans chiefe resort) the shores then sitting hie,
Which under water now so many fadoms lie:
And wallowing Porpice sport and lord it in the flood,
Where once the portly Oke, and large-limb'd Popler stood:
Of all the Forrests kind these two now onely left.
But Time, as guilty since to mans insatiate theft,
Transferd the English names of Townes and housholds hither,
With the industrious Dutch since soiourning together.

When wrathfull heaven the clouds so liberally bestow'd,
The Seas (then wanting roomth to lay their boystrous loade)
Upon the Belgian Marsh their pampred stomackes cast,
That peopled Cities sanke into the mightie wast.
The Flemings were inforc't to take them to their Ores,
To trie the Setting Maine to find out firmer shores;
When as this spacious Ile them entrance did allow,
To plant the Belgian stocke upon this goodly brow:
These Nations, that their tongues did naturally affect,
Both generallie forsooke the British Dialect:
As when it was decreed by all-fore-dooming Fate,
That ancient Rome should stoupe from her emperious state,
With Nations from the North then altogether fraught,
Which to her civill bounds their barbarous customes brought,
Of all her ancient spoyles and lastlie be forlorne,
From Tybers hallowed banks to old aBizantium borne:
Th'abundant Latine then old Latium lastly left,
Both of her proper forme and elegancie rest;
Before her smoothest tongue, their speech that did prefer,
And in her tables fixt their ill-shap't Character.

A divination strange the Dutch made-English have,
Appropriate to that place (as though some Power it gave)
By th'shoulder of a Ram from off the right side par'd,
Which usuallie they boile, the spade-boane beeing bar'd:
Which then the Wizard takes, and gazing there-upon,

Things long to come fore-showes, as things done long agon;
Scapes secretlie at home, as those abroad, and farre;
Murthers, adulterous stealths, as the euents of warre,
The raignes and death of Kings they take on them to know:
Which onelie to their skill the shoulder-blade doth show.

You goodlie sister Floods, how happy is your state!
Or should I more commend your features, or your Fate;
That Milford, which this Ile her greatest Port doth call
Before your equall Floods is lotted to your Fall!
Where was saile ever seene, or wind hath ever blowne,
Whence Penbrooke yet hath heard of Haven like her owne?
She bids Dungleddy dare Iberias proudest Road,
And chargeth her to send her challenges abroad
Along the coast of France, to proue if any bee
Her Milford that dare match: so absolute is shee.
And Clethy comming downe from Wrenyvaur her Sire
(A hill that thrusts his head into th'etheriall fire)
Her sisters part doth take, and dare avouch as much:
And Percily the proud, whom neerlie it doth touch,
Said, he would beare her out; and that they all should know.
And there-withall he struts, as though he scorn'd to show
His head belowe the Heaven, when he of Milford spake:
But there was not a Port the prize durst undertake.
So highlie Milford is in every mouth renownd,
Noe Haven hath ought good, in her that is not found:
Whereas the swelling surge, that with his fomie head,
The gentler looking Land with furie menaced,
With his encountring waue no longer there contends;
But sitting mildly downe like perfect ancient friends,
Unmou'd of any wind which way so ere it blow,
And rather seeme to smile, then knit an angry brow.
The ships with shattred ribs scarce creeping from the Seas,
On her sleeke bosome ride with such deliberate ease,
As all her passed stormes shee holds but meane and base,
So shee may reach at length this most delightfull place,
By nature with proud Cleeues invironed about,
To crowne the goodlie Road: where builds the Falcon stout,
Which we the Gentill call; whose fleet and active wings,
It seemes that Nature made when most shee thought on Kings:
Which manag'd to the lure, her high and gallant flight,
The vacant sportfull man so greatlie doth delight,
That with her nimble quills his soule doth seeme to houer,
And lie the verie pitch that lustie Bird doth couer;
That those proud Airies, bred whereas the scorching skie
Doth sindge the sandie Wyldes of spicefull Barbarie;
Or underneath our Pole, where Norwaies Forests wide
Their high clowd-touching heads in Winter snowes doe hide,

Out-brave not this our kind in mettle, nor exceed
The Falcon, which some-times the British Cleeues doe breed:
Which prey upon the Iles in the Vergiuian waste,
That from the British shores by Neptune are imbrac't;
Which stem his furious Tides when wildliest they doe raue,
And breake the big-swolne bulke of manie a boystrous waue:
As, calme when hee becomes, then likewise in their glorie
Doe cast their amorous eyes at many a Promontorie
That thrust their forehead forth into the smiling South;
As Rat and Sheepy, set to keepe calme Milfords mouth,
Expos'd to Neptunes power. So Gresholme farre doth stand:
Scalme, Stockholme, with Saint Bride, and Gatholme, neerer land
(Which with their veinie breasts intice the gods of Sea,
That with the lustie Iles doe reuell every day)
As Crescent-like the Land her bredth here inward bends,
From Milford, which she forth to old Meneuia sends;
Since, holy Davids seat; which of especiall grace
Doth lend that nobler name, to this unnobler place.
Of all the holy men whose fame so fresh remaines,
To whom the Britans built so many sumptuous Fanes,
This Saint before the rest their Patron still they hold:
Whose birth, their ancient Bards to Cambria long foretold;
And seated heere a See, his Bishoprick of yore,
Upon the farthest point of this unfruitfull shore;
Selected by himselfe, that farre from all resort
With contemplation seem'd most fitly to comport;
That, voyd of all delight, cold, barren, bleake, and dry,
No pleasure might allure, nor steale the wandring eye:
Where Ramsey with those Rockes, in ranke that ordered stand
Upon the furthest point of Davids ancient Land,
Doe raise their rugged heads (the Sea-mans noted markes)
Call'd, of their Mytred tops, The Bishop and his Clarkes;
Into that Chanell cast, whose raging current rores
Betwixt the British Sands, and the Hibernian shores:
Whose grimme and horrid face doth pleased Heaven neglect,
And beares bleake Winter still in his more sad aspect:
Yet Gwin and Nevern neere, two fine and fishfull brookes,
Do never stay their course, how sterne so ere he lookes;
Which with his shipping once should seeme to have commerst,
Where Fiscard as her flood, doth only grace the first.
To Newport fals the next: there we a while will rest;
Our next ensuing Song to wondrous things addrest.


THE SIXTH SONG

THE ARGUMENT

With Cardigan the Muse proceeds,
And tells what rare things Tivy breeds:
Next, proud Plynillimon shee plyes;
Where Severne, Wy, and Rydoll rise.
With Severne shee along doth goe,
Her Metamorphosis to showe;
And makes the wandring Wy declame
In honour of the British name:
Then musters all the watry traine
That those two Rivers entertaine:
And viewing how those Rillets creepe
From shore to the Vergiuian Deepe,
By Radnor and Mountgomery then
To Severne turnes her course agen:
And bringing all their Riverets in,
There ends; a new Song to begin.

Sith I must stem thy Streame, cleere Tivy, yet before
The Muse vouchsafe to seise the Cardiganian shore,
Shee of thy sourse will sing in all the Cambrian coast;
Which of thy Castors once, but now canst onelie boast
The Salmons, of all Floods most plentifull in thee.
Deere Brooke, within thy Banks if anie Powers there bee;
Then Neiads, or yee Nymphs of their like watrie kind
(Unto whose onelie care, great Neptune hath assign'd
The guidance of those Brooks wherein he takes delight)
Assist her: and whilst shee your dwelling shall recite,
Be present in her work: set her your graces view,
That to succeeding times them livelie shee may shew;
As when great Albions sonnes, which him a Sea-Nymph brought
Amongst the grisly Rocks, were with your beauties caught
(Whose onelie love surpriz'd those of the aPhlegrian size,
The Titanois, that once against high Heaven durst rise)
When as the hoarie woods, the climing hills did hide,
And couer'd everie Vale through which you gentlie glide;
Euen for those inly heats which through your loves they felt,
That oft in kindlie teares did in your bosomes melt,
To view your secret Bowres, such fauour let her win.

Then Tivy commeth downe from her capacious Lin,
Twixt Mirk and Brenny led, two handmaids, that doe stay
Their Mistres, as in State shee goes upon her way.

Which when Lanbeder sees, her wondrouslie shee likes:
Whose untam'd bosome so the beautious Tivy strikes,
As that the Forrest faine would have her there abide.
But shee (so pure a streame) transported with her pride

The offer idlie scorns; though with her flattering shade
The Syluan her entice with all that may perswade
A water-Nymph; yea, though great Thetis selfe shee were:
But nothing might preuaile, nor all the pleasures there
Her mind could ever moue one minutes staie to make.

Mild Mathern then, the next, doth Tivy ouer-take:
Which instantlie againe by Dittor is suppli'd.
Then, Keach and Kerry helpe: twixt which on either side,
To Cardigan shee comes, the Soueraigne of the Shere.
Now Tivy let us tell thy sundrie glories here.

When as the Salmon seekes a fresher streame to find
(Which hither from the Sea comes yeerely by his kind,
As he in season growes) and stems the watry tract
Where Tivy falling downe, doth make a Cataract,
Forc't by the rising Rocks that there her course oppose,
As though within their bounds they meant her to inclose;
Heere, when the labouring Fish doth at the foote arrive,
And finds that by his strength but vainlie he doth strive,
His taile takes in his teeth; and bending like a bowe,
That's to the compasse drawne, aloft himself doth throwe:
Then springing at his height, as doth a little wand,
That bended end to end, and fletted from the hand,
Farre off it selfe doth cast; so doth the Salmon vaut.
And if at first he faile, his second a Summersaut
Hee instantlie assaies; and from his nimble Ring,
Still yarking, never leaues, untill himselfe he fling,
Aboue the streamefull top of the surrounded heape.

More famous long agone, then for the Salmons leape,
For Beuers Tivy was, in her strong banks that bred,
Which else no other Brooke of Brittaine nourished:
Where Nature, in the shape of this now-perisht beast
His propertie did seeme t'have wondrouslie exprest;
Be'ing bodied like a Boat, with such a mightie taile
As seru'd him for a bridge, a helme, or for a saile,
When Kind did him commaund the Architect to play,
That his strong Castle built of branched twigs and clay:
Which, set upon the Deepe, but yet not fixed there,
Hee easelie could remoue as it he pleas'd to stere
To this side or to that; the workmanship so rare,
His stuffe where-with to build, first beeing to prepare,
A forraging he goes, to Groues or bushes nie,
And with his teeth cuts downe his Timber: which laid-by,
He turnes him on his back, his belly laid abroad,
When with what he hath got, the other doe him load,
Till lastlie by the weight, his burthen hee have found.

Then, with his mightie taile his carriage having bound
As Carters doe with ropes, in his sharpe teeth hee grip't
Some stronger stick: from which the lesser branches stript,
He takes it in the midst; at both the ends, the rest
Hard holding with their fangs, unto the labour prest,
Going backward, tow'rds their home their loaded carriage led,
From whom, those first heere borne, were taught the usefull Sled.
Then builded he his Fort with strong and several fights;
His passages contriv'd with such unusuall sleights,
That from the Hunter oft he issu'd undiscern'd,
As if men from this Beast to fortifie had learn'd;
Whose Kind, in her decay'd, is to this Ile unknowne.
Thus Tivy boasts this Beast peculiarly her owne.

But here why spend I time these trifles to areed?
Now, with thy former taske my Muse againe proceed,
To shewe the other Floods from the Cerettick shore
To the Verginian Sea contributing their store:
With Bidder first begin, that bendeth all her force
The Arron to assist, Arth holding on her course
The way the other went, with Werry which doth win
Faire Istwid to her ayde; who kindlie comming in,
Meets Rydoll at her mouth, that faire and princesse maid,
Plynillimons deere child, deliciouslie afraid,
As fits a Nymph so neere to Severne and her Queene.
Then come the sister Salks, as they before had seene
Those delicater Dames so trippinglie to read:
Then Kerry; Cletur next, and Kinver making head
With Enion, that her like cleere Levant brings by her.
Plynillimons high praise no longer Muse defer,
What once the Druids told, how great those Floods should bee
That here (most mightie Hill) derive themselues from thee.
The Bards with furie rapt, the British youth among,
Unto the charming Harpe thy future honor song
In brave and loftie straines; that in excesse of joy,
The Beldam and the Girle, the Grandsire and the Boy,
With shouts and yearning cries, the troubled ayre did load
(As when with crowned cuppes unto the Elian God
Those Priests his Orgyes held; or when the old world saw
Full Phoebes face eclipst, and thinking her to daw,
Whom they supposed falne in some inchanted swound,
Of beaten tinkling Brasse still ply'd her with the sound)
That all the Cambrian hills, which high'st their heads doe beare
With most obsequious showes of lowe subiected feare,
Should to thy greatnes stoupe: and all the Brooks that be,
Doe homage to those Floods that issued out of thee:
To princelie Severne first; next, to her sister Wye,
Which to her elders Court her course doth still apply.

But Rydoll, young'st, and least, and for the others pride
Not finding fitting roomth upon the rising side,
Alone unto the West directlie takes her way.
So all the neighboring Hills Plynillimon obey.
For, though Moylvadian beare his craggy top so hie,
As scorning all that come in compasse of his eye,
Yet greatlie is he pleas'd Plynillimon will grace
Him with a cheerfull looke: and fawning in his face,
His love to Severne showes us though his owne she were,
Thus comforting the Flood; O ever-during heire
Of Sabrine, Locryns child (who of her life bereft,
Her ever-living name to thee faire River left)
Brutes first begotten sonne, which Gwendelin did wed;
But soone th'unconstant Lord abandoned her bed
(Through his unchaste desire) for beautious Elstreds love,
Now, that which most of all her mightie hart did moue,
Her Father, Cornwalls Duke, great Corineus dead,
Was by the lustfull King unjustlie banished,
When shee, who to that time still with a smoothed brow
Had seem'd to beare the breach of Locrines former vow,
Perceiving stil her wrongs insufferable were;
Growne bigge with the reuenge which her full breast did beare,
And ayded to the birth with every little breath
(Alone shee beeing left the spoyle of love and death,
In labour of her griefe outrageously distract,
The utmost of her spleene on her false Lord to act)
Shee first implores their aide to hate him whom shee found;
Whose harts unto the depth she had not left to sound.
To Cornwall then shee sends her Country) for supplies:
Which all at ouer in Armes with Gwendelin arise.
Then with her warlike power, her husband shee pursu'd,
Whom his unlawfull love too vainlie did delude.

The fierce and iealous Queene, then voyde of all remorce,
As great in power or spirit, whilst hee neglects her force,
Him suddainlie surpriz'd, and from her irefull hart
All pittie cleane exil'd (whom nothing could convert)
The sonne of mightie Brute bereaued of his life;
Amongst the Britans here the first intestine strife,
Since they were put a land upon this promis'd shore.
Then crowning Madan King, whom shee to Locrine bore,
And those which seru'd his Sire to his obedience brought;
Not so with blood suffic'd, immediatly she sought
The mother and the child: whose beautie when shee saw,
Had not her hart been flint, had had the power to draw
A spring of pittying teares; when, dropping liquid pearle,
Before the cruell Queene, the Ladie and the Girle
Upon their tender knees begg'd mercie. Woe for thee

Faire Elstred, that thou should'st thy fairer Sabrine see,
As shee should thee behold the prey to her sterne rage
Whom kinglie Locrins death suffic'd not to asswage:
Who from the bordring Cleeues thee with thy Mother cast
Into thy christned Flood, the whilst the Rocks aghast
Resounded with your shriekes; till in a deadlie dreame
Your corses were dissolu'd into that crystall streame,
Your curles to curled waues, which plainlie still appeare
The same in water now, that once in locks they were:
And, as you wont to clip each others neck before,
Yee now with liquid armes embrace the wandring shore.

But leave we Severne heere, a little on pursue,
The often wandring Wye (her passages to view,
As wantonlie shee straines in her lascivious course)
And muster every flood that from her bountious sourse
Attends upon her Streame, whilst (as the famous bound
Twixt the Brecknokian earth, and the Radnorian ground)
Shee every Brooke receives. First, Clarwen commeth in,
With Clarwy: which to them their consort Eland win
To ayde their goodly Wye, which Ithon gets againe;
She Dulas drawes along: and in her watry traine
Clowedock hath recourse, and Comran, which she brings
Unto their wandring flood from the Radnorian Springs:
As Edwy her attends and Matchwy forward heaves
Her Mistresse. When at last the goodly Wye perceaves
Shee now was in that part of Wales, of all the rest
Which (as her very waste) in breadth from East to West,
In length from North to South, her midst is every way,
From Severns bordring banks into the either Sea,
Which shee might tearme the ham. The ancient Britans heere
The River calls to mind, and what those British were
Whilst Britain was her selfe, the Queene of all the West.

To whose old Nations praise whilst shee herselfe addrest,
From the Brecknokian bound when Irvon comming in,
Her Dulas, with Commarch, and Wevery that doth win,
Perswading her for them good matter to prouide.
The Wood-Nymphs so againe, from the Radnorian side,
As Radnor, with Blethaugh, and Knuckles Forrests, call
To Wye, and bad her now bestirre her for them all:
For, if shee stuck not close in their distressed Case,
The Britans were in doubt to under-goe disgrace.
That stronglie thus prouok't, shee for the Britans saies;
What spirit can lift you up, to that immortall praise
You worthilie deserue? by whom first Gaul was taught
Her knowledge: and for her, what Nation ever wrought
The conquest you atchiev'd? And, as you were most drad,

So yee (before the rest) in so great reverence had
Your Bards which sung your deeds, that whē sterne hosts have stood
With lifted hands to strike (in their inflamed blood)
One Bard but comming in, their murd'rous swords hath staid;
In her most dreadful voice as thundring Heaven had said,
Stay Britans: when he spake, his words so powrefull were.

So to her native Priests, the dreadlesse Druides here,
The neerest neighboring Gaul, that wiselie could discerne
Th' effect their doctrine wrought, it for their good to learne,
Her apt and pregnant Youth sent hither yeere by yeere,
Instructed in our Rites with most religious feare.
And afterward againe, when as our ancient fear
Her surcrease could not keepe, growne for her soile too great
(But like to casting Bees, so rising up in swarmes)
Our Cymbri with the Gaules, that their commixed Armes
Joyn'd with the German powers (those Nations of the North
Which ouer-spread the world) together issued forth:
Where, with our brazen swords, we stoutly fought, and long;
And after Conquests got, residing them among,
First planted in those parts our brave courageous blood:
Whose natures so adher'd unto their ancient blood,
As from them spring those Priests, whose praise so farre did sound,
Through whom that spacious Gaul was after so renown'd

Nor could the Saxons swords (which many a lingring yeere
Them sadlie did afflict, and that us Britans heere
Twixt Severne and this Sea) our mightie minds deject;
But that even they which fain'st our weaknes would detect,
Were forced to confesse, our wildest beasts that breed
Upon our mightie wastes, or on our Mountaines feed,
Were farre more sooner tam'd, than heere our Welch-men were;
Besides, in all the world no Nation is so deere.
As they unto their owne; that here within this Ile,
Or else in forraine parts, yea, forced to exile,
The noble Britan still his countryman releeues;
A Patriot, and so true, that it to death him greeues
To heare his Wales disgrac't: and on the Saxons swords
Oft hazardeth his life, ere with reprochefull words
His Language or his Leeke hee'le stand to heare abus'd.
Besides, the Britan is so naturallie infus'd
With true Poëtick rage, that in theira measures, Art
Doth rather seeme precise, then comlie; in each part
Their Metre most exact, in Verse of th'hardest kind.
And some to riming be so wondrouslie inclin'd,
Those Numbers they will hit, out of their genuine vaine,
Which many wise and learn'd can hardly creattaine.

O memorable Bards, of unmixt blood, which still
Posteritie shall praise for your so wondrous skill,
That in your noble Songs, the long Descents have kept
Of your great Heroës, else in Lethe that had slept,
With theirs whose ignorant pride your labours have disdain'd;
How much from time, and them, how bravelie have you gain'd!
Musician, Herault, Bard, thrice maist thou be renown'd,
And with three severall wreathes immortallie be crown'd;
Who, when to Penbrooke call'd before the English King,
And to thy powerfull Harpe commaunded there to sing,
Of famous Arthur told'st, and where hee was interr'd;
In which, those retchlesse times had long and blindlie err'd,
And Ignorance had brought the world to such a pass
As now, which scarce beleeues that Arthur ever was.
But when King bHenry sent th'reported place to view,
He found that man of men: and what thou said'st was true.

Heere then I cannot chuse but bitterlie exclame
Against those fooles that all Antiquitie defame,
Because they have found out, some credulous Ages layd
Slight fictions with the truth, whilst truth on rumor stayd;
And that one forward Time (perceiving the neglect
A former of her had) to purchase her respect,
With toyes then trimd her up, the drowsie world t'allure,
And lent her what it thought might appetite procure
To man, whose mind doth still varietie pursue;
And therefore to those things whose grounds were verie true,
Though naked yet and bare (not having to content
The weyward curious eare) gaue fictive ornament;
And fitter thought, the truth they should in question call,
Then coldlie sparing that, the truth should goe and all.
And surelie I suppose, that which this froward time
Doth scandalize her with to be her heynous crime,
That hath her most preseru'd: for, still where wit hath found
A thing most cleerlie true, it made that, fictions ground:
Which shee suppos'd might give sure colour to them both:
From which, as from a roote, this wondred error grow'th
At which our Criticks gird, whose judgements are so strict,
And he the bravest man who most can contradict
That which decrepit Age (which forced is to leane
Upon Tradition) tells; esteeming it so meane,
As they it quite reiect, and for some trifling thing
(Which Time hath pind to Truth) they all away will fling.
These men (for all the world) like our Precisions bee,
Who for some Crosse or Saint they in the window see
Will pluck downe all the Church: Soule-blinded sots that creepe
In durt, and never saw the wonders of the Deepe.
Therefore (in my conceit) most rightlie seru'd are they

That to the Roman trust (on his report that stay)
Our truth from him to learne, as ignorant of ours
As we were then of his; except t'were of his powers:
Who our wise Druides here unmercifullie slew;
Like whom, great Natures depths no men yet ever knew,
Nor with such dauntlesse spirits were ever yet inspir'd;
Who at their proud arrive th'ambitious Romans fir'd
When first they heard them preach the soules immortall state;
And euen in Romes despight, and in contempt of Fate,
Graspt hands with horrid death: which out of hate and pride
They slew, who through the world were reverenced beside.

To understand our state, no maruaile then though wee
Should so to Caesar seeke, in his reports to see
What ancientlie we were; when in our infant war,
Unskilfull of our tongue but by Interpreter,
Hee nothing had of ours which our great Bards did sing,
Except some few poore words; and those againe to bring
Unto the Latine sounds, and easiness they us'd,
By their most filed speech, our British most abus'd.
But of our former state, beginning, our descent,
The warres we had at home, the conquests where we went,
He never understood. And though the Romans here
So noble Trophies left, as verie worthie were
A people great as they, yet did they ours neglect,
Long rear'd ere they arriv'd. And where they doe obiect,
The Ruines and Records we show, be verie small
To proue our selues so great: euen this the most of all
(Gainst their obiection) seemes miraculous to mee,
That yet those should be found so generall as they bee;
The Roman, next the Pict, the Saxon, then the Dane,
All landing in this Ile, each like a horrid raine
Deforming her; besides the sacrilegious wrack
Of many a noble Booke, as impious hands should sack
The Center, to extirp all knowledge, and exile
All brave and ancient things, for ever from this Ile:
Expressing wondrous griefe, thus wandring Wye did sing.

But, backe, industrious Muse; obsequiously to bring
Cleere Severne from her sourse, and tell how she doth straine
Downe her delicious Dales; with all the goodly traine,
Brought forth the first of all by Brugan: which to make
Her party worthy note, next, Dulas in doth take.
Moylvadian his much love to Severne then to showe,
Upon her Southerne side, sends likewise (in a rowe)
Bright Biga, that brings on her friend and fellow Floyd;
Next, Dungum; Bacho then is busily imploy'd,
Tarranon, Carno, Hawes, with Becan, and the Rue,

In Severn's soueraine Bankes, that give attendance due.

Thus as she swoopes along, with all that goodly traine,
Upon her other Banke by Newtowne: so againe
Comes Dulas (of whose name so many Rivers bee,
As of none others is) with Mule, prepar'd to see
The confluence to their Queene, as on her course she makes:
Then at Mountgomery next cleere Kennet in she takes;
Where little Fledding fals into her broader Banke;
Forkt Vurnway, bringing Tur, and Tanot: growing ranke,
She plyes her towards the Poole, from the Gomerian feelds;
Then which in all our Wales, there is no country yeelds
An excellenter Horse, so full of naturall fire,
As one of Phoebus Steeds had beene that Stalyons sire
Which first their race begun; or of th'Asturian kind,
Which some have held to be begotten by the Wind,
Upon the Mountaine Mare; which strongly it receaues,
And in a little time her pregnant part upheaues.
But, leaue we this to such as after wonders long:
The Muse prepares herselfe unto another Song.


THE SEVENTH SONG

THE ARGUMENT

The Muse from Cambria comes againe,
To view the Forrest of faire Deane;
Sees Severne; when the Higre takes her,
How Fever-like the sicknes shakes her;
Makes mightie Maluerne speake his mind
In honour of the Mountaine kind;
Thence wasted with a merry gale,
Sees Lemster, and the Golden Vale;
Sports with the Nymphs, themselues that ply
At th'wedding of the Lug and Wy;
Viewing the Herefordian pride
Along on Severns setting side,
That small Wigornian part suruaies:
Where for a while herselfe shee staies.

HIgh matters call our Muse, inviting her to see
As well the lower Lands, as those were latelie shee
The Cambrian Mountaines clome, & (looking from aloft)
Survaid coy Severns course: but now to shores more soft
Shee shapes her prosperous saile; and in this loftie Song,
The Herefordian floods invites with her along,

That fraught from plentious Powse, with their superfluous waste,
Manure the batfull March, untill they be imbrac't
In Sabrins Soueraigne armes: with whose tumultuous waues
Shut up in narrower bounds, the Higre wildly raues;
And frights the strugling flocks, the neighbouring shores to flie,
A farre as from the Maine it comes with hideous cry,
And on the angry front the curled foame doth bring,
The billowes gainst the banks when fiercely it doth fling;
Hurles up the slimie ooze, and makes the scalie brood
Leape madding to the Land affrighted from the flood;
O returnes the toyling Bargē, whose steresman doth not lanch,
And thrusts the furrowing beake into her irefull panch:
As when we haplie see a sicklie woman fall
Into a fit of that when wee the Mother call,
When from the grieved wombe shee feeles the paine arise,
Breakes into grievous sighes, with intermixed cries,
Bereaved of her sense; and strugling still with those
That gainst her rising palne their utmost strength oppose,
Starts, tosses, tumbles, strikes, turnes, touses, spurnes and spraules,
Casting with furious lims her holders to the walles;
But that the horrid pangs torments the grieved so,
One well might muse frō whence this suddaine strength should grow.

Here (Queene of Forrests all, that West of Severne lie)
Her broad and bushie top Deane holdeth up so hie,
The lesser are not seene, shee is so tall and large.
And standing in such state upon the winding marge,
Within her hollow woods the Satyres that did wonne
In gloomie secret shades, not pierct with Sommers sunne,
Under a false pretence the Nymphs to entertaine,
Oft ravished the choice of Sabrius watry traine;
And from their Mistris banks them taking as a prey,
Unto their wooddie Caues have carried them away:
Then from her inner Groues for succour when they cri'd,
Shee retchlesse of their wrongs (her Satyres scapes to hide)
Unto their just complaint not once her eare enclines:
So fruitfull in her Woods, and wealthy in her Mines,
That Leden which her way doth through the Desert make,
Though neere to Deane ally'd, determin'd to forsake
Her course, and her cleere lims amongst the bushes hide,
Least by the Syluans (should she chance to be espide)
Shee might unmaidued goe unto her Soueraigne Flood:
So manie were the rapes done on the watry brood,
That Sabrine to her Sire (great Neptune) forc't to sue,
The ryots to represse of this outrageous crue,
His armed Orks hee sent her milder streame to keepe,
To drive them back to Deane that troubled all the Deepe.
Whilst Malverne (king of Hills) faire Severne ouer-lookes

(Attended on in state with tributatie Brookes)
And how the fertill fields of Hereford doe lie.
And from his many heads, with many an amorous eye
Beholds his goodlie site, how towards the pleasant rise,
Abounding in excesse, the Vale of Eusham lies,
The Mountaines every way about him that doe stand,
Of whom hee's daily seene, and seeing doth command;
On tiptoes set aloft, this proudlie uttereth hee:
Olympus, fayr'st of Hills, that Heaven art said to bee,
I not envie thy state, nor lesse my selfe doe make;
Nor to possesse thy name, mine owne would I forsake:
Nor would I, as thou doost, ambitiouslie aspire
To thrust my forked top into th'ethere all fire.
For, didst thou taste the sweets that on my face doe breathe,
Aboue thou wouldst nor seeke what I enjoy beneath:
Besides, the sundry soyles I everywhere survay,
Make me, if better nor, thy equall everie way.
And more, in our defence, to answere those, with spight
That tearme us barren rude, and voide of all delight;
Wee Mountaines, to the Land, like Worts or Wens to bee,
By which, fair'st living things disfigur'd oft they see;
This stronglie to performe, a well stuft braine would need.
And manie Hills there be, if they this Chuse would heed,
Having their rising tops familiar with the skie
(From whence all wit proceeds) that fitter were then I
The taske to under-rulde. As not a man that sees
Mounchdenny, Blorench hill, with Breadon, and the Clees,
And many more as great; and neerer me then they,
But thinks, in our defence they far much more could say.
Yet, falling to my lor, This stoutlie I maintaine
Gainst Forrests, Valleys, Fields, Groues, Rivers, Pasture, Plaine,
And all their flatter kind (so much that doe relie
Upon their feedings, flocks, and the infertilitie)
The Mountaine is the King: and he it is alone
Aboue the other soyles that Nature doth in throne
For Mountain be like Men of brave heroique mind,
With eyes erect to Heaven; of whence them selues they find;
Whereas the low lie Vale, as earthlie, like it selfe,
Doth never further looke then how to purchase pelfe.
And of their batfull sites, the Vales that boast them thus,
Nere had been what they are, had it not been for us:
For, from the rising banks that stronglie mound them in,
The Valley (as betwixt) her name did first begin:
And almost not a Brooke, if shee her banks doe fill,
But hath her plentious Spring from Mountaine or from Hill.
If Mead, or lower Slade, grieve at the roome we take,
Knowe that the snowe or raine, descending oft, doth make
The fruitfull Valley fat, with what from us doth glide,

Who with our Wintors waste maintaine their Sommers pride.
And to you lower Lands if terrible wee seeme,
And couer'd oft with clowds; it is your foggy steame
The powerfull Sunne exhales, that in the cooler day
Unto this Region comne, about our tops doth stay.
And, what's the Groue, so much that thinks her to be grac't,
If not aboue the rest upon the Mountaine plac't,
Where shee her curled head unto the eye may showe?
For, in the easie Vale if shee be set belowe,
What is shee but obscure? and her more dampie shade
And covert, but a Den for beasts of ravin made
Besides, wee are the Marks, which looking from an hie,
The trauailer beholds; and with a cheerfull eye
Doth thereby shape his course, and freshlie doth pursue
The way which long before lay tedious in his view.

What Forrest, Flood, or Field, that standoth not in awe,
Of Sina, or shall see the sight that Mountaine saw?
To none but to a Hill such grace was ever given:
As on his back tis said, great Atlas beares up Heaven.

So Latmus by the wise Endymion is renown'd,
That Hill, on whose high toplie was the first that found
Pale Phoebes wandring course; so skilfull in her Sphere,
As some stick not to say that he enjoy'd her there.

And those chaste maids, begot on Memoriebly loue,
Not Tempe onelie love delighting in their Groue;
Nor Helicon their Brooke, in whose delicious brims,
They oft are us'd to bathe their cloene and cry stall lims;
But high Parnassus have, their Mountaine, whereon they
Upon their golden Lutes continuallie doe play
Of these I more could tell, to proue the place our owne,
Then by his spatious Mape are by Ortillius showne.

For Mountaines this suffice. Which scarcelie had he told,
Along the fertill fields, when Melverne might behold
The Herefordian Floods, farre distant though they bee:
For great men, as we find, a great way off can see.
First, Frome with forhead cleare, by Bromyard that doth glide;
And taking Loden in, their mixed streames doe guide,
To meet their Soueraigne Lug, from the Radnorian Plaine
At Prestayn comming in; where hee doth entertaine
The Wadell, as along he under Derfold goes:
Her full and lustie side to whom the Forrest showes,
As to allure faire Lug, aboad with her to make.
Lug little Oney first, then Arro in doth take,
At Lemster, for her wooll whose Staple doth excell,

And seemes to ouer-match the golden Phrygian Fell.
Had this our Colchos been unto the Ancients knowne,
When Honor was her selfe, and in her glorie showne,
He then that did commaund the Infantry of Greece,
Had onely to our Ile adventur'd for this Floeoe.

Where lives the man so dull, on Britains furthest shore,
To whom did never found the name of Lemster Ore?
That with the Silke-wormes web for smalness doth compare:
Wherein, the Winder showes his workmanship so rare
As doth the Fleece excell, and mocks her looser clew;
As neatlie bottom'd up as Nature forth it drew;
Of each in high'st accompt, and reckoned here as fine,
As there th' Appulian fleece, or dainty Tarentyne.
From thence his lovely selfe for Wye he doth dispose,
To view the goodly flockes on each hand as he goes;
And makes his iourney short, with strange and sundry tales,
Of all their wondrous things; and, not the least, of Wales;
Of that prodigious Spring (him neighbouring as he past)
That little Fishes bones continually doth cast.
Whose reason whil'st he seekes industriously to knowe,
A great way he hath gon, and Hereford doth showe
Her rising Spires aloft; when as the Princely Wye,
Him from his Muse to wake, arrests him by and by.
Whose meeting to behold, with how well ordered grace
Each other entertaines, how kindly they embrace;
For joy, so great a shout the bordering Citie sent,
That with the sound thereof, which thorough Haywood went,
The Wood-Nymphs did awake that in the Forest won;
To know the sudden cause, and presently they ron
With lockes uncomb'd, for haste the lovely Wye to see
(The flood that grac't her most) this day should married be
To that more lovely Lug; a River of much fame,
That in her wandering bankes should lose his glorious name.
For Hereford, although her Wye she hold so deere,
Yet Lug (whose longer course doth grace the goodly Sheere,
And with his plentious Streame so many Brookes doth bring)
Of all hers that be North is absolutely King.

But Marcely, griev'd that he (the neerest of the rest,
And of the Mountaine kind) not bidden was a guest
Unto this nuptiall Feast, so hardly it doth take,
As (meaning for the same his station to forsake)
Inrag'd and mad with griefe, himselfe in two did rive;
The Trees and Hedges neere, before him up doth drive,
And dropping headlong downe, three dayes together fall:
Which, bellowing as he went, the Rockes did so appall,
That they him passage made, who Coats and Chappels crusht:

So violently he into his Valley rusht.
But Wye (from her deare Lug whom nothing can restraine,
In many a pleasant shade, her joy to entertaine)
To Rosse her course directs; and right hee name to showe,
Oft windeth in her way, as backe she meant to goe.
Meander, who is said so intricate to bee,
Hath not so many turns, nor crankling nookes as shee.

The Herefordian fields when welneare having past,
As she is going forth, two sister Brookes at last
That Soile her kindly sends, to guide her on her way;
Neat Gamar, that gets in swift Garran: which do lay
Their waters in one Banke, augmenting of her traine,
To grace the goodlie Wye, as she doth passe by Deane.

Beyond whose equall Spring unto the West doth lie
The goodly Golden Vale, whose lushious sents do flie
More free then Hyblas sweets; and twixt her bordering hils,
The aire with such delights and delicacie fils,
As makes it loth to stirre, or thence those smels to beare.
Th' Hesperides scarce had such pleasures as be there:
Which sometime to attaine, that mighty sonne of loue
One of his Labors made, and with the Dragon stroue,
That never clos'd his eies, the golden fruit to guard;
As if t'enrich this place, from others, Nature spar'd:
Banks crown'd with curled Groues, from cold to keepe the Plaine,
Fields batfull, flowrie Meades, in state them to maintaine;
Floods, to make fat those Meades, from Marble veines that spout,
To shew, the wealth within doth answer that without.
So brave a Nymph she is, in every thing so rare,
As to sit down by her, she thinkes there's none should dare.
And forth she sends the Doire, upon the Wye to wait.
Whom Munne by the way more kindly doth intreat
(For Eskle, her most lou'd, and Olcons onely sake)
With her to go along, till Wye she overtake.
To whom she condiscends, from danger her to shield,
That th'Monumethian parts from th'Herefordian field.

Which manly Malvern sees from furthest of the Sheere,
On the Wigornian waste when Northward looking neere,
On Corswood casts his eie, and on his home-born Chase,
Then constantly beholds, with an unusuall pase
Team with her tribute come unto the Cambrian Queene,
Neere whom in all this place a River's scarcely seene,
That dare auouch her name; Teame scorning any Spring
But what with her along from Shrepshire she doth bring,
Except one namelesse Streame that Maluern sends her in,
And Laughern though but small: when they such grace that win,

There thrust in with the Brookes inclosed in her Banke.
Teame lastly thither com'n with water is so ranke,
As though she would contend with Sabryne, and doth craue
Of place (by her desert) precedencie to have:
Till chancing to behold the others godlike grace,
So strongly is surpris'd with beauties in her face
By no meanes she could hold, but needsly she must showe
Her liking; and her selfe doth into Sabrine throwe.

Not farre from him againe when Maluern doth perceaue
Two hils, which though their heads so high they doe not heaue,
Yet duly do obserue great Maluern, and affoord
Him reverence: who againe, as fits a gratious Lord,
Upon his Subiects looks, and equall praise doth give
That Woodberry so nigh and neighbourlie doth live
With Abberley his friend, deseruing well such fame
That Saxton in his Maps forgot them not to name:
Which, though in their meane types small matter doth appeare,
Yet both of good account are reckned in the Shiere,
And highly grac't of Teame in his proud passing by.

When soone the goodlie Wyre, that wonted was so hie
Her statelie top to reare, ashamed to behold
Her straight and goodlie Woods unto the Fornace sold
(And looking on her selfe, by her decay doth see
The miserie wherein her sister Forrests bee)
Of Erisicthons end begins her to be thinke,
And of his cruell plagues doth wish they all might drinke
That thus have them dispoil'd: then of her owne despight;
That shee, in whom her Towne faire Beudley tooke delight,
And from her goodlie seat conceiv'd so great a pride,
In Severne on her East, Wyre on the setting side,
So naked left of woods, of pleasure, and forlorne,
As she that lov'd her most, her now the most doth scorne;
With endlesse griefe perplext, her stubborne breast shee strake,
And to the deafened ayre thus passionately spake;

You Driades, that are said with Oakes to live and die,
Wherefore in our distresse doe you our dwellings flie;
Upon this monstrous Age and not reuenge our wrong?
For cutting downe an Oake that justlie did belong
To one of Ceres Nymphes, in Thessaly that grew
In the Dodonean Groue (O Nymphes!) you could pursue
The sonne of Perops then, and did the Goddesse stirre
That villanie to wreake the Tyrant did to her:
Who, with a dreadfull frowne did blast the growing Graine:
And having from him rest what should his life maintaine,
Shee unto Scythia sent, for Hunger, him to gnawe,

And thrust her downe his throat, into his stanchlesse mawe:
Who, when nor Sea nor Land for him sufficient were,
With his deuouring teeth his wretched flesh did teare.

This did you for one Tree: but of whole Forrests they
That in these impious times have been the vile decay
(Whom I may justlie call their Countries deadly foes)
Gainst them you moue no Power, their spoyle unpunisht goes.
How manie grieved soules in future time shall starue,
For that which they have rapt their beastlie lust to serue!

Wee, sometime that the state of famous Britaine were,
For whom she was renown'd in Kingdoms farre and neere,
Are ransackt; and our Trees so hackt aboue the ground,
That where their lostie tops their neighboring Countries crown'd,
Their Trunkes (like aged folkes) now bare and naked stand,
As for reuenge to Heaven each held a withered hand:
And where the goodly Heards of high-palm'd Harts did gaze
Upon the passer by, there now doth onely graze
The gall'd-backe carrion Iade, and hurtfull Swine do spoile
Once to the Syluan Powers our consecrated soile.
This uttered she with griefe: and more she would have spoke:
When the Salopian floods her of her purpose broke,
And silence did enjoyne; a listning eare to lend
To Severne, which was thought did mighty things intend.


THE EIGHTH SONG

THE ARGUMENT

The goodly Severne bravely sings
The noblest of her British Kings;
At Caesars landing what we were,
And of the Roman Conquests here:
Then shewes, to her deare Britans fame,
How quicklie christned they became;
And of their constancie doth boast,
In sundry fortunes strangely tost:
Then doth the Saxons landing tell,
And how by them the Britans fell;
Cheeres the Salopian Mountaines hie,
That on the west of Severne lie;
Calls downe each Riveret from her Spring,
Their Queene upon her way to bring;
Whom downe to Bruge the Muse attends:
Where, leaving her, this Song shee ends.

To Salop when her selfe cleere Sabrine comes to showe,
And wisely her bethinks the way shee had to goe,
South-west-ward casts her course; & with an amorous eye
Those Countries whence shee came, survayeth (passing by)
Those Lands in Ancient times old Cambria claym'd her due,
For refuge when to her th'oppressed Britans flew;
By England now usurp't, who (past the wonted Meeres,
Her sure and soueraigne banks) had taken sundry Sheeres,
Which shee her Marches made: whereby those Hills of fame
And Rivers stood disgrac't; accounting it their shame,
That all without that Mound which Mercian Offa cast
To runne from North to South, athwart the Cambrian wast,
Could England not suffice, but that the stragling Wye,
Which in the hart of Wales was some-time said to lye,
Now onely for her bound proud England did prefer.
That Severne, when shee sees the wrong thus offred her,
Though by injurious Time deprived of that place
Which anciently shee held: yet loth that her disgrace
Should on the Britans light, the Hills and Rivers neere
Austerely to her calls, commaunding them to heare
In her deere childrens right (their Ancesters of yore,
Now thrust betwixt her selfe, and the Virginian shore,
Who drave the Giants hence that of the Earth were bred,
And of the spacious Ile became the soueraigne head)
What from autentique bookes shee liberally could say.
Of which whilst shee bethought her; West-ward every way,
The Mountaines, Floods, and Meeres, to silence them betake:
When Severne lowting lowe, thus grauely them bespake;

How mightie was that man, and honoured still to bee,
That gaue this Ile his name, and to his children three,
Three Kingdoms in the same? which, time doth now denie,
With his arrivall heere, and primer Monarchy.

Loëgria, though thou canst thy Locrine easely lose,
Yet Cambria, him, whom Fate her ancient Founder chose,
In no wise will forgoe; nay, should Albania leaue
Her Albanact for ayde, and to the Scythian cleaue.
And though remorselesse Rome, which first did us enthrall,
As barbarous but esteem'd, and stickt not so to call;
The ancient Britans yet a sceptred King obey'd
Three hundred yeeres before Romes great foundation laid;
And had a thousand yeeres an Empire strongly stood,
Ere Caesar to her shores here stemd the circling Flood;
And long before, borne Armes against the barbarous Hun,
Heere landing with intent the Ile to ouer-run:
And following them in flight, their Generall Humber drownd

In that great arme of Sea, by his great name renown'd;
And her great Builders had, her Citties who did reare
With Fanes unto her Gods, and Flamins every where,
Nor Troynouant alone a Citty long did stand;
But after, soone againe by Ebranks powerfull hand
Yorke lifts her Towers aloft: which scarcely finisht was,
But as they, by those Kings; so by Rudhudibras,
Kents first and famous Towne, with Winchester, arose:
And other, others built, as they fit places chose.

So Britaine to her praise, of all conditions brings;
The warlike, as the wise. Of her courageous Kings,
Brute Green-shield: to whose name we prouidence impute,
Divinely to revive the Land's first Conqueror, Brute.

So had she those were learn'd, endu'd with nobler parts:
As, he from learned Greece, that (by the liberall Arts)
To Stamford, in this Ile, seem'd Athens to transfer;
Wise Bladud, of her Kings that great Philosopher;
Who found our boyling Bathes; and in his knowledge hie,
Disdaining humane paths, heere practiced to flie.

Of justly vexed Leire, and those who last did tug
In worie then Civill warre, the a sonnes of Gorbodug
(By whose unnaturall strife the Land so long was tost)
I cannot stay to tell, not shall my Britaine boast;
But, of that man which did her Monarchy restore,
Her first imperiall Crowne of gold that ever wore,
And that most glorious type of soueraignty regain'd;
Mulmutius: who this Land in such estate maintain'd
As his great Bel-sire Brute from Albions heires it wonne.
This Grand-child, great as he, those foure proud Streets begun
That each way crosse this Ile, and bounds did them allow.
Like priviledge he lent the Temple and the Plow:
So studious was this Prince in his most forward zeale
To the Celestiall power, and to the Publique weale.
Bellinus he begot, who Dacia proud subdu'd;
And Brennus, who abroad a worthier warre pursu'd,
Asham'd of civill strife, at home heere leaving all:
And with such goodly Youth, in Germany and Gaul
As he had gather'd up, the Alpin Mountaines past,
And bravely on the banks of fatall Allia chas't
The Romans (that her streame distained with their gore)
And through proud Rome, display'd his British Ensigne bore:
There, ballancing his sword against her baser gold,
The Senators for slaues hee in her Forum sold.
At last, by power expell'd, yet proud of late successe,
His forces then for Greece did instantly addresse;

And marching with his men upon her fruitfull face,
Made Macedon first stoope; then Thessay, and Thrace;
His souldiers there enricht with all Peonia's spoyle;
And where to Greece he gaue the last and deadliest foyle,
In that most dreadfull fight, on that more dismall day,
O'rthrew their utmost prowesse at sad Thermopylæ,
And daring of her Gods, adventur'd to have tane
Those sacred things enshrin'd in wise Apollo's Fane:
To whom when thundring Heaven pronounc't her fearefulst word,
Against the Delphian Power he shak't his irefull sword.

As of the British blood, the native Cambri here
(So of my Cambria call'd) those valiant Cymbri were
(When Britaine with her brood so peopled had her seat,
The soyle could not suffice, it daily grew so great)
Of Denmarke who themselues did anciently possesse,
And to that straitned poynt, that utmost Chersonesse,
My Countries name bequeath'd; whence Cymbrica it tooke:
Yet long were not compriz'd within that little nooke,
But with those Almaine powers this people issued forth:
And like some boystrous wind arising from the North,
Came that unwieldie host; that, which way it did moue,
The very burthenous earth before it seem'd to shoue,
And onely meant to claime the Universe its owne.
In this terrestriall Globe, as though some world unknowne,
By pampred Natures store too prodigally fed
(And surfetting there-with) her surcrease vomited,
These roaming up and downe to seeke some setling roome,
First like a Deluge fell upon Illyricum,
And with his Roman powers Papyrius ouer-threw;
Then, by great Belus brought against those Legions, flew
Their forces which in France Aurelius Scaurus led;
And afterward againe, as bravely vanquished
The Consulls Capio, and stout Manlius on the Plaine,
Where Rhodanus was red with blood of Latines slaine.

In greatnes next succeeds Belinus worthy sonne,
Gurgustus: who soone left what his great Father wonne,
To Guyuteline his heire: whosea Queene, beyond her kind,
In her great husbands peace, to shew her upright mind,
To wise Mulmutius lawes, her Martian first did frame:
From which we ours derive, to her eternall fame.

So Britaine forth with these, that valiant Bastard brought,
Morindus, Danius sonne, which with that Monster fought
His subiects that deuour'd; to shew himselfe againe
Their Martyr, who by them selected was to raigne.

So Britaine likewise boasts her Elidure the just,
Who with his people was of such especiall trust,
That (Archigallo falne into their generall hate,
And by their powerfull hand depriv'd of kingly state)
Unto the Regall Chayre they Elidure aduanc't:
But long he had not raign'd, ere happily it chanc't,
In hunting of a Hart, that in the Forrest wild,
The late deposed King, himselfe who had exil'd
From all resort of men, just Elidure did meet;
Who much unlike himselfe, at Elidurus feet,
Him prostrating with teares, his tender breast so strooke,
That he (the British rule who lately on him tooke
At th'earnest peoples pray'rs) him calling to the Court,
There Archigallo's wrongs so lively did report,
Relating (in his right) his lamentable case,
With so effectuall speech imploring their high grace,
That him they reinthron'd; in peace who spent his dayes.

Then Elidure againe, crown'd with applausive praise,
As he a brother rais'd, by brothers was depos'd,
And put into the Towre; where miserably inclos'd,
Out-living yet their hate, and the Usurpers dead,
Thrice had the British Crowne set on his reverend head.

When more then thirty Kings in faire succession came
Unto that mighty Lud, in whose eternall name
Great London still shall live (by him rebuilded) while
To Citties she remaines the Soueraigne of this Ile.

And when commaunding Rome to Caesar gaue the charge,
Her Empire (but too great) still further to enlarge
With all beyond the Alpes; the aydes he found to passe
From these parts into Gaul, shew'd heere some Nation was
Undaunted that remain'd with Romes so dreadfull name,
That durst presume to ayde those shee decreed to tame.
Wherefore that matchlesse man, whose high ambition wrought
Beyond her Empires bounds, by shipping wisely sought
(Heere proling on the shores) this Iland to discry,
What people her possest, how fashion'd shee did lie:
Where scarce a Strangers foote defil'd her virgin breast,
Since her first Conqueror Brute heere put his powers to rest;
Onely some little Boats, from Gaul that did her feed
With tryfles, which shee tooke for nicenesse more then need:
But as another world, with all abundance blest,
And satisfi'd with what shee in her selfe possest;
Through her excessive wealth (at length) till wanton growne,
Some Kings (with others Lands that would enlarge their owne)
By innovating Armes an open passage made

For him that gap't for all (the Roman) to invade.
Yet with grim-visag'd Warre when he her shores did greet,
And terriblest did threat with his amazing Fleet,
Those British bloods he found, his force that durst assaile,
And poured from the Cleeues their shafts like showers of haile
Upon his helmed head; to tell him as he came,
That they (from all the world) yet feared not his name:
Which, their undaunted spirits soone made that Conqueror feele,
Oft ventring their bare breasts gainst his oft-bloodied steele;
And in their Chariots charg'd; which they with wondrous skill
Could turne in their swift'st course upon the steepest hill,
And wheele about his troopes for vantage of the ground,
Or else disranke his force where entrance might be found:
And from their Armed seats their thrilling Darts could throwe;
Or nimblie leaping downe, their valiant swords bestowe,
And with an active skip remount themselues againe,
Leaving the Roman horse behind them on the Plaine,
And beat him back to Gaul his forces to supply;
As they the Gods of Rome and Caesar did defie
Cassibalan renown'd, the Britans faithfull guide,
Who when th'Italian powers could no way be deny'd,
But would this Ile subdue; their forces to fore-lay,
Thy Forrests thou didst fell, their speedy course to stay:
Those armed stakes in Tames that stuckst, their horse to gore
Which boldly durst attempt to forrage on thy shore:
Thou such hard entrance heere to Caesar didst allow,
To whom (thy selfe except) the Westerne world did bow.
And more then Caesar got, three Emperours could not win,
Till the courageous sonnes of our Cunobelin
Sunke under Plautius sword, sent hither to discusse
The former Roman right, by Armes againe, with us.
Nor with that Consull joyn'd, Vespasian could prevaile
In thirty severall fights, nor make them stoope their saile.
Yea, had not his brave sonne, young Titus, past their hopes,
His forward Father fetcht out of the British troopes,
And quit him wondrous well when he was strongly charg'd,
His Father (by his hands so valiantly enlarg'd)
Had never more seene Rome; nor had he ever spilt
The Temple that wise sonne of faithfull David built,
Subverted those high walls, and lay'd that Cittie wast
Which God, in humane flesh, aboue all other grac't.

No maruaile then though Rome so great her conquest thought,
In that the Ile of Wight shee to subiection brought,
Our Belgae and subdu'd (a people of the West)
That latest came to us, our least of all the rest;
When Claudius, who that time her wreath imperiall wore,
Though scarce he shew'd himselfe upon our Southerne shore,

It scornd not in his stile; but, due to that his praise
Triumphall Arches claim'd, and to have yeerely Playes,
The noblest Nauall Crowne, upon his Palace pitcht;
As with the Oceans spoyle his Rome who had enricht.

Her Caradock (with cause) so Britaine may prefer;
Then whom, a braver spirit was nere brought forth by her:
For whilst here in the West the Britans gather'd head,
This Generall of the rest, his stoutaSilures led
Against Ostorius, sent by Oasar to this place
With Romes high fortune (then the high'st in Fortunes grace)
A long and doubtfull warre with whom he did maintaine,
Untill that houre wherein his valiant Britans slaine
Hee grievously beheld (o'represt with Roman power)
Himselfe wel-neere the last their wrath did not deuour.
When (for revenge, not feare) he fled (as trusting most,
Another day might win, what this had lately lost)
To Cartismandua, Queene ofbBrigants, for her ayde,
He to his foes, by her, most falsely was betray'd.
Who, as a spoyle of warre, t'adorne the Triumph sene
To great Ostorius due, when through proud Rome hee went,
That had herselfe prepar'd (as shee had all been eyes)
Our Caradock to view; who in his Countries guise,
Came with his bodie nak't, his haire downe to his waste,
Girt with a chaine of steele; his manly breast inchaste
With sundry shapes of Beasts. And when this Britaine saw
His wife and children bound as slaues, it could not awe
His manlinesse at all: but with a setled grace,
Undaunted with her pride, hee lookt her in the face:
And with a speech so graue as well a Prince became,
Himselfe and his redeem'd, to our eternal fame.

Then Romes great Tyrant next, the lasts adopted heire,
That brave Suetonius sent, the British Coasts to cleere;
The utter spoyle of Mon who strongly did pursue
(Unto whose gloomy strengths, th'reuolted Britans flew)
There entring, hee beheld what strooke him pale with dread:
The frantick British Froes, their haire disheuelled,
With fire-brands ran about, like to their furious eyes;
And from the hollow woods the fearlesse Druides;
Who with their direfull threats, and execrable vowes,
Inforc't the troubled Heaven to knit her angry browes.

And as heere in the West the Romans bravely wan,
So all upon the East the Britans ouer-ran:
The Colony long kept at Mauldon, overthrowne,
Which by prodigious signes was many times fore-showne,
And often had dismai'd the Roman souldiers: when

Brave Voadicia made with her resolued'st men
To Virolam; whose siege with fire and sword she pli'd,
Till leueld with the earth. To London as shee hy'd,
The Consull comming in with his auspicious ayde,
The Queene (to quit her yoke no longer that delay'd)
Him dar'd by dint of sword, it hers or his to try,
With words that courage show'd, and with a voice as hie
(In her right hand her Launce, and in her left her Shield,
As both the Battells stood prepared in the Field)
Incouraging her men: which resolute, as strong,
Upon the Roman rusht; and shee, the rest among,
Wades in that doubtfull warre: till lastly, when she saw
The fortune of the day unto the Roman draw,
The Queene (t'out-live her friends who highly did disdaine,
And lastly, for proud Rome a Triumph to remaine)
By poyson ends her dayes, unto that end prepar'd,
As lavishly to spend what Suetonius spar'd.

Him scarcely Rome recall'd, such glory having wonne,
But bravely to proceed, as erst she had begunne,
Agricola heere made her great Lieutenant then:
Who having setled Men, that man of all her men,
Appointed by the Powers apparantly to see
The wearied Britans sinke, and easely in degree
Beneath his fatall sword the Ordovies to fall
Inhabiting the West, those people last of all
Which stoutl'est him with-stood, renown'd for Martiall worth.

Thence leading on his powers unto the utmost North,
When all the Townes that lay betwixt our Trent and Tweed,
Suffic'd not (by the way) his wasteful fires to feed,
He there some Britans found, who (to rebate their spleene,
As yet with grieved eyes our spoyles not having seene)
Him at Mount Grampus met: which from his height beheld
Them lavish of their lives; who could not be compeld
The Roman yoke to beare: and Galgacus their guide
Amongst his murthered troupes there resolutely di'd.

Eight Roman Emperours raign'd since first that warre began;
Great Julius Caesar first, the last Domitian.
A hundred thirtie yeeres the Northerne Britans still,
That would in no wise stoupe to Romes imperious will,
Into the straitned Land with theirs retired farre,
In lawes and manners since from us that different are;
And with the Irish Pict, which to their ayde they drew
(On them oft breaking in, who long did them pursue)
A greater foe to us in our owne bowels bred,
Then Rome, with much expense that us had conquered.

And when that we great Romes so much in time were growne,
That shee her charge durst leaue to Princes of our owne,
(Such as, within our selues, our suffrage should elect)
Aviragus, borne ours, heere first she did protect;
Who faithfully and long, of labour did her ease.

Then he, our Flamins seats who turn'd to Bishops seas;
Great Lucius, that good King: to whom we chiefly owe
This happinesse we have, Christ crucifi'd to knowe.

As Britaine to her praise receiv'd the Christian faith,
After (that Word-made Man) our deere Redeemers death
Within two hundred yeeres; and his Disciples heere,
By their great Maister sent to preach him every where,
Most reverently receiv'd, their doctrine and preferd;
Interring him, c who earst the Sonne of God interd.

So Britans was she borne, though Italy her crown'd,
Of all the Christian world that Empresse most renown'd,
Constantius worthy wife who scorning worldly losse,
Her selfe in person went to seeke that sacred Crosse,
Whereon our Saviour di'd: which found, as it was sought,
From Salem unto Rome triumphantly she brought.

As when the Primer Church her Councells pleas'd to call,
Great Britains Bishops there were not the least of all;
Against the Arian Sect at Aries having roome,
At Sardica againe, and at Ariminum,

Now, when with various Fate five hundred yeeres had past,
And Rome of her great charge grew weary heere at last;
The Vandalls, Goths, and Huns, that with a powerfull head
All Italy and France had wel-neare over-spred,
To much-endanger'd Rome sufficient warning gaue,
Those forces that shee held, within herselfe to have.
The Roman rule from us then utterly remou'd.

Whilst, we, in sundry Fields, our sundry fortunes prou'd
With the remorselesse Pict, still wasting us with warre.
And twixt the froward Sire, licentious Vortiger,
And his too forward sonne, young Vortimer, arose
Much strife within our selues, whilst heere they interpose
By turns each others raignes; whereby, we weakned grow.
The warlike Saxon then into the Land we drew;
A Nation nurst in spoyle, and fitt'st to undergoe
Our cause against the Pict, our most inveterate foe.

When they, which we had hyr'd for souldiers to the shore,
Perceiv'd the wealthy Ile to wallow in her store,
And suttly had found out how we in feebled were;
They, under false pretence of amitie and cheere,
The British Peeres invite, the German Healths to view
At Stonehenge, where they them unmercifully slew.

Then, those of Brutes great blood, of Armoriek possest,
Extreamly griev'd to see their kinsmen so distrest,
Us offred to relieve, or else with us to die:
Wee, after, to requite their noble curtesie,
Eleven thousand mayds sent those our friends againe,
In wedlock to be linkt with them of Brute's high Straine;
That none with Brutes great blood, but Britans might be mixt:
Such friendship ever was the stock of Troy betwixt.
Out of whose ancient race, that warlike Arthur sprong:
Whose most renowned Acts shall sounded be as long
As Britains name is known: which spred themselues so wide,
As scarcely hath for fame left any roomth beside.

My Wales, then hold thine owne, and let thy Britains stand
Upon their right, to be the noblest of the Land.
Thinke how much better tis, for thee, and those of thine,
From Gods, and Heroës old to drawe your famous line,
Then from the Scythian poore; whence they themselues derive
Whose multitudes did first you to the Mountaines drive.
Nor let the spacious Mound of that great Mercian King
(Into a lesser roomth thy burlinesse to bring)
Include thee; when my Selfe, and my deere brother Dee,
By nature were the bounds first limited to thee.

Scarce ended shee her speech, but those great Mountaines neere,
Upon the Cambrian part that all for Brutus were,
With her high truths inflam'd, look't every one about
To find their severall Springs; and bad them get them out,
And in their fulness waite upon their soueraigne Flood,
In Britains ancient right so bravely that had stood.

When first the furious Teame, that on the Cambrian side
Doth Shropshire as a Meere from Hereford divide,
As worthiest of the rest; so worthily doth craue
That of those lesser Brooks the leading she might have;
The first of which is Clun, that to her Mistris came
Which of a Forrest borne that beares her proper name,
Unto the Golden Vale and anciently ally'd,
Of every thing of both, sufficiently supply'd,
The longer that she growes, the more renowne doth win:
And for her greater State, next Bradfield bringeth in,

Which to her wider banks resignes a weake streame.

When fiercely making forth, the strong and lustie Teame
A friendly Forest Nymph (nam'd Mockery) doth imbrace,
Her selfe that bravely beares; twixt whom and Bringwood Chase,
Her banks with many a wreath are curiously brdrcht,
And in their safer shades they long time her protect.

Then takes shee Oney in, and forth from them doth fling:
When to her further ayde, next Bowe, and Warren, bring
Cleere Quenny; by the way, which Stradbrooke up doth take:
By whose united powers, their Teame they mightier make;
Which in her lively course to Ludlowe comes at last,
Where Corue into her streame her selfe doth head-long cast.
With due attendance next, comes Ledwich and the Rhea.

Then speeding her, as though sent post unto the Sea,
Her native Shropshire leaues, and bids those Townes adiew,
Her onely soueraigne Queene, proud Severne to pursue.

When at her going out, those Mountaines of command
(The Clees, like louing Twinnes, and Stitterston that stand)
Trans-Severned, behold faire England tow'rds the rise,
And on their setting side, how ancient Cambria lies.
Then Stipperston a hill, though not of such renowne
As many that are set heere tow'rds the going downe,
To those his owne Allyes, that stood not farre away,
Thus in behalfe of Wales directly seem'd to say;

Deare Corndon, my delight, as thou art lov'd of mee,
And Breeden, as thou hop'st a Britaine thought to bee,
To Cortock strongly cleaue, as to our ancient friend,
And all our utmost strength to Cambria let us lend.
For though that envious Time iniuriously have wroong
From us those proper names did first to us belong,
Yet for our Country still, stout Mountaines let us stand.

Here, every neighbouring Hill held up a willing hand,
As freely to applaud what Stipperston decreed:
And Hockstow when she heard the Mountaines thus proceed,
With ecchoes from her Woods, her inward joyes exprest,
To heare that Hill she lov'd, which likewise lov'd her best,
Should in the right of Wales, his neighbouring Mountaines stirre,
So to aduance that place which might them both preferre;
That she from open shouts could scarce her selfe refraine.

When soone those other Rils to Severne which retaine,
And 't ended not on Teame, thus of themselues do showe

The seruice that to her they absolutely owe.
First Camlet commeth in, a Mountgomerian mayde,
Her source in Severns bankes that safely having layd,
Mele, her great Mistris next at Shrewsbury doth meet,
To see with what a grace she that faire towne doth greet;
Into what sundry gyres her wondered selfe she throwes,
And oft in-Iles the shore, as want only she flowes;
Of it, oft taking leaue, oft turnes, it to imbrace;
As though she onely were enamored of that place,
Her fore-intended course determined to leaue,
And to that most lov'd Towne eternally to cleaue:
With much ado at length, yet bidding it adue,
Her iourney towards the Sea doth seriously pursue.
Where, as along the shores she prosperously doth sweepe,
Small Maybrooke maketh-in, to her inticing Deepe.
And as she lends her eye to Bruge's loftie sight,
That Forest-Nymph milde Morffe doth kindly her inuite
To see within her shade what pastime she could make:
Where she, of Shropshire; I my leaue of Severne take.


THE NINTH SONG

THE ARGUMENT

The Muse heere Merioneth vaunts,
And her proud Mountaines highly chaunts.
The Hills and Brooks, to bravery bent,
Stand for precedence from Descent:
The Rivers for them shewing there
The wonders of their Pimblemere.
Proud Snowdon gloriously proceeds
With Cambria's native Princes deeds.
The Muse then through Carnarvan makes,
And Mon (now Anglesey) awakes
To tell her ancient Druides guise,
And manner of their Sacrifice.
Her Rillets shee together calls;
Then back for Flint and Denbigh falls.

Of all the Cambrian Shires their heads that beare so hie,
And farth'st survay their soyles with an ambitious eye,
Mervinia for her Hills, as for their matchlesse crowds,
The neerest that are said to kisse the wandring clowds,
Especiall Audience craues, offended with the throng,
That shee of all the rest neglected was so long:
Alleaging for her selfe; When through the Saxons pride,

The God-like race of Brute to Severns setting side
Were cruelly inforc't, her Mountaines did relieve
Those, whom deuouring warre else every-where did grieve.
And when all Wales beside (by Fortune or by might)
Unto her ancient foe resign'd her ancient right,
A constant Mayden still shee onely did remaine,
The last her genuine lawes which stoutly did retaine.
And as each one is prays'd for her peculiar things;
So onely shee is rich, in Mountaines, Meres, and Springs,
And holds her selfe as great in her superfluous wast,
As others by their Townes, and fruitfull tillage grac't.
And therefore, to recount her Rivers, from their Lins,
Abbridging all delayes, Mervinia thus begins;

Though Dovy, which doth far her neighboring Floods surmount
(Whose course, for hers alone Mountgomery doth account)
Hath Angell for her owne, and Keriog she doth cleere,
With Towin, Gwedall then, and Dulas, all as deere,
Those tributary streames she is maintain'd withall:
Yet, boldly may I say, her rising and her fall
My Country calleth hers, with many another Brooke,
That with their crystall eyes on the Vergiuian looke.
To Dovy next, of which Desunny sea-ward drives,
Lingorrill goes alone: but plentious Avon strives
The first to be at Sea; and faster her to hie,
Cleere Kessilgum comes in, with Hergum by and by.
So Derry, Moothy drawes, and Moothy calleth Caine,
Which in one channell meet, in going to the Maine,
As to their utmost power to lend her all their aydes:
So Atro by the arme Lanbeder kindly leads.
And Velenrid the like, obseruing th'others lawe,
Calls Cunnell; shee againe, faire Drurid forth doth draw,
That from their mother Earth, the rough Mervinia, pay
Their mixed plentious Springs, unto the lesser Bay
Of those two noble armes into the Land that beare,
Which through Gwinethia be so famous every where,
On my Carnarvan side by nature made my Mound,
As Dovy doth divide the Cardiganian ground.
The peatly Conwayes head, as that of holy Dee,
Renowned Rivers both, their rising have in mee:
So, Lauern and the Lue, themselues that head-long throwe
Into the spacious Lake, where Dee unmixt doth flowe.
Trowerrin takes his streame, here from a native Lin;
Which, out of Pimblemere when Dee him selfe doth win,
Along with him his Lord full curteously doth glide:
So Rudock riseth heere, and Cletor that doe guide
Him in his rugged path, and make his greatnes way,
Their Dee into the bounds of Denbigh to convay.

The loftie Hills, this while attentively that stood,
As to survey the course of every severall Flood,
Sent forth such ecchoing shoutes (which every way so shrill,
With the reverberate sound the spacious ayre did fill)
That they were easely heard through the Vergiuian Maine
To Neptunes inward Court; and beating there, constraine
That mightie God of Sea t'awake: who full of dread,
Thrice threw his three-forkt Mace about his griefly head,
And thrice aboue the Rocks his fore-head rays'd to see
Amongst the high-topt Hills what tumult it should bee.
So that with very sweat Cadoridric did drop,
And mighty Raran shooke his proud sky-kissing top,
Amongst the furious rout whom madnes did enrage;
Untill the Mountaine Nymphs, the tumult to asswage,
Upon a modest signe of silence to the throng,
Consorting thus, in prayse of their Mervinia, song;

Thrice famous Saxon King, on whom Time nere shall pray,
O Edgar! who compeldst our Ludwall hence to pay
Three hundred Wolues a yeere for trybute unto thee:
And for that tribute payd, as famous may'st thou bee,
O conquer'd British King, by whom was first destroy'd
The multitude of Wolues, that long this Land annoy'd;
Regardlesse of their rape, that now our harmlesse Flocks,
Securely heere may sit upon the aged Rocks;
Or wandring from their walks, and straggling here and there
Amongst the scattred Cleeues, the Lambe needs never feare;
But from the threatning storme to saue it selfe may creepe
Into that darksome Caue where once his foe did keepe:
That now the clambring Goat all day which having fed,
And clyming up to see the sunne goe downe to bed,
Is not at all in doubt her little Kid to lose,
Which grazing in the Vale, secure and safe she knowes.

Where, from these lofty hills which spacious Heaven doe threat,
Yet of as equall height, as thick by nature set,
We talke how wee are stor'd, or what wee greatly need,
Or how our flocks doe fare, and how our heards doe feed,
When else the hanging Rocks, and Vallyes dark and deepe,
The Sommers longest day would us from meeting keepe.

Yee Cambrian Shepheards then, whō these our Mountaines please,
And yee our fellow Nymphs, yee light Oreades,
Saint Hellens wondrous way, and Herberts let us goe,
And our divided Rocks with admiration showe.

Not meaning there to end, but speaking as they were,

A suddaine fearefull noyse surprised every eare.
The water-Nymphs (not farre) Lin-Teged that frequent,
With browes besmear'd with ooze, their locks with dewe besprent,
Inhabiting the Lake, in sedgy bowres belowe,
Their inward grounded griefe that onely sought to showe
Against the Mountaine kind, which much on them did take
Aboue their watry brood, thus proudly them bespake;

Tell us, ye haughtie Hills, why vainly thus you threat,
Esteeming us so meane, compar'd to you so great.
To make you know your selues, you this must understand,
That our great Maker layd the surface of the Land,
As levell as the Lake untill the generall Flood,
When ouer all so long the troubled waters stood:
Which, hurried with the blasts from angry Heaven that blew,
Upon huge massy heapes the loosened grauell threw:
From hence we would yee knew, your first beginning came.
Which, since, in tract of time, your selues did Mountaines name.
So that the earth, by you (to check her mirthfull cheere)
May alwaies see (from Heaven) those plagues that poured were
Upon the former world; as t'were by scarres to showe
That still shee must remaine disfigur'd with the blowe:
And by th'infectious slime that doomefull Deluge left,
Nature herselfe hath since of puritie beene reft;
And by the seeds corrupt, the life of mortall man
Was shortned. With these plagues yee Mountaines first began.

But, ceasing you to shame; What Mountaine is there found
In all your monstrous kind (seeke yee the Iland round)
That truly of him selfe such wonders can report
As can this spacious Lin, the place of our resort?
That when Dee in his course faine in her lap would lie,
Commixtion with her store, his streame shee doth deny,
By his complexion prou'd, as he through her doth glide.
Her wealth againe from his, she likewise doth divide:
Those White-fish that in her doe wondrously abound,
Are never seene in him; nor are his Salmons found
At any time in her: but as shee him disdaines;
So hee againe, from her, as wilfully abstaines.
Downe from the neighboring Hills, those plentious Springs that fall,
Nor Land-floods after raine, her never moue at all.
And as in Sommers heat, so alwaies is she one,
Resembling that great Lake which seemes to care for none:
And with sterne Eolus blasts, like Thetis waxing ranke,
Shee onely ouer-swells the surface of her bank.

But, whilst the Nymphs report these wonders of their Lake,
Their further cause of speech the mightie aSnowdon brake;

Least, if their watry kind should suffred be too long,
The licence that they tooke, might doe the Mountaines wrong.
For quickly he had found that straitned poynt of Land,
Into the Irish Sea which puts his powrefull hand,
Puft with their watry praise, grew insolently proud,
And needs would have his Rills for Rivers be allow'd:
Short Dorent, neer'st unto the utmost poynt of all
That th'Ile of Gelin greets, and Bardsey in her fall;
And next to her, the Sawe, the Gir, the Er, the May,
Must Rivers be at least, should all the world gaine-say:
And those, whereas the Land lyes East-ward, amply wide,
That goodly Conway grace upon the other side,
Borne neere upon her banks, each from her proper Lin,
Soone from their Mothers out, soone with their Mistris in.
As Ledder, her Allie, and neighbour Legwy; then
Goes Purloyd, Castell next, with Giffin, that agen
Obserue faire Conway's course: and though their race be short,
Yet they their Soueraigne Flood inrich with their resort.
And Snowdon, more then this, his proper Mere did note
(Still Delos like, wherein a wandring Ile doth floate)
Was peremptory growne upon his higher ground;
That Poole, in which (besides) the one-eyed fish are found,
As of her wonder proud, did with the Floods partake.

So, when great Snowdon saw, a Faction they would make
Against his generall kind; both parties to appease,
Hee purposeth to sing their native Princes praise.
For Snowdony, a Hill, imperiall in his seat,
Is from his mighty foote, unto his head so great,
That were his Wales distrest, or of his helpe had need,
Hee all her Flocks and Heards for many months could feed.
Therefore to doe some-thing were worthy of his name,
Both tending to his strength, and to the Britans fame,
His Country to content, a signall having made,
By this Oration thinks both Parties to perswade:

Whilst heere this generall Ile, the ancient Britans ow'd,
Their valiant deeds before by Severn have been show'd:
But, since our furious Foe, these powrefull Saxon swarmes
(As mercilesse in spoyle, as well approu'd in Armes)
Heere called to our ayde, Loëgria us bereft,
Those poore and scatter'd few of Brutes high linage left,
For succour hither came; where that unmixed race
Remaines unto this day, yet owners of this place:
Of whom no Flood nor Hill peculiarly hath song.
These, then, shall be my Theame: least Time too much should wrong
Such Princes as were ours, since sever'd we have been;
And as themselues, their fame be limited between

The Severne and our Sea, long pent within this place,
Till with the tearme of Welsh, the English now embase
The nobler Britains name, that welneere was destroy'd
With Pestilence and Warre, which this great Ile annoy'd;
Cadwallader that draue to the Armorick shore:
To which, drad Conan, Lord of Denbigh, long before,
His Countrymen from hence auspiciously convay'd:
Whose noble feates in warre, and never-fayling ay'd,
Got Maximus (at length) the victorie in Gaul,
Upon the Roman powers. Where, after Gratians fall,
Armorica to them the valiant Victor gaue:
Where Conan, their great Lord, as full of courage, draue
The Celts out of their seats, and did their roome supply
With people still from hence; which of our Colony
Was little Britaine call'd. Where that distressed King,
Cadwallader, himselfe awhile recomforting
With hope of Alans ayde (which there did him detaine)
Forewarned was in Dreames, that of the Britans raigne
A sempiternall end the angry Powers decreed,
A Recluse life in Rome injoyning him to lead.
The King resigning all, his sonne young Edwall left
With Alan: who, much griev'd the Prince should be bereft
Of Britains ancient right, rigg'd his unconquer'd Fleet;
And as the Generalls then, for such an Army meet,
His Nephew Juor chose, and Hiner for his pheere;
Two most undaunted spirits. These valiant Britans were
The first who West-sex wonne. But by the ling'ring warre,
When they those Saxons found t'have succour still from farre,
They tooke them to their friends on Severns setting shore:
Where finding Edwall dead, they purpos'd to restore
His sonne young Rodorick, whom the Saxon powers pursu'd:
But hee, who at his home heere scorn'd to be subdu'd,
With Aldred (that on Wales his strong invasion brought)
Garthmalack, and Pencoyd (those famous battailes) fought,
That North and South-wales sing, on the West-Sexians wonne.

Scarce this victorious taske his bloodied sword had done,
But at Mount Carno met the Mercians, and with wounds
Made Ethelbald to feele his trespasse on our bounds;
Prevail'd against the Pict, before our force that flew;
And in a valiant fight their King Dalargan slew.

Nor Conan's courage lesse, nor lesse prevail'd in ought
Renowned Rodoricks heire, who with the English fought
The Herefordian Field; as Ruthlands red with gore:
Who, to transfer the warre from this his native shore,
Marcht through the Mercian Townes with his reuengefull blade;
And on the English there such mighty hauock made.

That Offa (when he saw his Countries goe to wrack)
From bick'ring with his folke, to keepe us Britains back,
Cast up that mighty Mound of eighty miles in length,
Athwart from Sea to Sea. Which of the Mercians strength
A witnesse though it stand, and Offa's name doe beare,
Our courage was the cause why first he cut it there:
As that most dreadfull day at Gauelford can tell,
Where under eithers sword so many thousands fell
With intermixed blood, that neither knew their owne;
Nor which went Victor thence, unto this day is knowne.

Nor Kettles conflict then, lesse martiall courage show'd,
Where valiant Mervin met the Mercians, and bestow'd
His nobler British blood on Burthreds recreant flight.

As Rodorick his great sonne, his father following right,
Bare not the Saxons scornes, his Britans to out-brave;
At Gwythen, but againe to Burthred battell gaue;
Twice driving out the Dane when he invasion brought.
Whose no lesse valiant sonne, againe at Conway fought
With Danes and Mercians mixt, and on their hatefull head
Down-showr'd their dire reuenge whom they had murthered.

And, wer't not that of us the English would report
(Abusing of our Tongue in most malicious sort
As often-times they doe) that more then any, wee
(The Welsh, as they us tearme) love glorifi'd to bee,
Heere could I else recount the slaught'red Saxons gore
Our swords at Crosford spilt on Severns wandring shore;
And Griffith here produce, Lewellins valiant sonne
(May wee believe our Bards) who five pitcht Battels wonne;
And to reuenge the wrongs the envious English wrought,
His well-train'd martiall troupes into the Marches brought
As farre as Wor'ster walls: nor thence did he retire,
Till Powse lay wel-neere spent in our reuengefull fire;
As Hereford layd waste: and from their plentious soyles,
Brought back with him to Wales his prisoners and his spoyles.

Thus as we valiant were, when valour might us steed:
With those so much that dar'd, wee had them that decreed.
For, what Mulmutian lawes, or Martian, ever were
More excellent then those which our good Howell heere
Ordayn'd to gouerne Wales? which still with us remaine.

And when all-powerfull Fate had brought to passe againe,
That as the Saxons earst did from the Britains win;
Upon them so (at last) the Normans comming in,
Tooke from those Tyrants heere, what treacherously they got

(To the perfidious French, which th'angry Heavens allot)
Nere could that Conquerors sword (which roughly did decide
His right in England heere, and prostrated her pride)
Us to subiection stoope, or make us Britains beare
Th'unwieldy Norman yoke: nor basely could we feare
His Conquest, entring Wales; but (with stout courage) ours
Defi'd him to his face, with all his English powers.
And when in his revenge, proud Rufus hither came
(With vowes) us to subvert; with slaughter and with shame,
O're Severn him we sent, to gather stronger ayde.

So, when to Englands power, Albania hers had lay'd,
By Henry Beauclarke brought (for all his divelish wit,
By which he raught the Wreath) hee not prevail'd a whit:
And through our rugged straits when he so rudely prest,
Had not his proued Maile sate surely to his breast,
A skilfull British hand his life had him bereft,
As his sterne brothers hart, by Tirrills hand was cleft.

And let the English thus which vilifie our name,
If it their greatnes please, report unto our shame
The foyle our Gwyneth gaue at Flints so deadly fight,
To Maud the Empresse sonne, that there he put to flight;
And from the English power th'imperiall Ensigne tooke:
About his plumed head which valiant Owen shooke.

As when that King againe, his fortune to advance
Aboue his former foyle, procur'd fresh powers from France,
A surely-leveld shaft if Sent-cleare had not seene,
And in the very loose, not thrust himselfe betweene
His Soueraigne and the shaft, he our reuenge had tri'd:
Thus, to preserue the King, the noble subiect dy'd.

As Madock his brave sonne, may come the rest among;
Who, like the God-like race from which his Grandsires sprong,
Whilst heere his Brothers tyr'd in sad domestick strife,
On their unnaturall breasts bent eithers murtherous knife;
This brave aduenturous Youth, in hote pursute of fame,
With such as his great spirit did with high deeds inflame,
Put forth his well-rigg'd Fleet to seeke him forraine ground,
And sayled West so long, untill that world he found
To Christians then unknowne (saue this adventrous crue)
Long ere Columbus liv'd, or it Vesputius knew;
And put the now-nam'd Welsh on India's parched face,
Unto the endlesse praise of Brutes renowned race,
Ere the Iberian Powers had toucht her long-sought Bay,
Or any eare had heard the sound of Florida.
And with that Croggens name let th'English us disgrace;

When there are to be seene, yet, in that ancient place
Frō whence that name they fetch, their cōquer'd Grandsires Graues:
For which each ignorant sot, unjustly us depraves.

And when that Tyrant John had our subversion vow'd,
To his unbridled will our necks we never bow'd:
Nor to his mightie sonne; whose host wee did inforce
(His succours cutting off) to eate their war-like horse.

Untill all-ruling Heaven would have us to resigne:
When that brave Prince, the last of all the British Line,
Lewellin, Griffiths sonne, unluckily was slaine,
As Fate had spar'd our fall till Edward Longshanks raigne.
Yet to the stock of Brute so true wee ever were,
We would permit no Prince, unlesse a native here.
Which, that most prudent King perceiving, wisely thought
To satisfie our wills, and to Carnarvan brought
His Queene be'ing great with child, euen ready downe to lie;
Then to his purpos'd end doth all his powers apply.

Through every part of Wales hee to the Nobles sent,
That they unto his Court should come incontinent,
Of things that much concern'd the Country to debate:
But now behold the power of unauoyded Fate.

When thus unto his will he fitly them had wonne,
At her expected houre the Queene brought forth a sonne.
And to this great designe, all hapning as he would,
He (his intended course that clearkly manage could)
Thus queintly traines us on: Since he perceiv'd us prone
Here onely to be rul'd by Princes of our owne,
Our naturalnes therein he greatly did approue;
And publiquely protests, that for the ancient love
He ever bare to Wales, they all should plainly see,
That he had found out one, their soueraigne Lord to bee;
Com'n of the race of Kings, and (in their Country borne)
Could not one English word: of which he durst be sworne.
Besides, his upright heart, and innocence was such,
As that (he was assur'd) blacke Enuie could not tuch
His spotlesse life in ought. Poore we (that not espie
His subtilty herein) in plaine simplicity,
Soone bound ourselues by oath, his choice not to refuse:
When as that craftie King, his little childe doth chuse,
Yong Edward, borne in Wales, and of Carnaruan call'd.
Thus by the English craft, we Britans were enthrall'd:

Yet in thine owne behalfe, deare Country dare to say,
Thou long as powerfull wert as England every way.

And if she ouermuch should seeke thee to imbase,
Tell her thou art the Nurse of all the British race;
And he that was by Heaven appointed to unite
(After that tedious warre) the red Rose and the white,
A Tudor was of thine, and native of thy Mon,
From whom descends that King now sitting on her Throane.

This speech, by Snowdon made, so luckie was to please
Both parties, and them both with such content t'appease;
That as before they stroue for soueraignty and place,
They onely now contend, which most should other grace.

Into the Irish Sea, then all those Rilles that ronne,
In Snowdons praise to speake, immediatly begon;
Lewenny, Lynan next, then Gwelly gaue it out,
And Kerriog her compeere, soone told it all about:
So did their sister Nymphs, that into Mena straine;
The flood that doth divide Mon from the Cambrian Maine.
It Gorway greatly prais'd, and Seint it lowdly song.
So, mighty Snowdons speech was through Carnaruan rong;
That scarcely such a noise to Mon from Mena came,
When with his puissant troupes for conquest of the same,
On Bridges made of Boates, the Roman powers her sought,
Or Edward to her sacke his English Armies brought:
That Mona strangely stird great Snowdons praise to heare,
Although the stock of Troy to her was ever deare;
Yet (from her proper worth) as shee before all other
§ Was call'd (in former times) her Country Cambria's mother,
Perswaded was thereby her praises to pursue,
Or by neglect, to lose what to her selfe was due,
A signe to Neptune sent, his boystrous rage to slake;
Which suddainly becalm'd, thus of her selfe she spake;

What one of all the Iles to Cambria doth belong
(To Britaine, I might say, and yet not doe her wrong)
Doth equall me in soyle, so good for grasse and graine?
As should my Wales (where still Brutes ofspring doth remaine)
That mighty store of men, yet more of beasts doth breed,
By famine of by warre constrained be to need,
And Englands neighboring Shires their succour would denie;
My onely selfe her wants could plentiously supply.

What Iland is there sound upon the Irish coast,
In which that Kingdome seemes to be delighted most
(And seeke you all along the rough Vergiuian shore,
Where the incountring tydes outrageously doe rore)
That bowes not at my beck, as they to me did owe
The dutie subiects should unto their Soueraigne showe;

§ So that th'Eubonian Man, a kingdome long time knowne,
Which wisely hath been rul'd by Princes of her owne,
In my alliance joyes, as in th'Albanian Seas
The aArrans, and by them the scatt'red Eubides
Rejoyce euen at my name; and put on mirthfull cheere,
When of my good estate, they by the Sea-Nymphs heare.

Sometimes within my shades, in many an ancient wood,
Whose often-twined tops, great Phoebus fires withstood,
The fearelesse British Priests, under an aged Oake,
Taking a milk-white Bull, unstrained with the yoke,
And with an Axe of gold, from that loue-sacred tree
The Missleto cut downe; then with a bended knee
On th'unhew'd Altar layd, put to the hallowed fires:
And whilst in the sharpe flame the trembling flesh expires,
As their strong furie mou'd (when all the rest adore)
Pronouncing their desires the sacrifice before,
Up to th'eternall Heauen their bloodied hands did reare:
And, whilst the murmuring woods euen shuddred as with feare,
Preacht to the beardlesse youth, the soules immortall state;
To other bodies still how it should transmigrate,
That to contempt of death them strongly might excite.

To dwell in my blacke shades the Wood-gods did delight,
Untroden with resort that long so gloomy were,
As when the Roman came, it strooke him sad with feare
To looke upon my face, which then was call'd the Darke;
Untill in after time, the English for a marke
Gaue me this hatefull name, which I must ever beare,
And Anglesey from them am called every where.

My Brooks (to whose sweet brimmes the Syluans did resort,
In glyding through my shades, to mightie Neptunes Court,
Of their huge Oakes bereft) to Heauen so open lie,
That now ther's not a roote discern'd by any eye:
My Brent, a pretty Beck, attending Menas mouth,
With those her sister Rills, that beare upon the South,
Guint, forth along with her Lewenny that doth draw;
And next to them againe, the fat and moory Frawe,
§ Which with my Princes Court I some-time pleas'd to grace,
As those that to the West directly runne their race.
Smooth Allo in her fall, that Lynon in doth take;
Mathanon, that amaine doth tow'rds Moylroniad make,
The Sea-calfes to behold that bleach them on her shore,
Which Gweger to her gets, as to increase her store.
Then Dulas to the North that straineth, as to see
The Ile that breedeth Mice: whose store so lothsome bee,
That shee in Neptunes brack her blewish head doth hide.

When now the wearied Muse her burthen having ply'd,
Her selfe a while betakes to bathe her in the Sound;
And quitting in her course the goodly Monian ground,
Assayes the Penmenmaur, and her cleere eyes doth throwe
On Conway, tow'rds the East, to England back to goe:
Where finding Denbigh fayre, and Flint not out of sight,
Cryes yet afresh for Wales, and for Brutes ancient right.


THE TENTH SONG

THE ARGUMENT

The serious Muse her selfe applyes
To Merlins ancient prophecies,
At Dinas Emris; where hee show'd
How Fate the Britaines rule bestow'd.
To Conway next she turnes her tale,
And sings her Cluyds renowned Vale;
Then of Saint Winifrid doth tell,
And all the wonders of her Well;
Makes Dee, Bruit's historie pursue:
At which, shee bids her Wales Adieu.

Awhile thus taking breath, our way yet faire in view,
The Muse her former course doth seriously pursue.
From Penmens craggy height to try her saily wings,
Herselfe long having bath'd in the delicious Springs
(That trembling from his top through long-worne crannies creepe,
To spend their liquid store on the insatiate Deepe)
Shee meets with Conway first, which lyeth next at hand:
Whose precious orient Pearle that breedeth in her sand,
Aboue the other floods of Britaine doth her grace:
Into the Irish Sea which making out her race,
Supply'd by many a Mere (through many severall Rills
Into her bosome pour'd) her plentiously shee fills.
O goodly River! neere unto thy sacred Spring
Prophetique Merlin sate, when to the British King
The changes long to come, auspiciously he told.
Most happy were thy Nymphs, that wondring did behold,
His grauer wrinkled brow, amazed and did heare
The dreadfull words he spake, that so ambiguous were.
Thrice happy Brooks, I say, that (every way about)
Thy tributaries be: as is that Towne, where-out
Into the Sea thou fall'st, which Conway of thy name
Perpetually is call'd, to register thy fame.

For thou, cleere Conway, heard'st wise Merlin first relate
The Destinies Decree, of Britains future fate;
Which truly he fore-told proud Vortiger should lose:
As, when him from his seat the Saxons should depose:
The forces that should heere from Armorick arrive,
Yet farre too weake from hence the enemie to drive:
And to that mightie King, which rashly under-tooke
A strong-wall'd Tower to reare, those earthly spirits that shooke
The great foundation still, in Dragons horrid shape,
That dreaming Wisard told; making the Mountaine gape
With his most powerfull charmes, to view those Caverns deepe;
And from the top of Brith, so high and wondrous steepe,
Where Dinas Emris stood, shew'd where the Serpents fought,
The White that tore the Red; from whence the Prophet wrought
The Britains sad decay then shortly to ensue.

O! happy yee that heard the man who all things knew
Untill the generall Doome, through all the world admyr'd:
By whose Prophetick Sawes yee all became inspyr'd;
As well the forked Neage, that neer'st her Fountaine springs,
With her beloved maid, Melandidar, that brings
Her flowe, where Conway forth into the Sea doth slide
(That to their Mistris make from the Denbighian side)
As those that from the hills of proud Carnarvan fall.

This scarce the Muse had said, but Cluyd doth quickly call
Her great recourse, to come and gard her while shee glide
Along the goodly Vale (which with her wealthy pride
Much beautifies her banks; so naturally her owne,
That Dyffren Cluyd by her both farre and neere is knowne)
With high embatteld hills that each way is enclos'd
But onely on the North: and to the North dispos'd,
Fierce Boreas finds accesse to court the dainty Vale:
Who, whisp'ring in her eare with many a wanton tale,
Allures her to his love (his Leman her to make)
As one that in himselfe much suffreth for her sake.

The Orcades, and all those Eubides imbrac't
In Neptunes aged armes, to Neptune seeming chast,
Yet prostitute themselues to Boreas; who neglects
The Calidonian Downes, nor ought at all respects
The other in-land Dales, abroad that scattred lie,
Some on the English earth, and some in Albany;
But, courting Dyffren Cluyd, her beautie doth prefer.
Such dalliance as alone the North-wind hath with her,
Orithya not enjoy'd, from Thrace when hee her tooke,
And in his saylie plumes the trembling Virgin shooke:
But through the extreame love hee to this Vale doth beare,

Growes iealous at the length, and mightily doth feare
Great Neptune, whom he sees to smug his horrid face:
And, fearing least the God should so obtaine her grace,
From the Septentrion cold, in the breem freezing ayre,
Where the bleake North-wind keeps, still dominering there,
From Shetland stradling wide, his foote on Thuly sets:
Whence storming, all the vast Deucalidon hee threts,
And beares his boystrous waues into the narrower mouth
Of the Vergiuian Sea: where meeting, from the South,
Great Neptunes surlier tides, with their robustious shocks,
Each other shoulder up against the griesly Rocks;
As strong men when they meet, contending for the path:
But, comming neere the Coast where Cluyd her dwelling hath,
The North-wind (calme become) forgets his Ire to wreake,
And the delicious Vale thus mildly doth bespeake;

Deere Cluyd, th'aboundant sweets, that from thy bosome flowe,
When with my active wings into the ayre I throwe,
Those Hills whose hoarie heads seeme in the clouds to dwell,
Of aged become young, enamor'd with the smell
Of th'odoriferous flowers in thy most precious lap:
Within whose veluit leaues, when I my selfe enwrap,
They suffocate with sents; that (from my native kind)
I seeme some slowe perfume, and not the swistest wind.
With joy, my Dyffren Cluyd, I see thee bravely spred,
Survaying every part, from foote up to thy head;
Thy full and youthfull breasts, which in their meadowy pride,
Are brancht with rivery veines, Meander-like that glide.
I further note in thee, more excellent then these
(Were there a thing that more the amorous eye might please)
Thy plumpe and swelling wombe, whose mellowy gleabe doth beare
The yellow ripened sheafe, that bendeth with the care.

Whilst in this sort his sute he amorously preferd,
Moylvennill neere at hand, the North-wind ouer-heard:
And, vexed at the hart, that he a Mountaine great,
Which long time in his breast had felt loves kindly heat,
As one whom crystall Cluyd had with her beauty caught,
Is for that Rivers sake neere of his wits distraught,
With inly rage to heare that Valley so extold;
And yet that Brooke whose course so batfull makes her mould,
And one that lends that Vale her most renowned name,
Should of her meaner farre, be ouer-gone in fame.
Wherefore, Moylevennill will'd his Cluyd her selfe to showe:
Who, from her native Fount, as proudly shee doth flowe,
Her hand-maids Manian hath, and Hespin, her to bring
To Ruthin. Whose faire seate first kindly visiting,
To lead her thence in state, Lewenny lends her sourse:

That when Moylvennill sees his Rivers great recourse,
From his intrenched top is pleas'd with her supplies.
Claweddock commeth in, and Istrad likewise hies
Unto the Queene-like Cluyd, as shee to Denbigh drawes:
And on the other side, from whence the Morning dawes,
Downe from the Flintian hills, comes Wheler, her to beare
To sacred Asaph's See, his hallowed Temple; where
Faire Elwy having wonne her sister Aleds power,
They entertaine their Cluyd neere mighty Neptunes bower:
Who likewise is sustain'd by Senion, last that falls,
And from the Virgins Well doth wash old Ruthlands walls.
Moylvennill with her sight that never is suffic'd,
Now with excessive joy so strongly is surpriz'd,
That thus he proudly spake; On the Gwynethian ground
(And looke from East to West) what Country is there crown'd
As thou Tegenia art? that, with a Vale so rich
(Cut thorough with the Cluyd, whose graces me bewitch)
The fruitfulst of all Wales, so long hast honor'd bin:
As also by thy Spring, such wonder who dost win,
That naturally remote, sixe British miles from Sea,
And rising on the Firme, yet in the naturall day
Twice falling, twice doth fill, in most admired wise.
When Cynthia from the East unto the South doth rise,
That mighty Neptune flowes, then strangly ebs thy Well:
And when againe he sinks, as strangely shee doth swell;
Yet to the sacred fount of Winifrid gives place;
Of all the Cambrian Springs of such especiall grace,
That oft the Deuian Nymphs, as also those that keepe
Amongst the Corall-Groues in the Verginian Deepe,
Have left their watry bowers, their secret safe Retire,
To see her whom report so greatly should admire
(Whose waters to this day as perfect are and cleere,
As her delightfull eyes in their full beauties were,
A virgin while she liv'd) chaste Winifrid: who chose
Before her mayden-gem she forcibly would lose,
To have her harmlesse life by the leud Rapter spilt:
For which, still more and more to aggrauate his guilt,
The livelesse teares shee shed, into a Fountaine turne.
And, that for her alone the water should not mourne,
The pure vermillion bloud, that issu'd from her vaines,
Unto this very day the pearly Grauell staines;
As erst the white and red were mixed in her cheeke.
And, that one part of her might be the other like,
Her haire was turn'd to mosse; whose sweetnesse doth declare,
In livelinesse of youth the naturall sweets she bare:
And of her holy life the innocence to show,
What-ever living thing into this Well you throwe,
Shee strongly beares it up, not suffring it to sinke.

Besides, the wholesome use in bathing, or in drinke.
Doth the diseased cure, as thereto shee did leaue
Her vertue with her name, that time should not bereaue.

Scarce of this tedious tale Moylevennill made an end,
But that the higher Yale, whose beeing doth ascend
Into the pleasant East, his loftier head aduanc't.
This Region, as a man that long had been intranc't
(Whilst thus himselfe to please, the mightie Mountaine tells
Such farlies of his Cluyd, and of his wondrous Wells)
Stood thinking what to doe: least faire Tegenia, plac't
So admirably well, might hold her selfe disgrac't
By his so barren site, being Mountainous and cold,
To nothing more unlike then Dyffren's batfull mould;
And in respect of her, to be accounted rude.
Yale, for he would not be confounded quite by Cluyd
(And for his common want, to coyne some poore excuse)
Unto his proper praise, discreetly doth produce
A Valley, for a Vale, of her peculiar kind;
In goodnesse, breadth, and length, though Dyffren farre behind:
On this yet dare he stand, that for the naturall frame,
That figure of the Crosse, of which it takes the name,
Is equall with the best, which else excell it farre:
And by the power of that most sacred Character,
Respect beyond the rest unto herselfe doth win.

When now the sterner Dee doth instantly begin
His ampler selfe to showe, that (downe the verdant Dale)
Straines, in his nobler course along the rougher Yale,
T'inuite his fauouring Brookes: where from that spacious Lin
Through which he comes unmixt, first Alwin falleth in:
And going on along, still gathering up his force,
Gets Gerrow to his ayde, to hasten on his course.
With Christioneth next, comes Keriog in apace.
Out of the leaden Mines, then with her sullied face
Claweddock casts about where Gwenrow shee may greet,
Till like two louing friends they under Wrexam meet.
Then Alen makes approach (to Dee most inly deere)
Taking Tegiddog in; who, earnest to be there,
For haste, twice under earth her crystall head doth runne:
When instantly againe, Dee's holinesse begun,
By his contracted front and sterner waues, to show
That he had things to speake, might profit them to know;
A Brooke, that was suppos'd much business to have seene,
Which had an ancient bound twixt Wales and England been,
And noted was by both to be an ominous Flood,
That changing of his Foards, the future ill, or good,
Of either Country told; of eithers warre, or peace,

The sicknes, or the health, the dearth, or the increase:
And that of all the Floods of Britaine, he might boast
His streame in former times to have been honor'd most,
When as at Chester once king Edgar held his Court,
To whom eight lesser Kings with homage did resort:
That mightie Mercian Lord, him in his Barge bestow'd,
And was by all those Kings about the River row'd.
For which, the hallowed Dee so much upon him tooke.
And now the time was come, that this imperious Brooke,
The long traduced Brute determin'd to awake,
And in the Britains right thus boldly to them spake;

O yee the ancient race of famous Brute that bee,
And thou the Queene of Iles, great Britaine; why doe yee
Your Grand-sires God-like name (with a neglectfull eare)
In so reproachfull tearmes and ignominy heare,
By every one of late contemptuouslie disgra'ct;
That he whom Time so long, and strongly hath imbrac't,
Should be reiected quite? The reason vrged why,
Is by the generall foe thus answer'd by and by:
That Brutus, as you say, by Sea who hither came,
From whom you would suppose this Ile first tooke the name,
Meerelie fictitious is; nor could the Romans heare
(Most studious of the truth, and neer'st those times that were)
Of any such as hee: nay, they who most doe strive,
From that great stock of Troy their linage to derive,
In all the large descent of Iülus, never found
That Brute, on whom wee might our first beginning ground.

To this Assertion, thus I faithfully reply;
And as a friend to Truth, doe constantlie denie
Antiquitie to them, as neerer to those times;
Their writings to precede our ancient British Rimes:
But that our noble Bards which so divinely sung
That remnant of old Troy, of which the Britaines sprung,
Before those Romans were, as proofe we can produce;
And learning, long with us, ere t'was with them in use.
And they but idly talke, upbrayding us with lies.
That Geffray Monmouth, first, our Brutus did deuise,
Not heard of till his time our Aduersary saies:
When pregnantlie wee proue, ere that Historians dayes,
A thousand ling'ring yeeres, our Prophets cleerely song
The Britaine-founding Brute, most frequent them among.
From Taliessen wise (approued so with us,
That what he spake, was held to be oraculous,
So true his writings were) and such immortall men
As this now-waning world shall hardly heare agen
In our owne genuine tongue, that natives were of Wales

Our Geffray had his Brute. Nor were these idle tales
(As he may find, the truth of our descents that seekes)
Nor fabulous, like those deuised by the Greeks:
But from the first of Time, by Judges still were heard,
Discreetlie every a yeere correcting where they err'd.

And that whereon our Foe his greatest hold doth take,
Against the handled Cause and most doth seeme to make,
Is, that we shewe no Booke our Brutus to approue;
But that our idle Bards, as their fond rage did moue,
Sang what their fancies pleas'd. Thus doe I answere these;
That th'ancient British Priests, the fearlesse Druides,
That ministred the lawes, and were so trulie wise,
That they determin'd states, attending sacrifice,
To letters never would their mysteries commit,
For which the breasts of men they deem'd to be more fit.
Which questionlesse should seeme from judgement to proceed.
For, when of Ages past wee looke in bookes to read,
Wee retchlesly discharge our memory of those.
So when iniurious Time, such Monuments doth lose
(As what so great a Work, by Time that is not wrackt?)
Wee utterly forgoe that memorable act:
But when we lay it up within the minds of men,
They leaue it their next Age; that, leaues it hers agen:
So strongly which (me thinks) doth for Tradition make,
As if you from the world it altogether take,
You utterly subvert Antiquitie thereby.
For though Time well may proue that often shee doth lie,
Posteritie by her yet many things hath known,
That ere men learn'd to write, could no way have been shown:
For, if the spirit of God, did not our faith assure
The Scriptures be from Heaven, like Heaven, divinely pure,
Of Moses mightie works, I reverently may say
(I speake with godlie feare) Tradition put away,
In power of humane wit it easely doth not lie
To proue before the Flood the Genealogie.
Nor any thing there is that kindlier doth agree
With our descent from Troy (if things compar'd may be)
Then peopling of this place, neere to those Ages, when
Exiled by the Greeks, those poore world-wandring men
(Of all hope to returne into their Country reft)
Sought shores whereon to set that little them was left:
From some such God-like race we questionlesse did spring,
Who soone became so great heere once inhabiting.
So barbarous nor were wee as manie have us made,
And Caesars envious pen would all the world perswade,
His owne ambitious ends in seeking to aduance,
When with his Roman power arriving heere from France,

If hee the Britains found experienc't so in warre,
That they with such great skill could weeld their armed Carre;
And, as he still came on, his skilfull march to let,
Cut downe their aged Oakes, and in the Rivers set
The sharpe steele-poynted stakes, as hee the Foards should pass;
I faine would understand how this that Nation was
So ignorant hee would make, and yet so knowing warre.

But, in things past so long (for all the world) we are
Like to a man embarqu't, and travelling the Deepe:
Who sayling by some hill, or promontory steepe
Which juts into the Sea, with an amazed eye
Beholds the Cleeues thrust up into the lofty skie.
And th'more that hee doth looke, the more it drawes his sight;
Now at the craggy front, then at the wondrous weight:
But, from the passed shore still as the swelling saile
(Thrust forward by the wind) the floating Barque doth haile,
The mightie Giant-heape, so lesse and lesser still
Appeareth to the eye, untill the monstrous hill
At length shewes like a cloud; and further beeing cast,
Is out of kenning quite: So, of the Ages past;
Those things that in their Age much to be wondred were,
Still as wing-footed Time them farther off doth beare,
Doe lessen every howre. When now the mighty prease,
Impatient of his speech, intreat the Flood to cease,
And cry with one consent, the Saxon state to showe,
As angry with the Muse such labour to bestowe
On Wales, but England still neglected thus to be.

And having past the time, the honorable Dee
At Chester was arriv'd, and bad them all adieu:
When our intended course, with England we pursue.


THE ELEVENTH SONG

THE ARGUMENT

The Muse, her native earth to see,
Returnes to England ouer Dee;
Visits stout Cheshire, and there showes
To her and hers, what England owes;
And of the Nymphets sporting there
In Wyrrall, and in Delamere.
Weever, the great deuotion sings
Of the religious Saxon Kings;
Those Riverets doth together call,

That into him, and Mersey fall;
Thence bearing to the side of Peake,
This zealous Canto off doth breake.

With as unwearied wings, and in as high a gate
As when we first set forth, obseruing every state,
The Muse frō Cambria comes, with pinions summ'd and sound:
And having put her selfe upō the English ground,
First seiseth in her course the noblest Cestrian shore;
Of our great English bloods as carefull heere of yore,
As Cambria of her Brutes, now is, or could be then;
For which, our prouerbe calls her, Cheshire, chiefe of men.
And of our Countries, place of Palatine doth hold,
And thereto hath her high Regalities enrold:
Besides, in many Fields since Conquering William came,
Her people shee hath prou'd, to her eternall fame.
All, children of her owne, the Leader and the Led,
The mightiest men of boane, in her full bosome bred:
And neither of them such as cold penurious need
Spurs to each rash attempt; but such as soundly feed,
Clad in warme English cloth; and maym'd should they returne
(Whom this false ruthless world else frō their doores would spurne)
Have livelihood of their owne, their ages to sustaine.
Nor did the Tenants pay, the Land-lords charge maintaine:
But as abroad in warre, he spent of his estate;
Returning to his home, his hospitable gate
The richer and the poore stood open to receaue.
They, of all England, most to ancient customes cleaue,
Their Yeomanry and still endeuoured to uphold.
For rightly whilst her selfe brave England was of old,
And our courageous Kings us forth to conquests led,
Our Armies in those times (neere through the world so dred)
Of our tall Yeomen were, and foot-men for the most;
Who (with their Bills, and Bowes) may confidently boast,
Our Leopards they so long and bravely did advance
Aboue the Flower-delice, euen in the hart of France.

O! thou thrice happy Shire, confined so to bee
Twixt two so famous Floods, as Mersey is, and Dee.
Thy Dee upon the West from Wales doth thee divide:
Thy Mersey on the North, from the Lancastrian side,
Thy naturall sister Shire; and linkt unto thee so,
That Lancashire along with Cheshire still doth goe.
As tow'rds the Derbian Peake, and Moreland (which doe draw
More mountainous and wild) the high-crown'd Shutlingslawe
And Molcop be thy Mounds, with those proud hills whence roue
The lovely sister Brooks, the silvery Dane and Doue;
Cleere Doue, that makes to Trent; the other to the West.

But, in that famous Towne, most happy of the rest
(From which thou tak'st thy name) faire Chester, call'd of old
Carelegion; whilst proud Rome her conquests heere did hold
Of those her legions known the faithfull station then,
So stoutly held to tack by those neere North-wales men;
Yet by her owne right name had rather called bee,
As her the Britaine tearm'd, The Fortresse upon Dee,
Then vainly shee would seeme a Miracle to stand,
Th'imaginary worke of some huge Giants hand:
Which if such ever were, Tradition tells not who.

But, backe awhile my Muse: to Weever let us goe,
Which (with himselfe compar'd) each British flood doth scorne;
His fountaine and his fall, both Chesters rightly borne;
The Country in his course, that cleane through doth divide,
Cut in two equall shares upon his either side:
And, what the famous Flood farre more then that enriches,
The bracky Fountaines are, those two renowned Wyches,
The Nant-wyche, and the North; whose either brynie Well,
For store and sorts of Salts, make Weever to excell.
Besides their generall use, not had by him in vaine,
But in him selfe thereby doth holinesse retuine
Aboue his fellow Floods: whose healthfull vertues taught,
Hath of the Sea-gods oft, caus'd Weever to be sought.
For physick in their need: and Thetis oft hath seene,
When by their wanton sports her Ner'ides have beene
So sick, that Glaucus selfe hath failed in their cure:
Yet Weever, by his Salts, recovery durst assure.
And Amphitrite oft this Wisard River led
Into her secret walks (the Depths profound and dread)
Of him (suppos'd so wise) the hid euents to knowe
Of things that were to come, as things done long agoe.
In which he had beene prou'd most exquisite to bee;
And bare his fame so farre, that oft twixt him and Dee,
Much strife there hath arose in their prophetick skill.

But to conclude his praise, our Weever heere doth will
The Muse, his sourse to sing; as how his course he steres:
Who from his naturall Spring, as from his neighboring Meres
Sufficiently supply'd, shootes forth his siluer breast,
As though he meant to take directly toward the East;
Untill at length it proues he loytreth, but to play
Till Ashbrooke and the Lee o're-take him on the way,
Which to his iourneys end him earnestly doe haste:
Till having got to Wyche, hee taking there a taste
Of her most sauory Salt, is by the sacred tuch,
Forc't faster in his course, his motion quickned much
To North-wyche: and at last, as hee approacheth neere,

Dane, Whelock drawes, then Crock, from that black ominous Mere,
Accounted one of those that Englands wonders make;
Of neighbours, Black-mere nam'd, of strangers, Breretons-Lake;
Whose property seemes farre from Reasons way to stand:
For, neere before his death that's owner of the Land,
Shee sends up stocks of trees, that on the top doe float;
By which the world her first did for a wonder note.

His handmayd Howty next, to Weever holds her race:
When Peever with the helpe of Pickmere, make apace
To put-in with those streames his sacred steps that tread,
Into the mighty waste of Mersey him to lead.
Where, when the Rivers meet, with all their stately traine,
Proud Mersey is so great in entring of the Maine,
As hee would make a shewe for Empery to stand,
And wrest the three-forkt Mace from out grym Neptunes hand;
To Cheshire highly bound for that his watry store,
As to the grosser Loughs on the Lancastrian shore.
From hence he getteth Goyt downe from her Peakish spring,
And Bollen, that along doth nimbler Birkin bring
From Maxfields mightie wildes, of whose shagg'd Syluans shee
Hath in the Rocks been woo'd, their Paramour to bee:
Who in the darksome holes, and Cauerns kept her long,
And that proud Forrest made a party to her wrong.
Yet could not all intreat the pretty Brooke to stay;
Which to her sister streame, sweet Bollen, creeps away.
To whom, upon their road shee pleasantly reports
The many mirthfull iests, and wanton woodish sports
In Maxfield they have had; as of that Forrests fate:
Untill they come at length, where Mersey for more state
Assuming broder banks, himselfe so proudly beares,
That at his sterne approach, extended Wyrrall feares,
That (what betwixt his floods of Mersey, and the Dee)
In very little time deuoured he might bee:
Out of the foaming surge till Hilbre lifts his head,
To let the fore-land see how richly he had sped.
Which Mersey cheeres so much, that with a smyling brow
He fawnes on both those Floods; their amorous armes that throw
About his goodly neck, and bar'd their swelling breasts:
On which whilst lull'd with ease, his pleased cheeke he rests,
The Naiades, sitting neere upon the aged Rocks,
Are busied with their combes, to brayd his verdant locks,
Whilst in their crystall eyes he doth for Cupids looke:
But Delamere from them his fancie quickly tooke,
Who shewes her selfe all drest in most delicious flowers;
And sitting like a Queene, sees from her shady Bowers
The wanton Wood-Nymphs mixt with her light-footed Fawnes,
To lead the rurall routs about the goodly Lawnds,

As over Holt and Heath, as thorough Frith and Fell;
And oft at Barly-breake, and Prison-base, to tell
(In carrolds as they course) each other all the joyes,
The passages, deceits, the sleights, the amorous toyes
The subtile Sea-Nymphs had, their Wyrralls love to win.

But Weever now againe to warne them doth begin
To leaue these triviall toyes, which inly hee did hate,
That neither them beseem'd, nor stood with his estate
(Beeing one that gaue him selfe industriously to know
What Monuments our Kings erected long agoe:
To which, the Flood himselfe so wholly did apply,
As though upon his skill, the rest should all rely)
And bent himselfe to shewe, that yet the Britains bold,
Whom the laborious Muse so highly had extold,
Those later Saxon Kings exceld not in their deeds,
And therefore with their praise thus zealously proceeds;

Whilst, the celestiall Powers th'arrived time attend
When o're this generall Ile the Britaines raigne should end,
And for the spoyling Pict heere prosp'rously had wrought,
Into th'afflicted Land which strong invasion brought,
And to that proud attempt, what yet his power might want,
The ill-disposed Heavens, Brutes ofspring to supplant,
Their angry plagues downe-pour'd, insatiate in their waste
(Needs must they fall, whom Heaven doth to destruction haste.)
And that which lastly came to consummate the rest,
Those prouder Saxon powers (which liberally they prest
Against th'invading Pict, of purpose hired in)
From those which payd them wage, the Iland soone did win;
And sooner ouerspred, beeing Masters of the Field;
Those, first for whom they fought, too impotent to wield,
A Land within it selfe that had so great a Foe;
And therefore thought it fit them wisely to bestow:
Which ouer Severne heere they in the Mountaines shut,
And some upon that poynt of Cornwall sorth they put.
Yet forced were they there their stations to defend.

Nor could our men permit the Britains to descend
From Ioue or Mars alone; but brought their blood as hie,
From Woden, by which name they stiled Mercurie.
Nor were the race of Brute, which ruled heere before,
More zealous to the Gods they brought unto this shore
Then Hengists noble heyres; their Idols that to raise
Heere put their German names upon our weekly daies.

These noble Saxons were a Nation hard and strong,
On sundry Lands and Seas, in warfare nuzzled long;

Affliction throughly knew; and in proud Fortunes spight,
Euen in the iawes of Death had dar'd her utmost might:
Who under Hengist first, and Horsa, their braue Chiefes,
From Germany arriv'd, and with the strong reliefes
Of th'Angles and the Jutes, them ready to supply,
Which anciently had beene of their affinitie,
By Scythia first sent out, which could not giue them meat,
Were forc't to seeke a soyle wherein themselues to seat.
Them at the last on Dansk their lingring fortune draue,
Where Holst unto their troups sufficient harbor gaue.
These with the Saxons went, and fortunatly wan:
Whose Captaine, Hengist, first a kingdome heere began
In Kent; where his great heires, ere other Princes rose
Of Saxonies descent, their fulness to oppose,
With swelling Humbers side their Empire did confine.
And of the rest, not least renowned of their Line,
Good Ethelbert of Kent, th'first christned English King,
To preach the faith of Christ, was first did hither bring
Wise Augustine the Monke, from holy Gregory sent.
This most religious King, with most deuout intent
That mightie Fane to Paule, in London did erect,
And priviledges gave, this Temple to protect.

His equall then in zeale, came Ercombert againe,
From that first christned King, the second in that raigne.
The gluttony then us'd severely to suppresse,
And make men fit to prayer (much hindred by excesse)
That abstinence from flesh for forty dayes began,
Which by the name of Lent is knowne to every man.

As mighty Hengist heere, by force of Armes had done,
So Ella comming in, soone from the Britaines wonne
The Countries neighboring Kent: which lying from the Maine,
Directly to the South did properly obtaine
The Southerne Saxons name; and not the last thereby
Amongst the other raignes which made the Heptarchy:
So in the high descent of that South-Saxon King,
We in the bead-roule heere of our religious bring
Wise Ethelwald: alone who Christian not became,
But willing that his folke should all receive the name,
Saint Wilfrid (sent from Yorke) into his Realme receiv'd
(Whom the Northumbrian folke had of his See bereau'd)
And on the South of Thames, a seat did him afford,
By whom that people first receiv'd the saving Word,

As likewise from the loynes of Erehinwin (who rais'd
Th'East-Saxons kingdome first) brave Sebert may be prais'd:
Which, as that King of Kent, had with such cost and state

Built Paules; his Greatness so (this King to imitate)
Began the goodly Church of Westminster to reare:
The Primer English Kings so truly zealous were.

Then Sebba of his seed, that did them all surpasse,
Who fitter for a shryne then for a scepter was,
(Aboue the power of flesh, his appetite to sterue
That his desired Christ he strictly might obserue)
Euen in his height of life, in health, in body strong,
Perswaded with his Queene, a Lady faire and young,
To separate themselues, and in a sole estate,
After religious sort themselues to dedicate.

Whose Nephew Uffa next, inflam'd with his high praise
(Enriching that proud Fane his Grandsire first did raise)
Abandoned the world he found so full of strife,
And after liv'd in Rome a strict religious life.

Nor these our Princes heere, of that pure Saxon straine,
Which tooke unto themselues each one their severall raigne,
For their so godly deeds, deserued greater fame
Then th'Angles their Allies, that hither with them came;
Who sharing-out themselues a kingdome in the East,
With th'Easterne Angles name their circuit did invest,
By Vffa in that part so happily begun:
Whose successors the Crowne for martyrdome have won
From all before or since that ever suffred heere;
Redwalds religious sonnes: who for their Saviour deere,
By cruell heathenish hands unmercifully slaine,
Amongst us ever-more remembred shall remaine,
And in the roule of Saints must have a speciall roome,
Where Derwald to all times with Erpenwald shall come.

When in that way they went, next Sebert them succeeds,
Scarce seconded againe for sanctimonious deeds:
Who for a private life when he his rule resign'd,
And to his Cloyster long had strictly him confin'd,
A Corslet for his Cowle was glad againe to take
His Country to defend (for his religions sake)
Against proud Penda, com'n with all his Pagan power,
Those christned Angels then of purpose to deuour:
And suffring with his folke, by Penda's heathenish pride,
As hee a Saint had liv'd, a constant Martyr dy'd.

When, after it fell out, that Offa had not long
Held that by cruell force, which Penda got by wrong,
Adopting for his heire young Edmond, brought him in,
Euen at what time the Danes this Iland sought to win:

Who christned soone became, and as religious growne
As those most heathenish were who set him on his throne,
Did expiate in that place his predecessors guilt,
Which so much Christian blood so cruelly had spilt.
For, taken by the Danes, who did all tortures try,
His Saviour Jesus Christ to force him to deny;
First beating him with bats, but no advantage got,
His body full of shafts then cruelly they shot;
The constant martyr'd King, a Saint thus justly crown'd.
To whom euen in that place, that Monument renown'd
Those after-Ages built to his eternall fame.
What English hath not heard Saint Edmonds Buries name?

As of those Angles heere, so from their loynes againe,
Whose hands hew'd out their way to the West-Sexian raigne
(From Kenrick, or that claime from Cerdick to descend)
A partnership in fame great Ina might pretend
With any King since first the Saxons came to shore.
Of all those christned heere, who highlier did adore
The God-head, then that man? or more that did apply
His power t'advance the Church in true sincerity?
Great Glastenbury then so wondrously decay'd,
Whose old foundation first the ancient Britains lay'd,
He gloriously rebuilt, enriching it with plate,
And many a sumptuous Cope, to uses consecrate:
Ordayning godly lawes for gouerning this Land,
Of all the Saxon Kings the Solon hee shall stand.

From Otta (borne with him who did this Ile invade)
And had a conquest first of the Northumbrians made,
And tributarie long of mightier Hengist held,
Till Ida (after borne) the Kentish power expeld,
And absolutely sate on the Dierian seat,
But afterward resign'd to Ethelfrid the Great:
An Army into Wales who for invasion led,
At Chester and in fight their forces vanquished;
Into their utter spoyle, then publique way to make,
The long Religious house of goodly Bangor brake,
And slew a thousand Monks, as they deuoutly pray'd.
For which his cruell spoyle upon the Christians made
(Though with the just consent of Christian Saxons slaine)
His blood, the hethenish hands of Redwald did distaine.
That murtherers issue next, this kingdome were exil'd:
And Edwyn tooke the rule; a Prince as just and mild
As th'other faithlesse were: nor could time ever bring
In all the seauen-fold rule an absoluter King;
And more t'aduance the fayth, his utmost power that lent:
Who reordained Yorke a Bishops gouernment;

And so much lov'd the poore, that in the waies of trade,
Where Fountaines fitly were, hee Iron dishes made,
And fastned them with chaynes the way farer to ease,
And the poore Pilgrims thirst, there resting, to appease.

As Mercia, mongst the rest, sought not the least to raise
The saving Christian sayth, nor merits humbler praise.
Nor those that from the stem of Saxon Creda came
(The Britains who expulst) were any whit in fame,
For pietie and zeale, behind the others best;
Though heathenish Penda long and proudly did infest
The christned neighboring Kings, and forc't them all to bow;
Till Oswy made, to God, a most religious vow,
Of his aboundant grace would hee be pleas'd to grant,
That he this Panim Prince in battell might supplant,
A Recluse he would give his daughter and delight,
Sweet Alfled then in youth, and as the Morning, bright:
And having his request, hee gaue as hee obtayn'd;
Though his unnaturall hands succeeding Wulpher stayn'd
In his owne childrens blood, whom their deare mother had
Confirm'd in Christs beliefe, by that most reverent Chad:
Yet to embrace the fayth when after he began
(For the unnaturalst deed that e're was done by man)
If possible it were to expiate his guilt,
Heere many a goodly house to holy uses built:
And shee (to purge his crime on her deere children done)
A crowned Queene, for him, became a vased Nun.

What Age a godlier Prince then Etheldred could bring?
Or then our Kinred heere, a more religious King?
Both taking them the Cowle, th'one heere his flesh did tame,
The other went to Rome, and there a Monke became.

So, Ethelbald may well be set the rest among:
Who, though most vainly given when he was hot and young;
Yet, by the wise reproofe of godly Bishops brought
From those unstay'd delights by which his youth was caught,
Hee all the former Kings of Mercia did exceed,
And (through his Rule) the Church from taxes strongly freed.
Then to the Easterne sea, in that deepe watry Fen
(Which seem'd a thing so much impossible to men)
Hee that great Abby built of Crowland; as though hee
Would have no others worke like his foundation bee.

As, Offa greater farre then any him before:
Whose conquests scarcely were suffic'd with all the shore;
But ouer into Wales adventurously hee shot
His Mercia's spacious Meere, and Powsland to it got.

This King, euen in that place, where with rude heapes of stones
The Britains had interr'd their Proto-martyrs bones,
That goodly Abby built to Alban; as to showe
How much the sonnes of Brute should to the Saxons owe.

But when by powerfull heaven, it was decreed at last,
That all those seauen-fold Rules should into one be cast
(Which quickly to a head by Britriks death was brought)
Then Egbert, who in France had carefully been taught,
Returning home, was King of the West-Sexians made.
Whose people, then most rich and potent, him perswade
(As once it was of old) to Monarchize the Land.
Who following their advise, first with a warlike hand
The Cornish ouer-came; and thence, with prosperous sailes,
O're Severne set his powers into the hart of Wales;
And with the Mercians there, a bloody battell wag'd:
Wherein he wan their Rule; and with his wounds enrag'd,
Went on against the rest. Which, sadly when they sawe
How those had sped before, with most subiective awe
Submit them to his sword: who prosperously alone
Reduc't the seauen-fold Rule, to his peculiar throne
(Extirping other stiles) and gaue it Englands name
Of th'Angles, from whose race his nobler fathers came.

When scarcely Egbert heere an entire Rule began,
But instantly thecDane the Iland ouer-ran;
A people, that their owne those Saxons payd againe.
For, as the Britaines first they treacherously had slaine,
This third upon their necks a heavier burthen lay'd
Then they had upon those whom falsly they betray'd.
And for each others states, though oft they here did toyle,
A people from their first bent naturally to spoyle,
That crueltie with them from their beginning brought.
Yet when the Christian fayth in them had throughly wrought,
Of any in the world no story shall us tell,
Which did the Saxon race in pious deeds excell:
That in these drowsie times should I in publique bring
Each great peculiar Act of every godly King,
The world might stand amaz'd in this our Age to see
Those goodly Fanes of theirs, which irreligious wee
Let every day decay; and yet we onely live
By the great Freedoms then those Kings to these did give.

Wise Segbert (worthy praise) preparing us the seat
Of famous Cambridge first, then with endowments great
The Muses to maintaine, those Sisters thither brought.
By whose example, next, religious Alfred taught,
Renowned Oxford built t'Apollo's learned brood;

And on the hallowed banke of Isis goodly Flood,
Worthy the glorious Arts, did gorgeous Bowres prouide.
He into severall Shires the kingdome did divide.

So, valiant Edgar, first, most happily destroy'd
The multitudes of Wolues, that long the Land annoy'd.
And our good Edward heere, the Confessor and King
(Unto whose sumptuous Shrine our Monarchs offrings bring)
That cankred Euill cur'd, bred twixt the throat and iawes.
When Physick could not find the remedy nor cause,
And much it did afflict his sickly people heere,
Hee of Almightie God obtain'd by earnest pray'r,
This Tumour by a King might cured be alone:
Which he an heyre-loome left unto the English Throne.
So, our Saint Edward heere, for Englands generall use,
Our Countries Common lawes did faithfully produce,
Both from th'old British writ, and from the Saxon tongue.

Of Forrests, Hills, and Floods, when now a mighty throng
For Audience cry'd aloud; because they late had heard,
That some high Cambrian hills the Wrekin proudly dar'd
With words that very much had stirr'd his rancorous spleene.
Where, though cleere Severne set her Princely selfe betweene
The English and the Welsh, yet could not make them cease.
Heere, Weever, as a Flood affecting godly peace,
His place of speech resignes; and to the Muse refers
The hearing of the Cause, to stickle all these stirs.


THE TWELFTH SONG

THE ARGUMENT

The Muse, that part of Shropshire plyes
Which on the East of Severne lies:
Where mighty Wrekin from his hight,
In the proud Cambrian Mountaines spight,
Sings those great Saxons ruling here,
Which the most famous warriors were.
And as shee in her course proceeds,
Relating many glorious deeds,
Of Guy of Warwicks fight doth straine
With Colebrond, that renowned Dane,
And of the famous Battels tryde
Twixt Knute and Edmond-Ironside;
To the Staffordian fields doth roue;
Visits the Springs of Trent and Doue;

Of Moreland, Cank, and Needwood sings;
An end which to this Canto brings.

The haughty Cambrian Hills enamor'd of their praise
(As they who onely sought ambitiously to raise
The blood of god-like Brute) their heads do proudly beare:
And having crown'd themselues sole Regents of the Ayre
(An other warre with Heaven as though they meant to make)
Did seeme in great disdaine the bold affront to take,
That any petty hill upon the English side,
Should dare, not (with a crouch) to vale unto their pride.

When Wrekin, as a hill his proper worth that knew,
And understood from whence their insolencie grew,
For all that they appear'd so terrible in sight,
Yet would not once forgoe a iote that was his right.
And when they star'd on him, to them the like he gaue,
And answer'd glance for glance, and brave againe for brave:
That, when some other hills which English dwellers were,
The lustie Wrekin saw himselfe so well to beare
Against the Cambrian part, respectlesse of their power;
His eminent disgrace expecting every howre,
Those Flatterers that before (with many cheerfull looke)
Had grac't his goodly site, him utterly forsooke,
And muffled them in clowds, like Mourners vayl'd in black,
Which of their utmost hope attend the ruinous wrack:
That those delicious Nymphs, fayre Tearne and Rodon cleere
(Two Brooks of him belov'd, and two that held him deare;
Hee, having none but them, they having none but hee,
Which to their mutuall joy, might eithers obiect be)
Within their secret breasts conceived sundry feares,
And as they mixt their streames, for him so mixt their teares.
Whom, in their comming downe, when plainly he discernes,
For them his nobler hart in his strong bosome earnes:
But, constantly resolu'd, that (dearer if they were)
The Britains should not yet all from the English beare;
Therfore, quoth he, brave Flood, though forth by Cambria brought,
Yet as faire Englands friend, or mine thou would'st be thought
(O Severne!) let thine eare my just defence partake:
Which sayd, in the behalfe of th'English, thus he spake;

Wise Weever (I suppose) sufficiently hath said
Of those our Princes heere, which fasted, watcht, and pray'd,
Whose deepe deuotion went for others ventrous deeds:
But in this Song of mine, hee seriously that reads,
Shall find, ere I have done, the Britaine (so extold,
Whose height each Mountaine strives so mainly to up-hold)
Matcht with as valiant men, and of as cleane a might,

As skilfull to commaund, and as inur'd to fight.
Who, when their fortune will'd that after they should scorse
Blowes with the big-boan'd Dane, eschanging force for force
(When first he put from Sea to forrage on this shore,
Two hundred e yeeres distain'd with eithers equall gore;
Now this aloft, now that: oft did the English raigne,
And oftentimes againe depressed by the Dane)
The Saxons, then I say, themselues as bravely show'd,
As these on whom the Welsh such glorious praise bestow'd.

Nor could his angry sword, who Egbert ouer-threw
(Through which he thought at once the Saxons to subdue)
His kingly courage quell: but from his short retyre,
His reinforced troupes (newe forg'd with sprightly fire)
Before them draue the Dane, and made the Britaine runne
(Whom he by liberall wage here to his ayde had wonne)
Upon their recreant backs, which both in flight were slaine,
Till their huge murthered heapes manur'd each neighboring Plaine.

As, Ethelwolfe againe, his utmost powers that bent
Against those fresh supplies each yeere from Denmarke sent
(Which, proling up and downe in their rude Danish ores,
Heere put themselues by stealth upon the pestred shores)
In many a doubtfull fight much fame in England wan.
So did the King of Kent, courageous Athelstan,
Which heere against the Dane got such victorious daies.

So, we the Wiltshire men as worthily may praise,
That buckled with those Danes, by Ceorle and Osrick brought.

And Etheldred, with them nine sundry Fields that fought,
Recorded in his praise, the conquests of one yeere.
You right-nam'd English then, courageous men you were
When Redding ye regain'd, led by that valiant Lord:
Where Basrig ye out-brau'd, and Halden, sword to sword;
The most redoubted spirits that Denmarke heere addrest.

And Alured, not much inferior to the rest:
Who having in his dayes so many dangers past,
In seauen brave foughten Fields their Champion Hubba chac't,
And slew him in the end, at Abington, that day
Whose like the Sunne nere sawe in his diurnall way:
Where those, that from the Field sore wounded sadly fled,
Were wel-neere ouer-whelm'd with mountaines of the dead.
His force and fortune made the Foes so much to feare,
As they the Land at last did utterly forsweare.

And, when proud Rollo, next, their former powers repair'd

(Yea, when the worst of all it with the English far'd)
Whose Countries neere at hand, his force did still supply,
And Denmarke to her drew the strengths of Normandie,
This Prince in many a fight their forces still defy'd.
The goodly River Lee he wisely did divide,
By which the Danes had then their full-fraught Navies tew'd:
The greatnes of whose streame besieged Harford rew'd.
This Alfred whose fore-sight had politiquely found
Betwixt them and the Thames advantage of the ground,
A puissant hand thereto laboriously did put,
And into lesser Streames that spacious Current cut.
Their ships thus set on shore (to frustrate their desire)
Those Danish Hulkes became the food of English fire.

Great Alfred left his life: when Elflida up-grew,
That farre beyond the pitch of other women flew:
Who having in her youth of childing felt the woe,
Her Lords imbraces vow'd shee never more would know:
But differing from her sexe (as, full of manly fire)
This most courageous Queene, by conquest to aspire,
The puissant Danish powers victoriously pursu'd,
And resolutely heere through their thicke Squadron shew'd
Her way into the North. Where, Darby having wonne,
And things beyond beliefe upon the Enemy done,
Shee sav'd besieged Yorke; and in the Danes despight,
When most they were up-held with all the Eusterne might,
More Townes and Citties built out of her wealth and power,
Then all their hostile flames could any way deuour.
And, when the Danish heere the Country most destroy'd,
Yet all our powers on them not wholly were imploy'd;
But some we still reseru'd abroad for us to roame,
To fetch-in forraine spoyls, to helpe our losse at home.
And all the Land, from us, they never cleerely wan:
But to his endlesse praise, our English Athelstan,
In the Northumbrian fields, with most victorious might
Put Alaffe and his powers to more inglorious flight;
And more then any King of th'English him before,
Each way from North to South, from West to th'Easterne shore,
Made all the Ile his owne; his seat who firmly fixt,
The Calidonian hills, and Cathnes poynt betwixt,
And Constantine their King (a prisoner) hither brought;
Then ouer Severns banks the warlike Britains sought:
Where he their Princes forc't from that their strong retreat,
In England to appeare at his Imperiall seat.

But after, when the Danes, who never wearied were,
Came with intent to make a generall conquest here,
They brought with them a man deem'd of so wondrous might,

As was not to be matcht by any mortall wight:
For, one could scarcely beare his Ax into the field;
Which as a little wand the Dane would lightly wield:
And (to enforce that strength) of such a dauntlesse spirit,
A man (in their conceit) of so exceeding merit,
That to the English oft they offred him (in pride)
The ending of the warre by combate to decide:
Much scandall which procur'd unto the English name.
When, some out of their love, and some spurr'd on with shame,
By enuy some provokt, some out of courage, faine
Would under-take the Cause to combate with the Dane.
But Athelstan the while, in settled judgement found,
Should the Defendant fayle, how wide and deepe a wound
It likely was to leaue to his defensive warre.

Thus, whilst with sundry doubts his thoughts perplexed are,
It pleas'd all-powerfull Heaven, that Warwicks famous Guy
(The Knight through all the world renown'd for Chivalrie)
Arriv'd from forraine parts, where he had held him long.
His honorable Armes deuoutly having hong
In a Religious house, the offrings of his praise,
To his Redeemer Christ, his helpe at all assayes
(Those Armes, by whose strong proofe he many a Christian freed,
And bore the perfect marks of many a worthy deed)
Himselfe, a Palmer poore, in homely Russet clad
(And onely in his hand his Hermits staffe he had)
Tow'rds Winchester alone (so) sadly tooke his way,
Where Athelstan, that time the King of England lay;
And where the Danish Campe then strongly did abide,
Neere to a goodly Meade, which men there call the Hide.

The day that Guy arriv'd (when silent night did bring
Sleepe both on friend and foe) that most religious King
(Whose strong and constant hart, all grievous cares supprest)
His due deuotion done, betooke himselfe to rest.
To whom it seem'd by night an Angell did appeare,
Sent to him from that God whom hee invoak't by pray'r;
Commaunding him the time not idly to for-slowe,
But rathe as hee could rise, to such a gate to goe,
Whereas he should not faile to find a goodly Knight
In Palmers poore attyre: though very meanly dight,
Yet by his comely shape, and limmes exceeding strong,
He easely might him know the other folke among;
And bad him not to feare, but chuse him for the man.

No sooner brake the day, but up rose Athelstan;
And as the Vision show'd, he such a Palmer found,
With others of his sort, there sitting on the ground:

Where, for some poore repast they onely seem'd to stay,
Else ready to depart each one upon his way:
When secretly the King revealed to the Knight
His comfortable dreames that lately passed night:
With mild and princely words be speaking him; quoth hee,
Farre better you are knowne to Heaven (it seemes) then mee
For this great Action fit: by whose most drad command
(Before a world of men) it's lay'd upon your hand.
Then stout and valiant Knight, heere to my Court repaire,
Refresh you in my bathes, and mollifie your care
With comfortable wines and meats what you will aske:
And chuse my richest Armes to fit you for this taske.

The Palmer (gray with age) with countenance lowting lowe,
His head euen to the earth before the King doth bow,
Him softly answering thus; Drad Lord, it fits mee ill
(A wretched man) t'oppose high Heavens eternall will:
Yet my most soueraigne Liege, no more of me esteeme
Then this poore habit showes, a Pilgrim as I seeme;
But yet I must confesse, have seene in former dayes
The best Knights of the world, and scuffled is some frayes.
Those times are gone with me; and, beeing aged now,
Have offred up my Armes, to Heau'n and made my vow
Nere more to beare a Shield, nor my declining age
(Except some Palmers Tent, or homely Hermitage)
Shall ever enter roofe: but if, by Heaven and thee,
This Action be impos'd great English King on mee,
Send to the Danish Campe, their challenge to accept,
In some conuenient place proclaiming it be kept:
Where, by th' Almighties power, for England Ile appeare.

The King, much pleas'd in mind, assumes his wonted cheere,
And to the Danish power his choicest Herault sent.
When, both through Campe and Court, this Combat quickly went.
Which suddainly divulg'd, whilst every listning eare,
As thirsting after newes, desirous was to heare,
Who for the English side durst under-take the day;
The puissant Kings accord, that in the middle way
Betwixt the Tent and Towne, to eithers equall sight,
Within a goodly Mead, most fit for such a fight,
The Lists should be prepar'd for this materiall prize.

The day prefixt once com'n, both Dane and English rise,
And to th' appointed place th' unnumbred people throng:
The weaker female sex, old men, and children young
Into the windowes get, and up on stalls, to see
The man on whose brave hand their hope that day must bee.
In noting of it well, there might a man behold

More sundry formes of feare then thought imagine could.
One looks upon his friend with sad and heauy cheere,
Who seemes in this distresse a part with him to beare:
Their passions doe expresse much pittie mixt with rage.
Whilst one his wives laments is labouring to asswage,
His little infant neere, in childish gibbridge showes
What addeth to his griefe who sought to calme her woes.
One having climb'd some roofe, the concourse to discry,
From thence upon the earth deiects his humble eye,
As since he thither came hee suddainly had found
Some danger them amongst which lurkt upon the ground.
One stands with fixed eyes, as though he were agast:
Another sadly comes, as though his hopes were past.
This harkneth with his friend, as though with him to breake
Of some intended act. Whilst they together speake,
Another standeth neere to listen what they say,
Or what should be the end of this so doubtfull day.
One great and generall face the gathered people seeme:
So that the perfect'st sight beholding could not deeme
What lookes most sorrow show'd; their griefes so equall were.
Upon the heads of two, whose cheekes were joynd so neere
As if together growne, a third his chin doth rest:
Another lookes or'e his: and others, hardly prest,
Lookt underneath their armes. Thus, whilst in crowds they throng
(Led by the King himselfe) the Champion comes along;
A man well strooke in yeeres, in homely Palmers gray,
And in his hand his staffe, his reverent steps to stay,
Holding a comly pase: which at his passing by,
In every censuring tongue, as every serious eye,
Compassion mixt with feare, distrust and courage, bred.

Then Colebrond for the Danes came forth in irefull red;
Before him (from the Campe) an Ensigne first display'd
Amidst a guard of gleaues: then sumptuously array'd
Were twenty gallant youths, that to the warlike sound
Of Danish brazen Drums, with many a loftie bound,
Come with their Countries march, as they to Mars should dance.
Thus, forward to the fight, both Champions them advance:
And each without respect doth resolutely chuse
The weapon that he brought, nor doth his foes refuse.
The Dane prepares his Axe, that pond'rous was to feele,
Whose squares were layd with plates, and riveted with steele,
And armed downe along with pykes; whose hardned poynts
(Forc't with the weapons weight) had power to teare the joynts
Of Curas or of Mayle, or what-so-ere they tooke:
Which caus'd him at the Knight disdainfully to looke.

When our stout Palmer soone (unknowne for valiant Guy)

The cord from his straight loynes doth presently untie,
Puts off his Palmers weede unto his trusse, which bore
The staines of ancient Armes, but show'd it had before
Beene costly cloth of Gold; and off his hood he threw:
Out of his Hermits staffe his two-hand sword hee drew
(The unsuspected sheath which long to it had beene)
Which till that instant time the people had not seene;
A sword so often try'd. Then to himselfe, quoth hee,
Armes let me craue your ayde, to set my Country free:
And never shall my hart your help againe require,
But onely to my God to lift you up in pray'r.

Here, Colebrond forward made, and soone the Christian Knight
Encounters him againe with equall power and spight:
Whereas, betwixt them two, might easely have been seene
Such blowes, in publique throngs as used had they been,
Of many there the least might many men have slaine:
Which none but they could strike, nor none but they sustaine;
The most relentlesse eye that had the power to awe,
And so great wonder bred in those the Fight that saw,
As verily they thought, that Nature untill then
Had purposely reseru'd the utmost power of men,
Where strength still answerd strength, on courage courage grew.

Looke how two Lyons fierce, both hungry, both pursue
One sweet and selfe-same prey, at one another flie,
And with their armed pawes ingrappled dreadfully,
The thunder of their rage, and boystrous struggling, make
The neighboring Forrests round affrightedly to quake:
Their sad encounter, such. The mightie Colebrond stroke
A cruell blowe at Guy: which though hee finely broke,
Yet (with the weapons weight) his ancient hilt it split,
And (thereby lessened much) the Champion lightly hit
Upon the reverent brow: immediatly from whence
The blood dropt softly downe, as if the wound had sense
Of their much inward woe that it with griefe should see.

The Danes, a deadly blowe supposing it to bee,
Sent such an ecchoing shoute that rent the troubled ayre.
The English at the noise, wext all so wan with feare,
As though They lost the blood their aged Champion shed:
Yet were not these so pale, but th'other were as red;
As though the blood that fell, upon their cheekes had staid.

Here Guy, his better spirits recalling to his ayde,
Came fresh upon his foe; when mightie Colebrond makes
An other desperate stroke: which Guy of Warwick takes
Undauntedly aloft; and followed with a blowe

Upon his shorter ribs, that the excessive flowe
Stream'd up unto his hilts: the wound so gap't withall,
As though it meant to say, Behold your Champions fall
By this proud Palmers hand. Such claps againe and cryes
The joyfull English gaue as cleft the very skies.
Which comming on along from these that were without,
When those within the Towne receiv'd this cheerfull shout,
They answer'd them with like; as those their joy that knew.

Then with such eager blowes each other they pursue,
As every offer made, should threaten imminent death;
Untill, through heat and toyle both hardly drawing breath,
They desperately doe close. Looke how two Boares, being set
Together side to side, their threatning tusks doe whet,
And with their gnashing teeth their angry foame doe bite,
Whilst still they shouldring seeke, each other where to smite:
Thus stood those irefull Knights; till flying back, at length
The Palmer, of the two the first recouering strength,
Upon the left arme lent great Colebrond such a wound,
That whilst his weapons poynt fell wel-neere to the ground,
And slowly he it rais'd, the valiant Guy againe
Sent through his cloven scalpe his blade into his braine.
When downeward went his head, and up his heeles he threw;
As wanting hands to bid his Countrimen Adieu.

The English part, which thought an end he would have made,
And seeming as they much would in his praise have said,
He bad them yet forbeare, whilst he pursu'd his fame
That to this passed King next in succession came;
That great and puissant Knight (in whose victorious dayes
Those knight-like deeds were done, no lesse deseruing praise)
Brave Edmond, Edwards sonne, that Stafford having tane,
With as succesfull speed won Darby from the Dane.
From Lester then againe, and Lincolne at the length,
Draue out the Dacian Powers by his resistlesse strength:
And this his England cleer'd beyond that raging Flood,
Which that proud King of Hunnes once christned with his blood.
By which, great Edmonds power apparantly was showne,
The Land from Humber South recouering for his owne,
That Edgar after him so much disdain'd the Dane
Unworthy of a warre that should disturbe his raigne,
As generally he seem'd regardlesse of their hate.
And studying every way magnificence in State,
At Chester whilst he liv'd at more then kingly charge,
Eight tributary Kings there row'd him in his Barge:
His shores from Pirats sack the King that strongly kept:
A Neptune, whose proud sayles the British Ocean swept.

But after his decease, when his more hopefull sonne,
By cruell Stepdam's hate, to death was lastly done,
To set his rightfull Crowne upon a wrongfull head
(When by thy fatall curse, licentious Etheldred,
Through dissolutenes, sloth, and thy abhorred life,
As greeuous were thy sinnes, so were thy sorrowes rife)
The Dane, possessing all, the English forc't to beare
A heauier yoke then first those Heathen slaueries were;
Subiected, bought, and sold, in that most wretched plight,
As euen their thraldome seem'd their neighbors to affright.
Yet could not all their plagues the English height abate:
But euen in their low'st Eb, and miserablest state,
Courageously themselues they into action put,
And in one night, the throats of all the Danish cut.

And when in their revenge, the most insatiate Dane
Unshipt them on our shores, under their puissant Swane:
And swolne with hate and ire, their huge unweeldy force,
Came clustring like the Greeks out of the Woodden-horse:
And the Norfolcian Townes, the neer'st unto the East,
With sacriledge and rape did terriblest infest;
Those Danes yet from the shores we with such violence draue,
That from our swords, their ships could them but hardly saue.
And to renew the warre, that yeere ensuing, when
With fit supplies for spoyle, they landed heere agen,
And all the Southerne shores from Kent to Cornwall spred,
With those disordred troupes by Alaffe hither led,
In seconding their Swane, which cry'd to them for ayde;
Their multitudes so much sad Ethelred dismay'd,
As from his Country forc't the wretched King to flie.
An English yet there was, when England seem'd to lie
Under the heauiest yoke that ever kingdome bore,
Who washt his secret knife in Swane's relentlesse gore,
Whilst (swelling in excesse) his lavish Cups he ply'd.
Such meanes t'redeeme themselues th'afflicted Nation try'd.
And when courageous Knute, th'late murther'd Swanus sonne,
Came in t'reuenge that act on his great father done,
He found so rare a spirit that heere against him rose,
As though ordain'd by Heaven his greatnesse to oppose:
Who with him foot to foot, and face to face durst stand.
When Knute, which heere alone affected the Command,
The Crowne upon his head at faire South-hampton set:
And Edmond, loth to lose what Knute desir'd to get,
At London caus'd himselfe inaugurate to bee.
King Knute would conquer all, King Edmond would be free.

The kingdome is the Prize for which they both are prest:
And with their equall powers both meeting in the West,

The greene Dorsetian fields a deepe vermillion dy'd:
Where Gillingham gaue way to their great hostes (in pride)
Abundantly their blood that each on other spent.
But Edmond, on whose side that day the better went
(And with like fortune thought the remnant to suppresse
That Sarum then besieg'd, which was in great distresse)
With his victorious troupes to Salsbury retires:
When with fresh bleeding wounds, Knute, as with fresh desires,
Whose might though some-what maym'd, his mind yet unsubdu'd,
His lately conquering Foe, courageously pursu'd:
And finding out a way, sent to his friends with speed,
Who him supply'd with ayde: and being helpt at need,
Tempts Edmond still to fight, still hoping for a day.

Towards Worstershire their Powers both well upon their way,
There, falling to the Field, in a continuall fight
Two dayes the angry hosts still parted were by Night:
Where twice the rising Sunne, and twice the setting, saw
Them with their equall wounds their wearied breath to draw.

Great London to surprize, then (next) Canutus makes:
And thitherward as fast King Edmond Ironside takes.
Whilst Knute set downe his siege before the Easterne gate,
King Edmond through the West, past in tryumphall state.
But this courageous King, that scorned, in his pride,
A Towne should be besieg'd wherein he did abide,
Into the fields againe the valiant Edmond goes.
Kanutus, yet that hopes to winne what he did lose,
Provokes him still to fight: and falling backe where they
Might field-roomth find at large, their Ensignes to display,
Together flewe againe; that Brentford, with the blood
Of Danes and English mixt, discoloured long time stood.
Yet Edmond, as before, went Victor still away.

When soone that valiant Knute, whom nothing could dismay,
Recall'd his scattered troupes, and into Essex hies,
Where (as ill fortune would) the Dane with fresh supplies
Was lately come a-land, to whom brave Ironside makes;
But Knute to him againe as soone fresh courage takes:
And Fortune (as her selfe) determining to showe
That shee could bring an Eb, on valiant Edmonds Flowe,
And easely cast him downe from off the top of Chance,
By turning of her wheele, Canutus doth advance.
Where shee beheld that Prince which she had fauor'd long
(Euen in her proud despight) his murther'd troupes among
With sweat and blood besmear'd (Dukes, Earles, and Bishops slaine,
In that most dreadfull day, when all went to the Dane)
Through worlds of dangers wade; and with his Sword and Shield,

Such wonders there to act as made her in the Field
Ashamed of her selfe, so brave a spirit as he
By her unconstant hand should so much wronged be.

But, having lost the day, to Glocester hee drawes,
To raise a second power in his slaine souldiers cause.
When late-encourag'd Knute, whilst fortune yet doth last,
Who oft from Ironside fled, now followed him as fast.

Whilst thus in Civill Armes continually they toyle,
And what th'one strives to make, the other seeks to spoyle,
With threatning swords still drawne; and with obnoxious hands
Attending their reuenge, whilst either enemie stands,
One man amongst the rest from this confusion breaks,
And to the irefull Kings with courage boldly speakes;

Yet cannot all this blood your rauenous out-rage fill?
Is there no law, no bound, to your ambitious will,
But what your swords admit? as Nature did ordaine
Our lives for nothing else, but onely to maintaine
Your murthers, sack, and spoyle? If by this wastfull warre
The Land unpeopled lye, some Nation shall from farre,
By ruine of you both, into the Ile be brought,
Obtayning that for which you twaine so long have fought.
Unlesse then through your thirst of Emperie you meane
Both Nations in these broyles shall be extinguisht cleane,
Select you Champions fit, by them to proue your right,
Or try it man to man your selues in single fight.

When as those warlike Kings, prouokt with courage hie,
It willingly accept in person by and by.
And whilst they them prepare, the shapelesse concourse growes
In little time so great, that their unusuall flowes
Surrounded Severns banks, whose streame amazed stood,
Her Birlich to behold, in-Iled with her flood,
That with refulgent Armes then flamed; whilst the Kings,
Whose rage out of the hate of eithers Empire springs,
Both armed, Cap à Pe, upon their barred horse
Together fiercely flew; that in their violent course
(Like thunder when it speaks most horribly and lowd,
Tearing the ful-stuft panch of some congealed clowd)
Their strong hoofes strooke the earth: and with the fearfull shock,
Their speares in splinters flew, their Beuers both unlock.
Canutus, of the two that furthest was from hope,
Who found with what a Foe his fortune was to cope,
Cryes, noble Edmona, hold; Let us the Land divide.
Heere th'English and the Danes, from either equall side
Were Ecchoes to his words, and all aloud doe cry,

Courageous Kings divide; twere pitty such should die.

When now the neighboring Floods, will'd Wrekin to suppresse
His style, or they were like to surfet with excesse.
And time had brought about, that now they all began
To listen to a long told Prophecie, which ran
Of Moreland, that shee might live prosperously to see
A River borne of her, who well might reccon'd be
The third of this large Ile: which Saw did first arise
From Arden, in those dayes delivering prophecies.

The Druids (as some say) by her instructed were.
In many secret skills shee had been cond her lere.
The ledden of the Birds most perfectly shee knew:
And also from their flight strange Auguries shee drew;
Supreamest in her place: whose circuit was extent
From Avon to the Banks of Severne and to Trent:
Where Empresse like shee sate with Natures bounties blest,
And seru'd by many a Nymph; but two, of all the rest,
That Staffordshire calls hers, there both of high account.
The eld'st of which is Canke: though Needwood her surmount,
In excellence of soyle, by beeing richly plac't,
Twixt Trent and batning Doue; and, equally imbrac't
By their abounding banks, participates their store;
Of Britaines Forrests all (from th'lesse unto the more)
For finenesse of her turfe surpassing; and doth beare
Her curled head so high, that Forrests farre and neere
Oft grutch at her estate; her florishing to see,
Of all their stately tyers disrobed when they bee.
But (as the world goes now) ô wofull Canke the while,
As brave a Wood-Nymph once as any of this Ile;
Great Ardens eldest child: which, in her mothers ground
Before fayre Feck'nhams selfe, her old age might have crownd;
When as those fallow Deere, and huge-hancht Stags that graz'd
Upon her shaggy Heaths, the passenger amaz'd
To see their mighty Heards, with high-palmd heads to threat
The woods of o'regrowne Oakes; as though they meant to set
Their hornes to th'others heights. But now, both those and these
Are by vile gaine deuour'd: So abiect are our daies.
Shee now, unlike her selfe, a Neatheards life doth live,
And her deiected mind to Country cares doth give.

But Muse, thou seem'st to leaue the Morelands too too long:
Of whom report may speake (our mightie wastes among)
Shee from her chilly site, as from her barren feed,
For body, horne, and haire, as faire a Beast doth breed
As scarcely this great Ile can equall: then of her,
Why should'st thou all this while the prophecie defer?

Who bearing many Springs, which pretty Rivers grew,
Shee could not be content, untill shee fully knew
Which child it was of hers (borne under such a fate)
As should in time be rays'd unto that high estate.
(I faine would have you thinke, that this was long agoe,
When many a River, now that furiously doth flowe,
Had scarcely learn'd to creepe) and therefore shee doth will
Wise Arden, from the depth of her abundant skill,
To tell her which of these her Rills it was shee ment.
To satisfie her will, the Wisard answers; Trent.
For, as a skilfull Seer, the aged Forrest wist,
A more then usuall power did in that name consist,
Which thirty doth import; by which she thus divin'd,
There should be found in her, of Fishes thirty kind;
And thirty Abbeys great, in places fat and ranke,
Should in succeeding time be builded on her banke;
And thirtie severall Streames from many a sundry way,
Unto her greatnesse should their watry tribute pay.

This, Moreland greatly lik't: yet in that tender love,
Which shee had ever borne unto her darling Doue,
Shee could have wisht it his: because the daintie grasse
That growes upon his banke, all other doth surpasse.
But, subiect he must be: as Sow, which from her Spring,
At Stafford meeteth Penk, which shee along doth bring
To Trent by Tixall grac't, the Astons ancient seat;
Which oft the Muse hath found her safe and sweet retreat.
The noble Owners now of which beloved place,
Good fortunes them and theirs with honor'd titles grace:
May Heaven still blesse that House, till happy Floods you see
Your selues more grac't by it, then it by you can bee.
Whose bounty, still my Muse so freely shall confesse,
As when she shall want words, her signes shall it expresse.

So Blyth beares easely downe tow'rds her deere Soueraigne Trent:
But nothing in the world gives Moreland such content
As her owne darling Doue his confluence to behold
Of Floods in sundry straines: as, crankling Many-fold
The first that lends him force: of whose meandred waies,
And labyrinth-like turnes (as in the Mores shee straies)
Shee first receiv'd her name, by growing strangely mad,
Or'e-gone with love of Hanse, a dapper More-land Lad.
Who neere their crystall springs as in those wasts they playd,
Bewitcht the wanton hart of that delicious mayd:
Which instantly was turn'd so much from beeing coy,
That shee might seeme to doat upon the Morish boy.
Who closely stole a way (perceiving her intent)
With his deare Lord the Doue, in quest of Princely Trent,

With many other Floods (as, Churnet, in his traine
That draweth Dunsmore on, with Yendon, then cleere Taine,
That comes alone to Doue) of which, Hanse one would bee.
And for himselfe he faine of Many-fold would free
(Thinking this amorous Nymph by some meanes to beguile)
He closely under earth convayes his head awhile.
But, when the River feares some policie of his,
And her beloved Hanse immediatly doth miss,
Distracted in her course, improuidently rash,
Shee oft against the Cleeues her crystall front doth dash:
Now forward, then againe shee backward seemes to beare;
As, like to lose her selfe by straggling heere and there.
Hanse, that this while suppos'd him quite out of her sight,
No sooner thrusts his head into the cheerfull light,
But Many-fold that still the Run-away doth watch,
Him (ere he was aware) about the neck doth catch:
And, as the angry Hanse would faine her hold remoue,
They struggling tumble downe into their Lord, the Doue.

Thus though th' industrious Muse hath been imploy'd so long,
Yet is shee loth to doe poore little Smestall wrong,
That from her Wilfrunes Spring neere Hampton plyes, to pour
The wealth shee there receives, into her friendly Stowr.
Nor shall the little Bourne have cause the Muse to blame,
From these Staffordian Heathes that strives to catch the Tame:
Whom shee in her next Song shall greet with mirthfull cheere,
So happily arriv'd now in her native Shire.


THE THIRTEENTH SONG

THE ARGUMENT

This Song our Shire of Warwick sounds;
Revives old Ardens ancient bounds.
Through many shapes the Muse heere roues;
Now sporting in those shady Groues,
The tunes of Birds oft staies to heare:
Then, finding Herds of lustie Deare,
She Huntresse-like the Hart pursues;
And like a Hermit walks, to chuse
The Simples every where that growe;
Comes Ancors glory next to showe;
Tells Guy of Warwicks famous deeds;
To th' Vale of Red-horse then proceeds,
To play her part the rest among;
There shutteth up her thirteenth Song.

Upon the Mid-lands now th' industrious Muse doth fall;
That Shire which wee the hart of England well may call,
As shee her selfe extends (the midst which is decreed)
Betwixt S. Michaels Mount, and Barwick-bord'ring Tweed,
Brave Warwick; that abroad so long advanc't her Beare,
By her illustrious Earles renowned every where;
Aboue her neighboring Shires which alwaies bore her head.
My native Country then, which so brave spirits hast bred,
If there be vertue yet remaining in thy earth,
Or any good of thine thou breathd'st into my birth,
Accept it as thine owne whilst now I sing of thee;
Of all thy later Brood th'unworthiest though I bee.
Muse, first of Arden tell, whose foot-steps yet are found
In her rough wood-lands more then any other ground
That mighty Arden held euen in her height of pride;
Her one hand touching Trent, the other, Severns side.
The very sound of these, the Wood-Nymphs doth awake:
When thus of her owne selfe the ancient Forrest spake;

My many goodly sites when first I came to showe,
Here opened I the way to myne owne ouer-throwe:
For, when the world found out the fitnesse of my soyle,
The gripple wretch began immediatly to spoyle
My tall and goodly woods, and did my grounds inclose:
By which, in little time my bounds I came to lose.

When Britaine first her fields with Villages had fild,
Her people wexing still, and wanting where to build,
They oft dislodg'd the Hart, and set their houses, where
He in the Broome and Brakes had long time made his leyre.
Of all the Forrests heere within this mightie Ile,
If those old Britains then me Soueraigne did instile,
I needs must be the great'st; for greatnesse tis alone
That gives our kind the place: else were there many a one
For pleasantnes of shade that farre doth mee excell.
But, of our Forrests kind the quality to tell,
We equally partake with Wood-land as with Plaine,
Alike with Hill and Dale; and every day maintaine
The sundry kinds of beasts upon our copious wast's,
That men for profit breed, as well as those of chase.

Here Arden of her selfe ceast any more to showe;
And with her Sylvan joyes the Muse along doth goe.

When Phoebus lifts his head out of the Winters waue,
No sooner doth the Earth her flowerie bosome brave,
At such time as the Yeere brings on the pleasant Spring,

But Hunts-up to the Morne the feath'red Sylvans sing:
And in the lower Groue, as on the rising Knole,
Upon the highest spray of every mounting pole,
Those Quirristers are pearcht with many a speckled breast.
Then from her burnisht gate the goodly glittring East
Guilds every lofty top, which late the humorous Night
Bespangled had with pearle, to please the Mornings sight:
On which the mirthfull Quires, with their cleere open throats,
Unto the joyfull Morne so straine their warbling notes,
That Hills and Valleys ring, and euen the ecchoing Ayre
Seemes all compos'd of sounds, about them every where.
The Throstell, with shrill Sharps; as purposely he song
T'awake the lustlesse Sunne; or chyding, that so long
He was in comming forth, that should the thickets thrill:
The Woosell neere at hand, that hath a golden bill;
As Nature him had markt of purpose, t'let us see
That from all other Birds his tunes should different bee:
For, with their vocall sounds, they sing to pleasant May;
Upon his dulcet pype the Merle doth onely play.
When in the lower Brake, the Nightingale hard-by,
In such lamenting straines the joyfull howres doth ply,
As though the other Birds shee to her tunes would draw.
And, but that Nature (by her all-constraining law)
Each Bird to her owne kind this season doth invite,
They else, alone to heare that Charmer of the Night
(The more to use their eares) their voyces sure would spare,
That moduleth her tunes so admirably rare,
As man to set in Parts, at first had learn'd of her.

To Philomell the next, the Linet we prefer;
And by that warbling bird, the Wood-Larke place we then,
The Red-sparrow, the Nope, the Red-breast, and the Wren,
The Yellow-pate: which though shee hurt the blooming tree,
Yet scarce hath any bird a finer pype then shee.
And of these chaunting Fowles, the Goldfinch not behind,
That hath so many sorts descending from her kind.
The Tydie for her notes as delicate as they,
The laughing Hecco, then the counterfetting lay,
The Softer, with the (Shrill some hid among the leaues,
Some in the taller trees, some in the lower greaues)
Thus sing away the Morne, untill the mounting Sunne,
Through thick exhaled fogs, his golden head hath runne,
And through the twisted tops of our close Covert creeps
To kisse the gentle Shade, this while that sweetly sleeps.

And neere to these our Thicks, the wild and frightfull Heards,
Not hearing other noyse but this of chattering Birds,
Feed fairely on the Launds; both sorts of seasoned Deere:

Here walke, the stately Red, the freckled Fallowe there:
The Bucks and lusty Stags amongst the Rascalls strew'd,
As sometime gallant spirits amongst the multitude.

Of all the Beasts which we for our veneriall name,
The Hart amongst the rest, the Hunters noblest game:
Of which most Princely Chase sith none did ere report,
Or by description touch, t'expresse that wondrous sport
(Yet might have well beseem'd th'ancients nobler Songs)
To our old Arden heere, most fitly it belongs:
Yet shall shee not invoke the Muses to her ayde;
But thee Diana bright, a Goddesse and a mayd:
In many a huge-growne Wood, and many a shady Groue,
Which oft hast borne thy Bowe (great Huntresse) us'd to roue
At many a cruell beast, and with thy darts to pierce
The Lyon, Panther, Ounce, the Beare, and Tiger fierce;
And following thy fleet Game, chaste mightie Forrests Queene,
With thy disheueld Nymphs attyr'd in youthfull greene,
About the Launds hast scowr'd, and Wastes both farre and neere,
Brave Huntresse: but no beast shall proue thy Quarries heere;
Saue those the best of Chase, the tall and lusty Red,
The Stag for goodly shape, and statelinesse of head,
Is fitt'st to hunt at force. For whom, when with his hounds
The laboring Hunter tufts the thicke unbarbed grounds
Where harbor'd is the Hart; there often from his feed
The dogs of him doe find; or thorough skilfull heed,
The Huntsman by his slot, or breaking earth, perceaues,
Or entring of the thicke by pressing of the greaues
Where he hath gone to lodge. Now when the Hart doth heare
The often-bellowing hounds to vent his secret leyre,
He rouzing rusheth out, and through the Brakes doth drive,
As though up by the roots the bushes he would rive.
And through the combrous thicks, as fearefully he makes,
Hee with his branched head, the tender Saplings shakes,
That sprinkling their moyst pearle doe seeme for him to weepe;
When after goes the Cry, with yellings lowd and deepe,
That all the Forrest rings, and every neighbouring place:
And there is not a hound but falleth to the Chase.
Rechating with his horne, which then the Hunter cheeres,
Whilst still the lustie Stag his high-palm'd head up-beares,
His body showing state, with unbent knees upright,
Expressing (from all beasts) his courage in his flight.
But when th'approaching foes still following he perceives,
That hee his speed must trust, his usuall walke he leaues;
And or'e the Champaine flies: which when th'assembly find,
Each followes, as his horse were footed with the wind.
But beeing then imbost, the noble stately Deere
When he hath gotten ground (the kennell cast arere)

Doth beat the Brooks and Ponds for sweet refreshing soyle:
That seruing not, then proues if he his sent can foyle,
And makes amongst the Heards, and flocks of shag-wooll'd Sheepe,
Them frighting from the guard of those who had their keepe.
But when as all his shifts his safety still denies,
Put quite out of his walke, the wayes and fallowes tryes.
Whom when the Plow-man meets, his teame he letteth stand
T'assaile him with his goad: so with his hooke in hand,
The Shepheard him pursues, and to his dog doth halow:
When, with tempestuous speed, the hounds and Huntsmen follow;
Untill the noble Deere through toyle bereau'd of strength,
His long and sinewy legs then fayling him at length,
The Villages attempts, enrag'd, not giving way
To any thing hee meets now at his sad decay.
The cruell rauenous hounds and bloody Hunters neer,
This noblest beast of Chase, that vainly doth but feare,
Some banke or quick-set finds: to which his hanch oppos'd,
He turnes upon his foes, that soone have him inclos'd.
The churlish throated hounds then holding him at bay,
And as their cruell fangs on his harsh skin they lay,
With his sharp-poynted head he dealeth deadly wounds.

The Hunter, comming in to helpe his wearied hounds,
He desperatly assailes; untill opprest by force,
He who the Mourner is to his owne dying Corse,
Upon the ruthlesse earth his precious teares lets fall.

To Forrests that belongs; but yet this is not all:
With solitude what sorts, that here's not wondrous rife?
Whereas the Hermit leades a sweet retyred life,
From Villages replete with ragg'd and sweating Clownes,
And from the lothsome ayres of smoky cittied Townes.
Suppose twixt noone and night, the Sunne his halfe-way wrought
(The shadowes to be large, by his descending brought)
Who with a feruent eye lookes through the twyring glades,
And his dispersed rayes commixeth with the shades,
Exhaling the milch dewe, which there had tarried long,
And on the ranker grasse till past the noone-sted hong;
When as the Hermet comes out of his homely Cell,
Where from all rude resort he happily doth dwell:
Who in the strength of youth, a man at Armes hath been;
Or one who of this world the vilenesse having seene,
Retyres him from it quite; and with a constant mind
Mans beastliness so loathes, that flying humane kind,
The black and darksome nights, the bright and gladsome dayes
Indifferent are to him, his hope on God that staies.
Each little Village yeelds his short and homely fare:
To gather wind-falne sticks, his great'st and onely care;

Which every aged tree still yeeldeth to his fire.

This man, that is alone a King in his desire,
By no proud ignorant Lord is basely ouer-aw'd,
Nor his false prayse affects, who grosly beeing claw'd,
Stands like an itchy Moyle; nor of a pin he wayes
What fooles, abused Kings, and humorous Ladies raise.
His free and noble thought, nere envies at the grace
That often times is given unto a Baud most base,
Nor stirres it him to thinke on the Impostour vile,
Who seeming what hee's not, doth sensually beguile
The sottish purblind world: but absolutely free,
His happy time he spends the works of God to see,
In those so sundry hearbs which there in plenty growe:
Whose sundry strange effects he onely seeks to knowe.
And in a little Maund, beeing made of Oziars small,
Which serueth him to doe full many a thing withall,
He very choicely sorts his Simples got abroad.

Heere finds he on an Oake Rheume-purging Polipode;
And in some open place that to the Sunne doth lye,
He Fumitorie gets, and Eye-bright for the eye:
The Yarrow, where-with-all he stops the wound-made gore:
The healing Tutsan then, and Plantan for a sore.
And hard by them againe he holy Vervaine finds,
Which he about his head that hath the Megrim binds.
The wonder-working Dill hee gets not farre from these,
Which curious women use in many a nice disease.
For them that are with Newts, or Snakes, or Adders stong,
He seeketh out an hearbe that's called Adders-tong;
As Nature it ordain'd, its owne like hurt to cure,
And sportive did her selfe to niceties invre.
Valerian then he crops, and purposely doth stampe,
T'apply unto the place that's haled with the Crampe.
As Century, to close the wideness of a wound:
The belly hurt by birth, by Mugwort to make sound.
His Chickweed cures the heat that in the face doth rise.

For Physick, some againe he inwardly applyes.
For comforting the Spleene and Liver, gets for iuce,
Pale Hore-hound, which he holds of most especiall use.
So Saxifrage is good, and Harts-tongue for the Stone,
With Agrimony, and that hearbe we call S. John.
To him that hath a flux, of Sheepheards purse he gives,
And Mous-eare unto him whom some sharpe rupture grieves.
And for the laboring wretch that's troubled with a cough,
Or stopping of the breath, by fleagme that's hard and tough,
Campana heere he crops, approoued wondrous good:

As Comfrey unto him that's brused, spetting blood;
And from the Falling-ill, by Five-leafe doth restore,
And Melancholy cures by soueraigne Hellebore.

Of these most helpfull hearbs yet tell we but a few,
To those unnumbred sorts of Simples here that grew.
Which justly to set downe, euen Dodon short doth fall;
Nor skilfull Gerard, yet, shall ever find them all.

But from our Hermit heere the Muse we must inforce,
And zealously proceed in our intended course:
How Arden of her Rills and Riverets doth dispose;
By Alcester how Alne to Arro easely flowes;
And mildly beeing mixt, to Avon hold their way:
And likewise tow'rd the North, how lively-tripping Rhea,
T'attend the lustier Tame, is from her Fountaine sent:
So little Cole and Blyth goe on with him to Trent.
His Tamworth at the last, he in his way doth win:
There playing him awhile, till Ancor should come in,
Which trifleth twixt her banks, obseruing state, so slowe,
As though into his armes she scorn'd her selfe to throwe:
Yet Arden will'd her Tame to serue her on his knee;
For by that Nymph alone, they both should honor'd be.
The Forrest so much falne from what she was before,
That to her former height Fate could her not restore;
Though oft in her behalfe, the Genius of the Land
Importuned the Heavens with an auspicious hand.
Yet granted at the last (the aged Nymph to grace)
They by a Ladies birth would more renowne that place
Then if her Woods their heads aboue the Hills should seat;
And for that purpose, first made Couentry so great
(A poore thatcht Village then, or scarcely none at all,
That could not once have dream'd of her now stately wall)
And thither wisely brought that goodly Virgin-band,
Th'eleuen thousand maids, chaste Vrsula's Commaund,
Whom then the Britaine Kings gaue her full power to presse,
For matches to their friends in Britanny the lesse.
At whose departure thence, each by her just bequest
Some speciall vertue gaue, ordayning it to rest
With one of their owne sex, that there her birth should have,
Till fulnesse of the time which Fate did choicely saue;
Untill the Saxons raigne, when Couentry at length,
From her small, meane regard, recouered state and strength,
By Leofrick her Lord yet in base bondage held,
The people from her Marts by tollage who expeld:
Whose Dutchesse, which desir'd this tribute to release,
Their freedome often begg'd. The Duke, to make her cease,
Told her that if shee would his losse so farre inforce,

His will was, shee should ride starke nak't upon a horse
By day light through the street: which certainly he thought,
In her heroïck breast so deeply would have wrought,
That in her former sute she would have left to deale.
But that most princely Dame, as one deuour'd with zeale,
Went on, and by that meane the Cittie cleerly freed.

The first part of whose name, Godiua, doth forereed
Th' first syllable of hers, and Goodere halfe doth sound;
For by agreeing words, great matters have been found.
But further then this place the mysterie extends.
What Arden had begun, in Ancor lastly ends:
For in the British tongue, the Britaines could not find,
Wherefore to her that name of Ancor was assign'd:
Nor yet the Saxons since, nor times to come had known,
But that her beeing heere, was by this name fore-shown,
As prophecying her. For, as the first did tell
Her Sir-name, so againe doth Ancor lively spell
Her Christned title Anne. And as those Virgins there
Did sanctifie that Place: so holy Edith heere
A Recluse long time liv'd, in that faire Abbey plac't
Which Alured enricht, and Powlesworth highly grac't.
A Princesse being borne, and Abbesse, with those Maids,
All Noble like her selfe, in bidding of their Beads
Their holinesse bequeath'd, upon her to descend
Which there should after live: in whose deere selfe should end
Th'intent of Ancors name, her comming that decreed,
As hers (her place of birth) faire Couentry that freed.

But whilst about this tale smooth Ancor tryfling stayes,
Unto the lustier Tame as loth to come her waies,
The Flood intreats her thus; Deere Brooke, why doost thou wrong
Our mutuall love so much, and tediously prolong
Our mirthfull mariage-howre, for which I still prepare?
Haste to my broader banks, my joy and onely care.
For as of all my Floods thou art the first in fame;
When frankly thou shalt yeeld thine honor to my name,
I will protect thy state: then doe not wrong thy kind.
What pleasure hath the world that heere thou maist not find?

Hence, Muse, divert thy course to Dunsmore, by that Crosse
Where those two mightie waies, the Watling and the Fosse,
Our Center seeme to cut. (The first doth hold her way,
From Douer, to the farth'st of fruitfull Anglesey:
The second South and North, from Michaels utmost Mount,
To Cathnesse, which the furth'st of Scotland wee account.)
And then proceed to showe, how Avon from her Spring,
By Newnhams Fount is blest; and how she, blandishing,

By Dunsmore drives along. Whom Sow doth first assist,
Which taketh Shirburn in, with Cune, a great while mist;
Though Coventry from thence her name at first did raise,
Now florishing with Fanes, and proud Piramides;
Her walls in good repaire, her Ports so bravely built,
Her halls in good estate, her Crosse so richly gilt,
As scorning all the Townes that stand within her view:
Yet must shee not be griev'd, that Cune should claime her due.

Tow'rds Warwick with this traine as Avon trips along,
To Guy-cliffe beeing come, her Nymphs thus bravely song;
To thee renowned Knight, continuall prayse wee owe,
And at thy hallowed Tombe thy yeerely Obijts showe;
Who, thy deere Phillis name and Country to advance,
Left'st Warwicks wealthy seate: and sayling into France,
At Tilt, from his proud Steed, Duke Otton threw'st to ground:
And with th'invalewed Prize of Blanch the beautious crown'd
(The Almaine Emperors heire) high acts didst there atchieve:
As Lovaine thou againe didst valiantly relieve.
Thou in the Soldans blood thy worthy sword imbru'dst;
And then in single fight, great Amerant subdu'dst.
T'was thy Herculian hand, which happily destroy'd
That Dragon, which so long Northumberland annoy'd;
And slew that cruell Bore, which waste our wood-lands layd,
Whose tusks turn'd up our Tilths, and Dens in Medowes made:
Whose shoulder-blade remaines at Couentry till now;
And, at our humble sute, did quell that monstrous Cow
The passengers that us'd from Dunsmore to affright.
Of all our English (yet) ô most renowned Knight,
That Colebrond ouercam'st: at whose amazing fall
The Danes remou'd their Campe from Winchesters sieg'd wall.
Thy statue Guy-cliffe keepes, the gazers eye to please;
Warwick, thy mighty Armes (thou English Hercules)
Thy strong and masly sword, that never was controld:
Which, as her ancient right, her Castle still shall hold.

Scarce ended they their Song, but Avons winding streame,
By Warwick, entertaines the high complection'd Leame:
And as she thence along to Stratford on doth straine,
Receiveth little Heile the next into her traine:
Then taketh in the Stour, the Brooke, of all the rest
Which that most goodly Vale of Red-horse loveth best;
A Vally that enjoyes a verie great estate,
Yet not so famous held as smaller, by her fate:
Now, for Report had been too partiall in her praise,
Her just conceived greefe, faire Red-horse thus bewraies;

Shall every Vale be heard to boast her wealth? and I,

The needie Countries neere that with my Corne supply
As bravely as the best, shall onely I endure
The dull and beastly world my glories to obscure;
Neere way-lesse Ardens side, sith my rety'rd aboad
Stood quite out of the way from every common road?
Great Eushams fertill Gleabe, what tongue hath not extold?
As though to her alone belongd the Garbe of Gold.
Of Beuers batfull earth, men seeme as though to faine,
Reporting in what store shee multiplies her graine:
And folke such wondrous things of Alsburie will tell,
As though Aboundance stroue her burthened wombe to swell.
Her roome amongst the rest, so White-horse is decreed:
Shee wants no setting forth: her brave Pegasian Steed
(The wonder of the West) exalted to the skies:
My Red-horse of you all contemned onely lies.
The fault is not in me, but in the wretched time:
On whom, upon good cause, I well may lay the crime:
Which as all noble things, so mee it doth neglect.
But when th'industrious Muse shall purchase me respect
Of Countries neere my site, and win me forraine fame
(The Eden of you all deseruedly that am)
I shall as much be praysd for delicacie then,
As now in small account with vile and barbarous men.
For, from the loftie Edge that on my side doth lye,
Upon my spacious earth who casts a curious eye,
As many goodly seates shall in my compasse see,
As many sweet delights and rarities in mee
As in the greatest Vale: from where my head I couch
At Cotswolds Countries foot, till with my heeles I touch
The North-hamptonian fields, and fatning Pastures; where
I ravish every eye with my inticing cheere.
As still the Yeere growes on, that Ceres once doth load
The full Earth with her store; my plentious bosome strow'd
With all aboundant sweets: my frim and lustie flanke
Her bravery then displayes, with Meadowes hugely ranke.
The thick and well-growne fogge doth matt my smoother slades,
And on the lower Leas, as on the higher Hades
The daintie Clover growes (of grasse the onely silke)
That makes each Vdder strout abundantly with milke.

As an unlettred man, at the desired sight
Of some rare beautie moou'd with infinite delight,
Not out of his owne spirit, but by that power divine,
Which through a sparkling eye perspicuously doth shine,
Feeles his hard temper yeeld, that hee in passion breakes,
And things beyond his height, transported strangely speaks:
So those that dwell in mee, and live by frugall toyle,
When they in my defence are reasoning of my soyle,

As rapted with my wealth and beauties, learned growe,
And in wel-fitting tearmes, and noble language, showe
The Lordships in my Lands, from Rolright (which remaines
A witnesse of that day we wonne upon the Danes)
To Tawcester wel-neere: twixt which, they use to tell
Of places which they say doe Rumneys selfe excell.
Of Dasset they dare boast, and give Wormlighton prize,
As of that fertill Flat by Bishopton that lies.

For showing of my bounds, if men may rightly ghesse
By my continued forme which best doth me expresse,
On either of my sides and by the rising grounds,
Which in one fashion hold, as my most certaine Mounds,
In length neere thirtie miles I am discern'd to bee.
Thus Red-horse ends her tale; and I therewith agree
To finish heere my Song: the Muse some ease doth aske,
As wearied with the toyle in this her serious taske.


THE FOURTEENTH SONG

THE ARGUMENT

Her sundry straines the Muse to proue,
Now sings of homely Country love;
What moane th'old Heardsman Clent doth make,
For his coy Wood-Nymph Feckn'hams sake;
And, how the Nymphs each other greet,
When Avon and brave Severne meet.
The Vale of Eusham then doth tell,
How farre the Vales doe Hills excell.
Ascending, next, faire Cotswolds Plaines,
Shee reuels with the Shepheards swaines;
And sends the daintie Nymphes away,
Gainst Tame and Isis Wedding day.

At length, attain'd those Lands that South of Severne lye,
As to the varying Earth the Muse doth her apply,
Poore Sheep-hook and plaine Goad, she many times doth sound:
Then in a Buskind strain she instantly doth bound.
Smooth as the lowly streame, shee softly now doth glide:
And with the Mountaines straight contendeth in her pride.
Now back againe I turne, the Land with mee to take,
From the Staffordian heaths as Stour her course doth make.
Which Clent, from his proud top, contentedly doth view:
But yet the aged Hill, immoderatly doth rew
His loved Feckn'hams fall, and doth her state bemoane;

To please his amorous eye, whose like the world had none.
For, from her very youth, he (then an aged Hill)
Had to that Forrest-Nymph a speciall lyking still:
The least regard of him who never seemes to take,
But suffreth in herselfe for Salwarp's onely sake;
And on that River doats, as much as Clent on her.

Now, when the Hill perceiv'd, the Flood she would prefer,
All pleasure he forsakes; that at the full-bagd Cow,
Or at the curle-fac't Bull, when venting he doth low,
Or at th'unhappy wags, which let their Cattell stray,
At Nine-holes on the heath whilst they together play,
He never seemes to smile; nor ever taketh keepe
To heare the harmlesse Swaine pype to his grazing sheepe:
Nor to the Carters tune, in whistling to his Teame;
Nor lends his listning eare (once) to the ambling Streame,
That in the euening calme against the stones doth rush
With such a murmuring noyse, as it would seeme to hush
The silent Meads asleepe; but, voyd of all delight,
Remedilesly drown'd in sorrow day and night,
Nor Licky his Allie and neighbour doth respect:
And there-with beeing charg'd, thus answereth in effect;
That Lickey to his height seem'd slowly but to rise,
And that in length and bredth he all extended lyes,
Nor doth likes other hills to suddaine sharpnesse mount,
That of their kingly kind they scarce can him account;
Though by his swelling soyle set in so high a place,
That Malverns mightie selfe he seemeth to out-face.

Whilst Clent and Licky thus, doe both expresse their pride,
As Salwarpe slips along by Feck'nhams shady side,
That Forrest him affects in wandring to the Wych:
But he, himselfe by Salts there seeking to enrich,
His Feck'nham quite forgets; from all affection free.

But she, that to the Flood most constant meanes to be,
More prodigally gives her woods to those strong fires
Which boyle the source to Salts. Which Clent so much admires,
That love, and her disdaine, to madness him prouoke:
When to the Wood-Nymph thus the iealous Mountaine spoke;

Fond Nymph, thy twisted curles, on which were all my care,
Thou lett'st the Furnace waste; that miserably bare
I hope to see thee left, which so doost mee despise;
Whose beauties many a morne have blest my longing eyes:
And, till the wearie Sunne sunk downe unto the West,
Thou still my obiect wast, thou once my onely best,
The time shall quickly come, thy Groues and pleasant Springs,

Where to the mirthfull Merle the warbling Mavis sings,
The painfull laborers hand shall stock the roots, to burne;
The branch and body spent, yet could not serue his turne.
Which when, most wilfull Nymph, thy chaunce shal be to see,
Too late thou shalt repent thy small regard of mee.

But Saltwarpe downe from Wyche his nimbler feet doth ply,
Great Severne to attend, along to Teuksbury,
With others to partake the joy that there is seene,
When beautious Avon comes unto her soueraigne Queene.
Heere downe from Eushams Vale, their greatnesse to attend,
Comes Swilliat sweeping in, which Cotswold downe doth send:
And Garran there arrives, the great recourse to see.
Where thus together met, with most delightfull glee,
The cheerfull Nymphs that haunt the Valley rank and lowe
(Where full Pomona seemes most plentiously to flowe,
And with her fruitery swells by Pershore, in her pride)
Amongst the batfull Meads on Severns either side,
To these their confluent Floods, full Boaules of Pery brought:
Where, to each others health past many a deep-fetcht draught,
And many a sound Carouse from friend to friend doth goe,
Thus whilst the mellowed Earth with her owne juice doth flowe,
Inflamed with excesse the lustie pampred Vale,
In praise of her great selfe, thus frames her glorious tale;

I doubt not but some Vale enough for us hath said,
To answer them that most with basenesse us upbray'd;
Those high presumptuous Hills, which bend their utmost might,
Us onely to deiect, in their inveterate spight:
But I would have them thinke, that I (which am the Queene
Of all the British Vales, and so have ever beene
Since Gomers Giant-brood inhabited this Ile,
And that of all the rest, my selfe may so enstile)
Against the highest Hill dare put my selfe for place,
That ever threatned Heaven with the austerest face.
And for our praise, then thus; What Fountaine send they forth
(That finds a Rivers name, though of the smallest worth)
But it invales it selfe, and on it either side
Doth make those fruitfull Meads, which with their painted pride
Imbroader his proud Banke? whilst in lascivious Gyres
He swiftly sallieth out, and suddainly retyres
In sundry works and trailes, now shallowe, and then deepe,
Searching the spacious shores, as though it meant to sweepe
Their sweets with it away, with which they are repleat.
And men, first building Townes, themselues did wisely seat
Still in the bountious Vale: whose burthened Pasture beares
The most aboundant swathe, whose Gleabe such goodly cares,
As to the weightie sheafe with sythe or sickle cut,

When as his hardned hand the Labourer comes to put,
Sinks him in his owne sweat, which it but hardly wields:
And on the Corne-strew'd Lands, then in the stubble fields,
There feed the Heards of Neat, by them the Flocks of Sheep,
Seeking the scatt'red Corne upon the ridges steepe:
And in the furrowe by (where Ceres lyes much spild)
Th'unweldy larding Swine his mawe then having fild,
Lies wallowing in the myre, thence able scarce to rise.
When as those monstrous Hills so much that us despise
(The Mountaine, which forsooth the lowly Valley mocks)
Have nothing in the world upon their barren Rocks,
But greedy clambring Goats, and Conies, banisht quite
From every fertill place; as Rascals, that delight
In base and barren plots, and at good earth repine.
And though in Winter we to moysture much incline,
Yet those that be our owne, and dwell upon our Land,
When twixt their burly Stacks, and full-stuft Barnes they stand,
Into the softer Clay as easely they doe sinke,
Pluck up their heavie feet, with lighter spirits, to thinke
That Autumne shall produce, to recompence their toyle,
A rich and goodly croppe from that unpleasant soyle.
And from that envious Foe which seekes us to depraue,
Though much against his will this good we cleerly have,
We still are highly prais'd, and honor'd by his hight,
For, who will us survey, their cleere and judging sight
May see us thence at full: which else the searchingst eye,
By reason that so flat and leuelied we lie,
Could never throughly view, our selues nor could we showe.

Yet more; what lofty Hills to humble Valleys owe,
And what high grace they have which neere to us are plac't,
In Breedon may be seene, beeing amorously imbrac't
In cincture of mine armes. Who though he doe not vaunt
His head like those that looke as they would Heaven supplant:
Yet let them wisely note, in what excessive pride
He in my bosome sits; while him on every side
With my delicious sweets and delicates I trym.
And when great Malvern looks most terrible and grym,
Hee with a pleased brow continually doth smile.

Heere Breedon, having heard his praises all the while,
Grew insolently proud; and doth upon him take
Such state, as he would seeme but small account to make
Of Malvern, or of Mein. So that the wiser Vale,
To his instruction turnes the processe of her tale.
T'avoyd the greaters wrath, and shunne the meaners hate,
Quoth shee, take my advice, abandon idle state;
And by that way I goe, doe thou thy course contrive:

Give others leaue to vaunt, and let us closely thrive.
Whilst idly but for place the loftie Mountaines toyle,
Let us have store of graine, and quantity of soyle.
To what end serue their tops (that seeme to threat the skie).
But to be rent with stormes? whilst we in safety lie.
Their Rocks but barren be, and they which rashly clime,
Stand most in Envies sight, the fairest prey for Time.
And when the lowely Vales are clad in Sommers greene,
The grisled Winters snowe upon their heads is seene.
Of all the Hills I knowe, let Mein thy patterne bee:
Who though his site be such as seemes to equall thee,
And destitute of nought that Arden him can yeeld;
Nor of th'especiall grace of many a goodly field;
Nor of deere Cliffords seat (the place of health and sport)
Which many a time hath been the Muses quiet Port.
Yet brags not he of that, nor of himselfe esteemes
The more for his faire site; but richer then he seemes,
Clad in a gowne of Grasse, so soft and wondrous warme,
As him the Sommers heat, nor Winters cold can harme.
Of whom I well may say, as I may speake of thee;
From either of your tops, that who beholdeth mee,
To Paradise may thinke a second hee had found,
If any like the first were ever on the ground.

Her long and zealous speech thus Eusham doth conclude:
When straight the active Muse industriously pursu'd
This noble Countries praise, as matter still did rise.
For Gloster in times past her selfe did highly prize,
When in her pride of strength she nourisht goodly Vines,
And oft her cares represt with her delicious Wines.
But, now th'All-cheering Sun the colder soyle deceaues,
And us (heere tow'rds the Pole) still falling South-ward leaues:
So that the sullen earth th'effect thereof doth proue;
According to their Books, who hold that he doth moue
From his first Zeniths poynt; the cause we feele his want.
But of her Vines depriv'd, now Gloster learnes to plant
The Peare-tree every where: whose fruit shee straines for iuce,
That her pur'st Pery is, which first shee did produce
From Worstershire, and there is common as the fields;
Which naturally that soyle in most aboundance yeelds.

But the laborious Muse, which still new worke assaies,
Here sallyeth through the slades, where beautious Severne playes,
Untill that River gets her Glosters wished sight:
Where, she her streame divides, that with the more delight
Shee might behold the Towne, of which shee's wondrous proud:
Then takes shee in the Frome, then Cam, and next the Strowd,
As thence upon her course she wantonly doth straine.

Supposing then her selfe a Sea-god by her traine,
Shee Neptune-like doth float upon the bracky Marsh.
Where, least shee should become too combersome and harsh,
Faire Micklewood (a Nymph, long honor'd for a Chase,
Contending to have stood the high'st in Severns grace,
Of any of the Dryad's there bordring on her shore)
With her coole amorous shades, and all her Sylvan store,
To please the goodly Flood imployes her utmost powers,
Supposing the proud Nymph might like her woody Bowers.

But Severne (on her way) so large and head-strong grew,
That shee the Wood-Nymph scornes, and Avon doth pursue;
A River with no lesse then goodly Kings-wood crown'd,
A Forrest and a Flood by eithers fame renown'd;
And each with others pride and beautie much bewitcht;
Besides, with Bristowes state both wondrously enricht.
Which soone to Severne sent th'report of that faire Road
(So burthened still with Barks, as it would ouer-load
Great Neptune with the weight) whose fame so farre doth ring.
When as that mightie Flood, most bravely florishing,
Like Thetis goodlie selfe, maiestically glides;
Upon her spacious breast tossing the surgefull Tydes,
To have the River see the state to which shee growes,
And how much to her Queene the beautious Avon owes.

But, noble Muse, proceed immediatly to tell
How Eushams fertile Vale at first in liking fell
With Cotswold, that great King of Shepheards: whose proud site
When that faire Vale first saw, so nourisht her delight,
That him she onely lov'd: for wisely shee beheld
The beauties cleane throughout that on his sur-face dweld:
Of just and equall height two banks arising, which
Grew poore (as it should seeme) to make some Valley rich:
Betwixt them thrusting out an Elbowe of such height,
As shrowds the lower soyle; which, shadowed from the light,
Shootes forth a little Groue, that in the Sommers day
Invites the Flocks, for shade that to the Covert stray.
A Hill there holds his head, as though it told a tale,
Or stooped to looke downe, or whisper with a Vale;
Where little purling winds like wantons seeme to dally,
And skip from Bank to Banke, from Valley trip to Valley.
Such sundry shapes of soyle where Nature doth deuise,
That she may rather seeme fantasticall, then wise.

T'whom Sarum's Plaine gives place: though famous for her Flocks,
Yet hardly doth she tythe our Cotswolds wealthy locks.
Though Lemster him exceed for finenesse of her ore,
Yet quite he puts her downe for his aboundant store.

A match so fit as hee, contenting to her mind,
Few Vales (as I suppose) like Eusham hapt to find:
Nor any other Wold, like Cotswold ever sped,
So faire and rich a Vale by fortuning to wed.
Hee hath the goodly Wooll, and shee the wealthy Graine:
Through which they wisely seeme their houshold to maintaine.
He hath pure wholesome Ayre, and daintie crystall Springs.
To those delights of his, shee daily profit brings:
As to his large expense, she multiplies her heapes:
Nor can his Flocks deuour th'aboundance that shee reaps;
As th'one with what it hath, the other stroue to grace.

And, now that every thing may in the proper place
Most aptly be contriv'd, the Sheepe our Wold doth breed
(The simplest though it seeme) shall our description need,
And Shepheard-like, the Muse thus of that kind doth speak;
No browne, nor sullyed black the face or legs doth streak,
Like those of Moreland, Cank, or of the Cambrian hills
That lightly laden are: but Cotswold wisely fills
Her with the whitest kind: whose browes so woolly be,
As men in her faire Sheepe no emptiness should see.
The Staple deepe and thick, through, to the very graine,
Most strongly keepeth out the violentest raine:
A body long and large, the buttocks equall broad;
As fit to under-goe the full and weightie load.
And of the fleecie face, the flanke doth nothing lack,
But every-where is stor'd; the belly, as the back.
The faire and goodly Flock, the Shepheards onely pride,
As white as Winters snowe, when from the Rivers side
He drives his new-washt Sheepe; or on the Sheering day,
When as the lusty Ram, with those rich spoyles of May
His crooked hornes hath crown'd; the Bell-weather, so brave
As none in all the Flock they like themselues would have.

But Muse, returne to tell, how there the Sheepheards King,
Whose Flock hath chanc't that yeere the earliest Lambe to bring,
In his gay Bauldrick sits at his lowe grassie Bord,
With Flawns, Curds, Clowted-creame, and Country dainties stor'd:
And, whilst the Bag-pipe playes, each lustie iocund Swaine
Quaffes Sillibubs in Kans, to all upon the Plaine,
And to their Country-Girles, whose Nosegayes they doe weare.
Some Roundelayes doe sing: the rest, the burthen beare.

But Cotswold, be this spoke to th'onely praise of thee,
That thou of all the rest, the chosen soyle should'st bee,
Faire Isis to bring-forth (the Mother of great Tames)
With those delicious Brooks, by whose immortall streames
Her greatnesse is begunne: so that our Rivers King,

When he his long Descent shall from his Bel-sires bring,
Must needs (Great Pastures Prince) derive his stem by thee,
From kingly Cotswolds selfe, sprung of the third degree:
As th'old worlds Heroës wont, that in the times of yore,
On Neptune, Ioue, and Mars, themselues so highly bore.

But easely from her source as Isis gently dades;
Unto her present ayde, downe through the deeper slades,
The nimbler footed Churne, by Cisseter doth slide;
And first at Greeklade gets preheminence, to guide
Queene Isis on her way, ere shee receive her traine.
Cleere Colne, and lively Leech, so downe from Cotswolds Plaine,
At Leechlade linking hands, come likewise to support
The Mother of great Tames. When, seeing the resort,
From Cotswold Windrush scowres; and with her selfe doth cast
The Traine to ouer-take, and therefore hies her fast
Through the Oxfordian fields; when (as the last of all
Those Floods, that into Tames out of our Cotswold fall,
And farth'st unto the North) bright Enload forth doth beare.
For, though it had been long, at length she came to heare
That Isis was to Tame in wedlock to be ti'd:
And therefore shee prepar'd t'attend upon the Bride;
Expecting, at the Feast, past ordinarie grace.

And beeing neere of kinne to that most Spring-full place,
Where out of Blockleys banks so many Fountaines flowe,
That cleane throughout his soyle proud Cotswold cannot showe
The like: as though from farre, his long and many Hills,
There emptied all their vaines, where-with those Founts hee fills,
Which in the greatest drought so brimfull still doe float,
Sent through the rifted Rocks with such an open throat,
As though the Cleeues consum'd in humor; they alone,
So crystalline and cold, as hardneth stick to stone.

But whilst this while we talke, the farre divulged fame
Of this great Bridale tow'rd, in Phoebus mightie name
Doth bid the Muse make haste, and to the Bride-house speed;
Of her attendance there least they should stand in need.

THE FIFTEENTH SONG

THE ARGUMENT

The guests heere to the Bride-house hie.
The goodly Vale of Al'sbury
Sets her sonne (Tame) forth, brave as May,

Upon the joyfull Wedding day:
Who, deckt up, tow'rds his Bride is gone.
So lovely Isis comming on,
At Oxford all the Muses meet her,
And with a Prothalamion greet her.
The Nymphs are in the Bridall Bowres,
Some strowing sweets, some sorting flowres:
Where lustie Charwell himselfe raises,
And sings of Rivers, and their praises.
Then Tames his way tow'rd Windsore tends.
Thus, with the Song, the Mariage ends.

Now Fame had through this Ile divulg'd, in every eare,
The long-expected day of Mariage to be neere,
That Isis, Cotswolds heire, long woo'd was lastly wonne,
And instantly should wed with Tame, old Chiltern's sonne.
And now that Wood-mans wife, the mother of the Flood,
The rich and goodly Vale of Alsbury, that stood
So much upon her Tame, was busied in her Bowres,
Preparing for her sonne, as many sutes of Flowres,
As Cotswold for the Bride, his Isis, lately made;
Who for the lovely Tame, her Bridegroome, onely staid.

Whilst every crystall Flood is to this business prest,
The cause of their great speed and many thus request;
O! whither goe yee Floods? what suddaine wind doth blowe,
Then other of your kind, that you so fast should flowe?
What busines is in hand, that spurres you thus away?
Faire Windrush let me heare, I pray thee Charwell say:
They suddainly reply, What lets you should not see
That for this Nuptiall feast wee all prepared bee?
Therefore this idle chat our eares doth but offend:
Our leysure serues not now these trifles to attend.

But whilst things are in hand, old Chiltern (for his life)
From prodigall expense can no way keepe his wife;
Who feedes her Tame with Marle, in Cordiall-wise prepar'd,
And thinks all idly spent, that now she onely spar'd
In setting forth her sonne: nor can shee thinke it well,
Unlesse her lavish charge doe Cotswold's farre excell.
For, Alsbury's a Vale that walloweth in her wealth,
And (by her wholesome ayre continually in health)
Is lustie, frim, and fat, and holds her youthfull strength.
Besides her fruitfull earth, her mightie breadth and length,
Doth Chiltern fitly match: which mountainously hie,
And beeing very long, so likewise shee doth lie;
From the Bedfordian fields, where first she doth begin,
To fashion like a Vale, to th'place where Tame doth win

His Isis wished Bed; her soyle throughout so sure,
For goodnesse of her Gleabe, and for her Pasture pure,
That as her Graine and Grasse, so shee her Sheepe doth breed,
For burthen and for boane all other that exceed:
And shee, which thus in wealth aboundantly doth flowe,
Now cares not on her Child what cost shee doe bestowe.
Which when wise Chiltern saw (the world who long had try'd,
And now at last had layd all garish pompe aside;
Whose hoare and chalkie head discry'd him to be old,
His Beechen woods bereft that kept him from the cold)
Would faine perswade the Vale to hold a steddy rate;
And with his curious Wife, thus wisely doth debate:

Quoth hee, you might allow what needeth, to the most:
But where as lesse will serue, what meanes this idle cost?
Too much, a surfet breeds, and may our Child annoy:
These fat and lushious meats doe but our stomacks cloy.
The modest comly meane, in all things likes the wise,
Apparrell often shewes us womanish precise.
And what will Cotswold thinke when he shall heare of this?
Hee'll rather blame your waste, then praise your cost iwiss.

But, women wilfull be, and shee her will must have,
Nor cares how Chiltern chides, so that her Tame be brave.
Alone which tow'rds his Love shee easely doth convay:
For the Oxonian Ouze was lately sent away
From Buckingham, where first he finds his nimbler feet;
Tow'rds Whittlewood then takes: where, past the noblest Street,
Hee to the Forrest gives his farewell, and doth keepe
His course directly downe into the German Deepe,
To publish that great day in mightie Neptunes Hall,
That all the Sea-gods there might keep it festivall.

As wee have told how Tame holds on his euen course,
Returne we to report, how Isis from her sourse
Comes tripping with delight, downe from her daintier Springs;
And in her princely traine, t'attend her Marriage, brings
Cleere Churnet, Colne, and Leech, which first she did retaine,
With Windrush: and with her (all out-rage to restraine
Which well might offred be to Isis as shee went)
Came Yenload with a guard of Satyres, which were sent
From Whichwood, to await the bright and God-like Dame.
So, Bernwood did bequeath his Satyres to the Tame,
For Sticklers in those stirres that at the Feast should bee.

These preparations great when Charwell comes to see,
To Oxford got before, to entertaine the Flood,
Apollo's ayde he begs, with all his sacred brood,

To that most learned place to welcome her repaire.
Who in her comming on, was wext so wondrous faire,
That meeting, strife arose betwixt them, whether they
Her beauty should extoll, or shee admire their Bay.
On whom their severall gifts (to amplifie her dowre)
The Muses there bestowe; which ever have the power
Immortall her to make. And as shee past along,
Those modest Thespian Maids thus to their Isis song;

Yee Daughters of the Hills, come downe from every side,
And due attendance give upon the lovely Bride:
Goe strewe the paths with flowers by which shee is to passe.
For be yee thus assur'd, in Albion never was
A beautie (yet) like hers: where have yee ever seene
So absolute a Nymph in all things, for a Queene?
Give instantly in charge the day by wondrous faire,
That no disorderd blast attempt her braided haire.
Goe, see her State prepar'd, and every thing be fit,
The Bride-chamber adorn'd with all beseeming it.
And for the princely Groome, who ever yet could name
A Flood that is so fit for Isis as the Tame?
Yee both so lovely are, that knowledge scarce can tell,
For feature whether hee, or beautie shee excell:
That ravished with joy each other to behold,
When as your crystall wasts you closely doe enfold,
Betwixt your beautious selues you shall beget a Sonne,
That when your lives shall end, in him shall be begunne.
The pleasant Surryan shores shall in that Flood delight,
And Kent esteeme her selfe most happy in his sight.
The Shire that London loves, shall onely him prefer,
And give full many a gift to hold him neer to her.
The Skeld, the goodly Mose, the rich and Viny Rheine,
Shall come to meet the Thames in Neptunes watry Plaine.
And all the Belgian Streames and neighboring Floods of Gaul,
Of him shall stand in awe, his tributaries all.
As of fayre Isis thus, the learned Virgins spake,
A shrill and suddaine brute this Prothalamion brake;
That White-horse, for the love she bare to her Ally,
And honored sister Vale, the bountious Alsbury,
Sent Presents to the Tame by Ock her onely Flood,
Which for his Mother Vale, so much on greatnesse stood.

From Oxford, Isis hasts more speedily, to see
That River like his birth might entertained bee:
For, that ambitious Vale, still striving to commaund,
And using for her place continually to stand,
Proud White-horse to perswade, much busines there hath been
T'acknowledge that great Vale of Eusham for her Queen.

And but that Eusham is so opulent and great,
That thereby shee herselfe holds in the soueraigne seat,
This White-horse all the Vales of Britaine would or'e beare,
And absolutely sit in the imperiall Chaire;
And boasts as goodly Heards, and numerous Flocks to seed;
To have as soft a Gleabe, as good increase of seed;
As pure and fresh an ayre upon her face to flowe,
As Eusham for her life: and from her Steed doth showe,
Her lustie rising Downes, as faire a prospect take
As that imperious Wold: which her great Queene doth make
So wondrously admyr'd, and her so farre extend.
But, to the Mariage, hence, industrious Muse descend.

The Naïads, and the Nymphs extreamly ouer-joy'd,
And on the winding banks all busily imploy'd,
Upon this joyfull day, some dainty Chaplets twine:
Some others chosen out, with fingers neat and fine,
Brave Anadems doe make: some Bauldricks up do bind:
Some, Garlands: and to some, the Nosegaies were assign'd;
As best their skill did serue. But, for that Tame should be
Still man-like as him selfe, therefore they will that he
Should not be drest with Flowers, to Gardens that belong
(His Bride that better fitte) but onely such as sprong
From the replenisht Meads, and fruitfull Pastures neere.
To sort which Flowers, some sit; some making Garlands were;
The Primrose placing first, because that in the Spring
It is the first appeares, then onely florishing;
The azur'd Hare-bell next, with them, they neatly mixt:
T'allay whose lushious smell, they Woodbind plac't betwixt.
Amongst those things of sent, there prick they in the Lilly:
And neere to that againe, her sister Daffadilly.
To sort these Flowers to showe, with th'other that were sweet,
The Cowslip then they couch, and th'Oxslip, for her meet:
The Columbine amongst they sparingly doe set,
The yellow King-cup, wrought in many a curious fret,
And now and then among, of Eglantine a spray,
By which againe a course of Lady-smocks they lay:
The Crow-flower, and there-by the Clover-flower they stick,
The Daysie, ouerall those sundry sweets so thick,
As Nature doth her selfe; to imitate her right:
Who seems in that her pearle so greatly to delight,
That every Plaine therewith she powdreth to beholde:
The crimsin Darnell Flower, the Blew-bottle, and Gold:
Which though esteem'd but weeds; yet for their dainty hewes,
And for their sent not ill, they for this purpose chuse.

Thus having told you how the Bridegroome Tame was drest,
Ile shew you, how the Bride, faire Isis, they invest;

Sitting to be attyr'd under her Bower of State,
Which scornes a meaner sort, then fits a Princely rate.
In Anadems for whom they curiously dispose
The Red, the dainty White, the goodly Damask Rose,
For the rich Ruby, Pearle, and Amatist, men place
In Kings Emperiall Crownes, the circle that enchase.
The brave Carnation then, with sweet and soueraigne power
(So of his colour call'd, although a Iuly-flower)
With th'other of his kinde, the speckled and the pale:
Then th'odoriferous Pink, that sends forth such a gale
Of sweetnes; yet in sents, as various as in sorts.
The purple Violet then, the Pansie there supports:
The Mary-gold aboue t'adorne the arched Bar:
The dubble Daysie, Thrift, the Button-batcheler,
Sweet William, Sops in wine, the Campion: and to these,
Some Lauander they put, with Rosemary and Bayes:
Sweet Marjoram, with her like, sweet Basill rare for smell,
With many a flower, whose name were now too long to tell:
And rarely with the rest, the goodly Fower-delice.

Thus for the nuptiall houre, all fitted point-deuice,
Whilst some still busied are in decking of the Bride,
Some others were again as seriously imploy'd
In strewing of those hearbs, at Bridalls us'd that be;
Which every where they throwe with bountious hands and free.
The healthfull Balme and Mint, from their full laps doe fly,
The sent-full Camomill, the verdurous Costmary.
They hot Muscado oft with milder Maudlin cast:
Strong Tansey, Fennell coole, they prodigally waste:
Cleere Isop, and therewith the comfortable Thyme,
Germander with the rest, each thing then in her prime;
As well of wholesome hearbs, as every pleasant flower,
Which Nature here produc't, to fit this happy houre.
Amongst these strewing kinds, some other wilde that growe,
As Burnet, all abroad, and Meadow-wort they throwe.

Thus all things falling out to every ones desire,
The ceremonies done that Mariage doth require,
The Bride and Bridegroome set, and serv'd with sundry cates,
And every other plac't, as fitted their estates;
Amongst this confluence great, wise Charwell here was thought
The first to cheare the guests: who throughly had been taught
In all that could pertaine to Court-ship, long agon,
As comming from his Sire, the fruitfull Helidon,
He trauelleth to Tames; where passing by those Townes
Of that rich Country neere, whereas the mirthfull clownes,
With Taber and the pipe, on holydayes doe use,
Upon the May-pole Greene, to trample out their shooes:

And having in his eares the deepe and solemne rings,
Which sound him all the way, unto the learned Springs,
Where he, his Soueraigne Ouze most happily doth meet,
And him, the thrice-three maids, Apollos ofspring, greet
With all their sacred gifts: thus, expert being growne
In musicke; and besides, a curious Maker knowne:
This Charwell (as I said) the first these Floods among,
For silence having call'd, thus to th'assembly song;

Stand fast ye higher Hills: low vallies easily lie:
And Forrests that to both you equally apply
(But for the greater part, both wilde and barren be)
Retire ye to your wastes; and Rivers only we,
Oft meeting let us mixe: and with delightfull grace,
Let every beautious Nymph, her best lov'd Flood imbrace,
An Alien be he borne, or neer to her owne Spring,
So from his native Fount he bravely flourishing,
Along the flowry Fields, licentiously do straine,
Greeting each curled groue, and circling every Plaine;
Or hasting to his fall, his sholy grauell scowr's,
And with his Crystall front, then courts the climing Towres.

Let all the world be Judge, what Mountaine hath a name,
Like that from whose proud foot, their springs some Flood of Fame:
And in the Earth's suruay, what seat like that is set,
Whose Streets some ample Streame, aboundantly doth wet?
Where is there Haven found, or Harbour, like that Road,
Int'which some goodly Flood, his burthen doth unload?
By whose rank swelling Streame, the far-fetcht forraine fraught,
May up to In-land Townes conueniently be brought.
Of any part of Earth, we be the most renown'd;
That countries very oft, nay, Empires oft we bound.
As Rubicon, much fam'd, both for his Fount and Fall,
The ancient limit held, twixt Italy and Gaule.
Europe and Asia keep on Tanais either side.
Such honor have we Floods, the World (euen) to divide.
Nay: Kingdoms thus we proue are christened oft by us;
Iberia takes her name of Crystall Iberus.
Such reverence to our kinde the wiser Ancients gaue,
As they suppos'd each Flood a Deity to have:

But with our fame at home returne we to proceed.
In Britanne here we find, our Severne, and our Tweed,
The tripartited Ile doe generally divide,
To England, Scotland, Wales, as each doth keep her side.
Trent cuts the Land in two, so equally, as tho
Nature it pointed-out, to our great Brute to show
How to his mightie Sonnes the Iland he might share.

A thousand of this kinde, and neerer, I will spare;
Where if the state of Floods, at large I list to show,
I proudly could report how Pactolus doth throwe
Up graines of perfect gold; and of great Ganges tell,
Which when full India's showers inforceth him to swell,
Gilds with his glistering sands the ouer-pampered shore:
How wealthy Tagus first by tumbling down his ore,
The rude and slothfull Moores of old Iberia taught,
To search into those hills, from which such wealth he brought.
Beyond these if I pleas'd, I to your praise could bring,
In sacred Tempe, how (about the hoofe-plow'd Spring)
The Heliconian Maides, upon that hallowed ground,
Recounting Heavenly Hymnes eternally are crown'd.
And as the earth doth us in her owne bowels nourish;
So every thing, that growes by us, doth thrive and flourish.
To godly vertuous men, we wisely likened are:
To be so in themselues, that do not only care;
But by a sacred power, which goodnesse doth awaite,
Doe make those vertuous too, that them associate.

By this, the wedding ends, and brake up all the Showe:
And Tames, got, borne, and bred, immediately doth flowe,
To Windsor-ward amaine (that with a wondring eye,
The Forrest might behold his awfull Emperie)
And soon becometh great, with waters wext so rank,
That with his wealth he seemes to retch his widned Bank:
Till happily attayn'd his Grandsire Chilterns grounds,
Who with his Beechen wreaths this king of Rivers crownes.
Amongst his holts and hils, as on his way he makes,
At Reading once arriv'd, cleere Kennet overtakes:
Her Lord the stately Tames, which that great flood againe,
With many signes of joy doth kindly entertaine.
Then Loddon next comes in, contributing her store;
As still we see, The much runnes ever to the more.

Set out with all this pompe, when this Emperiall Streame,
Himselfe establisht sees, amidst his watry Realme,
His much-lov'd Henly leaues, and proudly doth pursue
His Wood nymph Windsors feate, her lovely site to view.
Whose most delightful face when once the River sees,
Which shewes her selfe attir'd in tall and stately trees,
He in such earnest love with amorous gestures wooes,
That looking still at her, his way was like to loose;
And wandring in and out so wildly seems to goe,
As headlong he himselfe into her lap would throw.

Him with the like desire the Forrest doth imbrace,
And with her presence strives her Tames asmuch to grace.

No Forrest, of them all, so fit as she doth stand.
When Princes, for their sports, her pleasures will command,
No Wood-nymph as her selfe such troupes hath ever seene,
Nor can such Quarries boast as have in Windsor beene.
Nor any ever had so many solemne dayes;
So brave assemblies viewd, nor took so rich assaies.

Then, hand in hand, her Tames the Forrest softly brings,
To that supreamest place of the great English Kings,
§ The Garters Royall seate, from him who did aduance
That Princely Order first, our first that conquered France;
The Temple of Saint George, wheras his honored Knights,
Upon his hallowed day, obserue their ancient rites:
Where Eaton is at hand to nurse that learned brood,
To keepe the Muses still neere to this Princely Flood;
That nothing there may want, to beawtifie that seate,
With every pleasure stor'd: And here my Song compleate.


THE SIXTEENTH SONG

THE ARGUMENT

Olde Ver, neere to Saint Albans, brings
Watling to talk of auncient things;
What Verlam was before she fell,
And many more sad ruines tell.
Of the foure old Emperiall Waies,
The course they held, and too what Seas;
Of those seauen Saxon Kingdomes here,
Their sites, and how they bounded were.
Then Pure-vale vants her rich estate:
And Lea bewraies her wretched Fate.
The Muse, led on with much delight,
Delivers Londons happy site;
Showes this loose Ages leud abuse:
And for this time there staies the Muse.

The Brydall of our Tame and Princely Isis past:
And Tamesis their sonne, begot, and wexing fast,
Inuiteth Crystall Colne his wealth on him to lay,
Whose beauties had intic't his Soueraine Tames to stay,
Had he not been inforc't, by his unruly traine.
For Brent, a pretty Brook, allures him on againe,
Great London to salute, whose hie-rear'd Turrets throng
To gaze upon the Flood, as he doth passe along.
Now, as the Tames is great, so most transparent Colne

Feeles, with excessive joy, her amorous bosome swolne,
That Ver of long esteem'd, a famous auncient Flood
(Upon whose aged Bank olde Verlamchester stood,
Before the Roman rule) here glorify'd of yore,
Unto her cleerer banks contributed his store;
Enlarging both her streame, and strengthening his renowne,
Where the delicious Meads her through her course doe crown.
This Ver (as I have said) Colnes tributary brook,
On Verlams ruin'd walles as sadly he doth look,
Neere Holy Albans Towne, where his rich shrine was set,
Old Watling in his way the Flood doth over-get.
Where after reverence done, Ver quoth the Ancient Street
Tis long since thou and I first in this place did meet.
And so it is quoth Ver, and we have liv'd to see
Things in farre better state then at this time they be:
But he that made, amend: for much their goes amisse.
Quoth Watling, gentle flood, yea so in truth it is:
And sith of this thou speakst; the very sooth to say,
Since Great Mulmutius, first, made me the noblest Way,
The soyle is altered much: the cause I pray thee showe.
The time that thou hast liv'd, hath taught thee much to knowe.
I faine would understand, why this delightfull place,
In former time that stood so hie in Natures grace
(Which bare such store of graine, and that so wondrous great,
That all the neighboring Coast was cald the soyle of wheate)
Of later time is turn'd a hotte and hungry sand,
Which scarce repayes the seed first cast into the the Land.
At which the silent brooke shrunk-in his siluer head,
And fain'd as he away would instantly have fled;
Suspecting, present speech might passed griefe renew.
Whom Watling thus againe doth seriously pursue;
I pray thee be not coy, but answere my demand:
The cause of this (deer Flood) I faine would understand.
Thou saw'st when Verlam once her head aloft did beare
(Which in her cinders now lies sadly buried heere)
With Alablaster, Tuch, and Porphery adorn'd,
When (welneare) in her pride great Troynouant she scorn'd.
Thou sawest great-burthen'd Ships through these thy valleyes pass,
Where now the sharp-edg'd Sithe sheeres up the spyring grasse:
That where the vgly Seale and Porpose us'd to play,
The Grashopper and Ant now lord it all the day:
Where now Saint Albans stands was called Holme-hurst then;
Whose sumptuous Fane we see neglected now agen.

This rich and goodly Fane which ruind thou doest see,
Quoth Ver, the motive is that thou importun'st me:
But to another thing thou cunningly doest flie,
And reason seem'st to vrge of her sterilitie.

With that he fetcht a sigh, and ground his teeth in rage;
Quoth Ver euen for the sin of this accursed Age.
Behold that goodly Fane, which ruind now doth stand,
To holy Albon built, first Martyr of the Land;
Who in the faith of Christ from Rome to Britanne came,
And dying in this place, resign'd his glorious Name.
In memory of whom, (as more then halfe Divine)
Our English Offa rear'd a rich and sumptuous shrine
And Monastary heere: which our succeeding kings,
From time to time endow'd with many goodly things.
And many a Christian Knight was buried heere, before
The Norman set his foote upon this conquered shore;
And after those brave spirits in all those balefull stowres,
That with Duke Robert went against the Pagan powers,
And in their Countries right at Cressy those that stood,
And that at Poyters bath'd their bilbowes in French blood;
Their valiant Nephewes next at Agin-court that fought,
Whereas rebellious France upon her knees was brought:
In this religious house at some of their returns,
When nature claym'd her due, here plac't their hallowed vrnes:
Which now deuowring Time, in his so mighty waste,
Demolishing those walls, hath utterly defac't.
So that the earth to feele the ruinous heaps of stones,
That with the burth'nous weight now presse their sacred boanes,
Forbids this wicked brood, should by her fruits be fed;
As loathing her owne womb, that such loose children bred.
Herewith transported quite, to these exclaimes he fell:
Lives no man, that this world her grievous crimes dare tell?
Where be those noble spirits for ancient things that stood?
When in my prime of youth I was a gallant flood;
In those free golden dayes, it was the Satyres use
To taxe the guilty times, and raile upon abuse:
But soothers find the way preferment most to win;
Who seruing Great mens turnes, become the bauds to sin.

When Watling in his words that tooke but small delight,
Hearing the angry Brook so cruelly to bite;
As one that faine would drive these fancies from his mind,
Quoth he, Ile tell thee things that sute thy gentler kind.
My Song is of my selfe, and my three sister Streets,
Which way each of us runne, where each her fellow meets,
Since us, his Kingly Waies, Mulmutius first began,
From Sea, againe to Sea, that through the Iland ran.
Which that in mind to keep posterity might have,
Appointing first our course, this priviledge he gave,
That no man might arrest, or debtors goods might seize
In any of us fowre his militarie Waies.
And though the Fosse in length exceed me many a mile,

That holds from shore to shore the length of all the Ile,
From where Rich Cornwall points, to the Iberian Seas,
Till colder Cathnes tells the scattered Orcades,
I measuring but the bredth, that is not halfe his gate;
Yet, for that I am grac't with goodly Londons state,
And Tames and Severne both since in my course I crosse,
And in much greater trade; am worthier farre then Fosse.
But ô unhappie chance! through times disastrous lot,
Our other fellow Streets lie utterly forgot:
As Icning, that set out from Yarmouth in the East,
By the Iceni then being generally possest,
Was of that people first tearm'd Icning in her race,
Upon the Chiltern here that did my course imbrace:
Into the dropping South and bearing then outright,
Upon the Solent Sea stopt on the Ile-of-Wight.

And Rickneld, forth that raught from Cambria's farther shore,
Where South-Wales now shoots forth Saint David's Promontore.
And, on his mid-way neere, did me in England meet;
Then in his oblique course the lusty stragling Street
Soone overtook the Fosse; and toward the fall of Tine,
Into the Germane Sea dissolu'd at his decline.

Here Watling would have ceast, his tale as having tolde:
But now this Flood that faine the Street in talke would hold,
Those ancient things to heare, which well old Watling knew,
With these entising words, her fairely forward drew.

Right Noble Street, quoth he, thou hast liv'd long, gone farre,
Much trafique had in peace, much trauailed in warre;
And in thy larger course suruay'st as sundry grounds
(Where I poore Flood am lockt within these narrower bounds,
And like my ruin'd selfe these ruins only see,
And there remains not one to pittie them or me)
On with thy former speech: I pray thee somwhat say.
For, Watling, as thou art a military Way,
Thy story of old Streets likes me so wondrous well,
That of the ancient folk I faine would heare thee tell.

With these perswasive words, smooth Ver the Watling wan:
Stroking her dusty face, when thus the Street began;

When once their seaven-fold Rule the Saxons came to reare,
And yet with halfe this Ile sufficed scarcely were,
Though from the Inland part the Britans they had chas't,
Then understand how heere themselues the Saxons plac't.

Where in Great Britans state foure people of her owne

Were by the severall names of their abodes well knowne
(As, in that horne which juttes into the Sea so farre,
Wherein our Deuonshire now, and furthest Cornewall are,
The old Daumonij dwelt: so hard againe at hand,
The Durotriges sat on the Dorsetian Sand:
And where from Sea to Sea the Belgae forth were let,
Even from Southhamptons shore, through Wilt and Sommerset,
The Attrebates in Bark unto the Bank of Tames,
Betwixt the Celtick sleeue and the Sabrinian streames)
The Saxons there set down one Kingdome: which install'd,
And being West, they it their Westerne kingdom call'd.
So Eastward where by Tames the Trinobants were set,
To Trinouant their Towne, for that their name in debt,
That London now we tearme, the Saxons did possesse,
And their East kingdome call'd, as Essex doth expresse;
The greatest part thereof, and still their name doth beare;
Though Middlesex therein, and part of Hartford were;
From Colne upon the West, upon the East to Stour,
Where mighty Tames himselfe doth into Neptune pour.

As to our farthest Rise, where forth those Fore-lands leane,
Which beare their chaulky browes into the German Maine,
The Angles which arose out of the Saxon race,
Allur'd with the delights and fitnes of that place,
Where the Iceni liv'd did set their kingdome downe,
From where the wallowing Seas those queachy Washes drowne
That Ely doe in-Ile, to martyred Edmonds Ditch,
Till those Norfolcian shores vast Neptune doth intich:
Which (farthest to the East of this divided Ile)
Th'East Angles kingdome, then, those English did instile.

And Sussex seemeth still, as with an open mouth,
Those Saxons Rule to shew that of the utmost South
The name to them assum'd, who rigorously expeld
The Kentish Britans thence, and those rough wood-lands held
From where the goodly Tames the Surrian grounds doth sweep,
Untill the smiling Downes salute the Celtick Deep.

Where the Dobuni dwelt, their neighbouring Cateuclani,
Cornavij more remote, and where the Coritani,
Where Dee and Mersey shoot into the Irish Sea;
(Which welneere o're this part, now called England, lay,
From Severne to the Ditch that cuts New-Market Plaine,
And from the Banks of Tames to Humber, which containe
So many goodly shires of Mersey, Mercia hight)
Their mightier Empire, there, the middle English pight.
Which farthest though it raught, yet there it did not end:
But Offa, king thereof, it after did extend

Beyond the Bank of Dee; and by a Ditch he cut
Through Wales from North to South, into wide Mercia put
Welneere the halfe thereof: and from three peoples there,
To whom three speciall parts divided justly were
(The Ordouices, now which North-Wales people be,
From Cheshire which of old diuided was by Dee:
And from our Marchers now, that were Demetae then;
And those Silures call'd, by us the South-Wales men)
Beyond the Severne, much the English Offa took,
To shut the Britans up, within a little nooke.

From whence, by Merseyes Banks, the rest a kingdome made:
Where, in the Britanes Rule (before) the Brigants sway'd;
The powerfull English there establisht were to stand:
Which, North from Humber set, they tearm'd North-humberland;
Two Kingdomes which had been, with severall thrones install'd.
Bernitia hight the one; Diera th'other call'd.
The first from Humber stretcht unto the Bank of Tine:
Which River and the Frith the other did confine.
Bernitia beareth through the spacious Yorkish bounds,
From Durham down along to the Lancastrian Sounds,
With Mersey and cleere Tine continuing to their fall,
To England-ward within the Pict's renowned Wall,
And did the greater part of Cumberland containe:
With whom the Britans name for ever shall remaine;
Who there amongst the rocks and mountaines lived long,
When they Loegria left, inforc't through powerfull wrong.
Diera ouer Tine, into Albania lay,
To where the Frith falls out into the German Sea.

This said, the aged Street sagd sadly on alone:
And Ver upon his course, now hasted to be gone
T'accompany his Colne: which as she gently glides,
Doth kindly him imbrace: whom soon this hap betides;
As Colne come on along, and chanc't to cast her eye
Upon that neighbouring Hill where Harrow stand so hie,
She Peryvale perceiv'd prankt up with wreaths of wheat,
And with exulting tearmes thus glorying in her seat;
Why should not I be coy, and of my Beauties nice,
Since this my goodly graine is held of greatest price?
No manchet can so well the courtly palat please,
As that made of the meale fetcht from my fertill Leaze.
Their finest of that kind, compared with my wheate,
For whitenesse of the Bread, doth look like common Cheate.
What Barly is there found, whose faire and bearded eare
Makes stouter English Ale, or stronger English Beere.
The Oate, the Beane, and Pease, with me but Pulses are;
The course and browner Rye, no more then Fitch and Tare.

What seed doth any soyle, in England bring, that I
Beyond her most increase yet cannot multiply.
Besides; my sure abode next goodly London is,
To vent my fruitfull store, that me doth never misse.
And those poore baser things, they cannot put away,
How ere I set my price, nere on my chap-men stay.

When presently the Hill, that maketh her a Vale,
With things he had in hand, did interrupt her tale,
With Hampsted being falne and Hie-gate at debate;
As one before them both, that would aduance his State,
From either for his height to beare away the praise,
Besides that he alone rich Peryvale suruaies.
But Hampsted pleads, himselfe in Simples to have skill,
And therefore by desert to be the noblest Hill;
As one, that on his worth and knowledge doth rely
In learned Physicks use, and skilfull Surgerie;
And challengeth, from them, the worthiest place her owne,
Since that old Watling once, o're him, to passe was knowne.

Then Hie-gate boasts his Way; Which men do most frequent;
His long-continued fame; his hie and great descent;
Appointed for a gate of London to have been,
When first the mighty Brute, that City did begin.
And that he is the Hill, next Enfield which hath place,
A Forrest for her pride, though titled but a Chase.
Her Purlewes, and her Parks, her circuit full as large,
As some (perhaps) whose state requires a greater charge.
Whose Holts that view the East, do wistly stand to look
Upon the winding course of Lee's delightfull Brook.
Where Mimer comming in, inuites her Sister Beane,
Amongst the chalky Bankst increase their Mistresse traine;
Whom by the dainty hand, obsequiously they lead
(By Hartford gliding on, through many a pleasant Mead.
And comming in hir course, to crosse the common Fare,
For kindnes she doth kisse that hospitable Ware.)
Yet scarsely comfort Lee (alasse!) so woe begonne,
Complaining in her course, thus to her selfe alone;
How should my beauty now give Waltham such delight,
Or I poore silly Brook take pleasure in her sight?
Antiquity (for that it stands so far from view,
And would her doating dreames should be believ'd for true)
Dare lowdly lie for Colne, that somtimes Ships did passe,
To Verlam by by her Streame, when Verlam famous was;
But, by these later times, suspected but to faine,
She Planks and Anchors shews, her errour to maintaine;
Which were, indeeds, of Boats, for pleasure there to rowe
Upon her (then a Lake) the Roman Pompe to showe,

When Rome her forces here did every yeere supply,
And at old Verlam kept a warlike Colony.
But I distressed Lee, whose course doth plainely tell,
That what of Colne is said, of me none could refell,
Whom Alfred but too wise (poore River) I may say
(When he the cruell Danes, did cunningly betray,
Which Hartford then besieg'd, whose Nauy there abode,
And on my spacious brest, before the Castle road)
By vantage of my soyle, he did divide my Streame
That they might ne're returne to Neptunes watry Realme.
And, since, distressed Lee I have been left forlorne
A by-word to each Brook, and to the World a scorne.

When Sturt, a Nymph of hers (whose saith she oft had prov'd,
And whom, of all her traine, Lee most intirely lov'd)
Least so excessive greefe, her Mistresse might inuade,
Thus (by faire gentle speech) to patience doth perswade:

Though you be not so great to others as before,
Yet not a iot for that dislike your selfe the more.
Your ense is not alone, nor is (at all) so strange;
Sith every thing on earth subiects it selfe to change.
Where rivers sometime ran, is firme and certaine ground:
And where before were Hills, now standing Lakes are found.
And that which most you vrge your beauty to dispoile,
Doth recompence your Bank, with quantitie of soyle,
Beset with ranks of Swans that, in their wonted pride,
Do prune their snowy plumes upon your pleasant side.
And Waltham wooes you still, and smiles with wonted cheere:
And Tames as at the first, so still doth hold you deer.

To much beloved Lee, this scarcely Sturt had spoke,
But goodly Londons sight their further purpose broke:
When Tames his either Banks, adorn'd with buildings faire,
The City to salute doth bid the Muse prepare.
Whose Turrets, Fanes, and Spyres, when wistly she beholds,
Her wonder at the site, thus strangely she unfolds:
At thy great Builders wit, who's he but wonder may?
Nay: of his wisedom, thus, ensuing times shall say;
O more then mortall man, that did this Towne begin!
Whose knowledge found the plot, so fit to set it in.
What God, or Heavenly power was harbourd in thy breast,
From whom with such successe thy labours should be blest?
Built on a rising Bank, within a Vale to stand,
And for thy healthfull soyle, chose grauell mixt with sand.
And where faire Tames his course into a Crescent casts
(That, forced by his Tydes, as still by her he hasts,
He might his surging waues into her bosome send)

Because too farre in length, his Towne should not extend.

And to the North and South, upon an equall reach,
Two Hils their euen Banks do somewhat seeme to stretch,
Those two extreamer Winds from hurting it to let;
And only leuell lies upon the Rise and Set.
Of all this goodly Ile, where breathes most cheerefull aire
And every way there-to the wayes most smooth and faire;
As in the fittest place, by man that could be thought,
To which by Land, or Sea, prouision might be brought.
And such a Road for Ships scarce all the world commands,
As is the goodly Tames, neer where Brute's City stands.
Nor any Haven lies to which is more resort,
Commodities to bring, as also to transport:
Our Kingdome that enricht (through which we flourisht long)
E're idle Gentry up in such aboundance sprong.
Now pestring all this Ile: whose disproportion drawes
The publique wealth so drie, and only is the cause
Our gold goes out so fast, for foolish foraine things,
Which upstart Gentry still into our Country brings;
Who their insatiate pride seek chiefly to maintaine
By that, which only serues to uses vile and vaine:
Which our plaine Fathers carst would have accounted sinne,
Before the costly Coach, and silken stock came in;
Before that Indian weed so strongly was imbrac't;
Wherin, such mighty summes we prodigally waste;
That Merchants long train'd up in Gayn's deceitfull schoole,
And subtly having learn'd to sooth the humorous soole,
Present their painted toyes unto this frantique gull,
Disparaging our Tinne, our Leather, Corne, and Wooll;
When Forrainers, with ours them warmly cloath and feed,
Transporting trash to us, of which we nere had need.

But whilst the angry Muse, thus on the Time exclames,
Sith every thing therin consisteth in extreames;
Lest she inforc't with wrongs, her limits should transcend,
Here of this present Song she briefly makes an end.


THE SEVENTEENTH SONG

THE ARGUMENT

To Medway, Tames a suter goes,
But fancies Mole, as forth he slowes.
Her Mother, Homesdale, holds her in:
She digs through Earth, the Tames to win.

Great Tames, as King of Rivers, sings
The Catalogue of th'English Kings.
Thence the light Muse, to th' Southward soares,
The Surrian and Sussexian shores;
The Forrests and the Downes suruaies,
With Rillets running to those Seas;
This Song of hers then cutteth short,
For things to come, of much import.

At length it came to passe, that Isis and her Tame
Of Medway understood, a Nymph of wondrous fame;
And much desirous were, their princely Tames shuld proue
If (as a wooer) he could win her Maiden-love;
That of so great descent, and of so large a Dower,
Might well-allie their House, and much increase his power:
And striving to preferre their Sonne, the best they may,
Set forth the lusty Flood, in rich and brave array,
Bankt with imbrodered Meads, of sundry sutes of flowres,
His brest adorn'd with Swans, oft washt with siluer showres:
A traine of gallant Floods, at such a costly rate
As might beseeme their care, and fitting his estate.

Attended and attyr'd magnificently thus,
They send him to the Court of great Oceanus,
The Worlds huge wealth to see; yet with a full intent,
To wooe the lovely Nymph, faire Medway as he went.
Who to his Dame and Sire, his duty scarce had done,
And whil'st they sadly wept at parting of their Sonne,
See what the Tames befell, when t'was suspected least.

As still his goodly traine yet every houre increast,
And from the Surrian shores cleere Wey came down to meet
His Greatnes, whom the Tames so gratiously doth greet,
That with the Fearne-crown'd Flood he Minion-like doth play:
Yet is not this the Brook, entiseth him to stay.
But as they thus, in pompe, came sporting on the shole,
Gainst Hampton-Court he meets the soft and gentle Mole.
Whose eyes so pierc't his breast, that seeming to foreslowe
The way which he so long, intended was to go,
With trifling up and down, he wandreth here and there;
And that he in her sight, transparent might appeare,
Applyes himselfe to Fords, and setteth his delight
On that which most might make him gratious in her sight.

Then Isis and the Tame from their conjoyned bed,
Desirous still to learne how Tames their son had sped
(For greatly they had hop't, his time had so been spent,
That he ere this had won the goodly heyre of Kent)

And sending to enquire, had newes return'd againe
(By such as they imploy'd, on purpose in his traine)
How this their only heyre, the Iles emperiall Flood,
Had loytered thus in love, neglectfull of his good.

No marvaile (at the newes) though Ouse and Tame were sad,
More comfort of their sonne expecting to have had.
Nor blame them, in their looks much sorrow through they show'd:
Who fearing least he might thus meanely be bestow'd,
And knowing danger still increased by delay,
Employ their utmost power, to hasten him away.
But Tames would hardly on: oft turning back to show,
From his much loved Mole how loth he was to go.

The mother of the Mole, old Homesdale, likewise beares
Th'affection of her childe, as ill as they do theirs:
Who nobly though deriv'd, yet could have been content,
Thave matcht her with a Flood, of farre more mean descent.
But Mole respects her words, as vaine and idle dreames,
Compar'd with that high joy, to be belou'd of Tames:
And head-long holds her course, his company to win.
But, Homesdale raised Hills, to keep the straggler in;
That of her daughters stay she need no more to doubt:
(Yet never was there help, but love could finde it out.)
Mole digs her selfe a Path, by working day and night
(According to her name, to shew her nature right)
And underneath the Earth, for three miles space doth creep:
Till gotten out of sight, quite from her mothers keep,
Her foreintended course the wanton Nymph doth run;
As longing to imbrace old Tame and Isis son.

When Tames now understood, what paines the Mole did take,
How farre the louing Nymph aduentur'd for his sake;
Although with Medway matcht, yet never could remoue
The often quickning sparks of his more ancient love.
So that it comes to passe, when by great Natures guide
The Ocean doth returne, and thrusteth-in the Tide;
Up tow'rds the place, where first his much-lov'd Mole was seen,
He ever since doth flow, beyond delightfull Sheene.

Then Wandal commeth in, the Moles beloved mate,
So amiable, faire, so pure, so delicate,
So plump, so full, so fresh, her eyes so wondrous cleer:
And first unto her Lord, at Wandsworth doth appeare,
That in the goodly Court, of their great soueraigne Tames,
There might no other speech be had amongst the Streames,
But only of this Nymph, sweet Wandal, what she wore;
Of her complection, grace, and how herselfe she bore.

But now this mighty Flood, upon his voiage prest
(That found how with his strength, his beauties still increast,
From where, brave Windsor stood on tip-toe to behold
The faire and goodly Tames, so farre as ere he could,
With Kingly houses Crown'd, of more then earthly pride,
Upon his either Banks, as he along doth glide)
With wonderfull delight, doth his long course pursue,
Where Orlands, Hampton Court, and Richmond he doth view,
Then Westminster the next great Tames doth entertaine;
That vaunts her Palace large, and her most sumptuous Fane:
The Lands tribunall seate that challengeth for hers,
The crowning of our Kings, their famous sepulchers.
Then goes he on along by that more beautious Strand,
Expressing both the wealth and bravery of the Land.
(So many sumptuous Bowres, within so little space,
The All-beholding Sun scarce sees in all his race.)
And on by London leads, which like a Crescent lies,
Whose windowes seem to mock the Star-befreckled skies;
Besides her rising Spyres, so thick themselues that show,
As doe the bristling reeds, within his Banks that growe.
There sees his crouded Wharfes, and people-pestred shores,
His Bosome ouer-spread, with shoales of labouring ores:
With that most costly Bridge, that doth him most renowne,
By which he cleerely puts all other Rivers downe.

Thus furnished with all that appertain'd to State,
Desired by the Floods (his Greatnes which awayt)
That as the rest before, so somewhat he would sing.
Both worthy of their praise, and of himselfe thier King;
A Catalogue of those, the Scepter heer that swayd,
The Princely Tames recites, and thus his Song he laid;

As Bastard William first, by Conquest hither came,
And brought the Norman Rule, upon the English name:
So with a redious warre, and almost endlesse toyles.
Throughout his troubled raigne, here held his hard-got spoyles.
Deceasing at the last, through his unsetled State,
Left (with his ill-got Crown) unnaturall debate.
For, dying at his home, his eldest sonne abroad
(Who, in the Holy-warre, his person then bestow'd)
His second Rufus next usurpt the wronged raigne:
And by a fatall dart, in his New Forrest slaine,
Whilst in his proper right religious Robert slept,
Through craft into the Throne, the younger Bean-cleark crept.
From whom his Scepter, then, whil'st Robert stroue to wrest,
The other (of his power that amply was possest)
With him in battell joyn'd: and, in that dreadfull day

(Where Fortune shew'd her selfe all humane power to sway)
Duke Robert went to wrack; and taken in the flight,
Was by that cruell King depriv'd of his sight,
And in close prison put; where miserably he dy'd:

But Henries whole intent was by just Heaven deny'd.
For, as of light, and life, he that sad Lord bereft;
So his, to whom the Land, he purpos'd to have left,
The raging Seas deuowr'd, as hitherward they saild.

When, in this Line direct, the Conquerors issue faild,
Twixt Henries Daughter Mauld, the Almayne Emperours Bride
(Which after to the Earle of Aniou was affi'd)
And Stephen Earle of Bloys, the Conquerors Sisters son,
A fierce and cruell war immediately begun;
Who with their severall powers, arrived here from France,
By force of hostile Armes, their Titles to aduance.
But, Stephen, what by coyne, and what by forraine strength,
Through Worlds of danger gain'd the glorious goale at length.

But, left without an heyre, the Empresse issue next,
No Title else on foote; upon so faire pretext,
The second Henry soon upon the Throne was set,
(Which Mauld to Ieffrey bare) the first Plantaginet.
Who held strong wars with Wales, that his subiection spurn'd:
Which oftentimes he beat; and, beaten oft, return'd:
With his sterne Children vext: who (whil'st he stroue t'aduance
His right within this Ile) rays'd war on him in France.
With his hie fame in fight, what colde brest was not fir'd?
Through all the Westerne world, for wisedome most admyr'd.

Then Richard got the Rule, his most renowned sonne.
Whose courage, him the name of Cure De Lion won.
With those first earthly Gods, had this brave Prince been borne,
His daring hand had from Alcides shoulders torne
The Nemean Lyon's hyde: who in the Holy-land
So dreadfull was, as though from Ioue and Neptunes hand,
The thundring three-forkt Fire, and Trident he had reft,
And him to rule their charge they only then had left.
Him John againe succeeds; who, having put-away
Yong Arthur (Richards sonne) the Scepter took to sway.
Who, of the common-wealth first hauock having made,
His sacrilegious hands upon the Churches laid,
In cruelty and rape continuing out his raigne;
That his outrageous lust and courses to restraine,
The Baronage were forc't defensive Armes to raise,
Their daughters to redeeme, that he by force would seise.
Which the first Civill warre in England here begun.

And for his sake such hate his sonne young Henry won,
That to depose their Prince, th'reuengefull people thought:
And from the Line of France yong Lewes to have brought,
To take on him our Rule: but, Henry got the Throne,
By his more forcefull friends: who, wise and puissant growne,
The generall Charter seiz'd: that into slavery drew
The freest borne English blood. Of which such discord grew,
And in the Barons breasts so rough combustions rais'd,
With much expence of blood as long was not appeaz'd,
By strong and tedious gustsheld up on either side,
Betwixt the Prince and Peeres, with equall power and pride.
He knew the worst of warre, matcht with the Barons strong;
Yet victor liv'd, and raign'd both happily and long.

This long-liv'd Prince expyr'd: the next succeeded; he,
Of us, that for a God might well related be.
Our Long shanks, Scotlands scourge: who to the Oreads raught
His Scepter, and with him from wilde Albania brought
The reliques of her Crowne (by him first placed here)
The seat on which her Kings inaugurated were.
He tam'd the desperate Welsh, that out so long had stood,
And made them take a Prince, sprong of the English blood.
This Ile, from Sea to Sea, he generally controld,
And made the other parts of England both to holde.

This Edward, first of ours, a second then ensues;
Who both his Name and Birth, by loosenes, did abuse:
Faire Ganimeds and Fools who rais'd to Princely places;
And chose not men for wit, but only for their faces.
In parasites and knaues, as he repos'd his trust,
Who sooth'd him in his wayes apparantly unjust;
For that preposterous sinne wherein he did offend,
In his posteriour parts had his preposterous end.

A third then, of that name, amends for this did make:
Who from his idle sire seem'd nought at all to take.
But as his Grand-sire did his Empires verge aduance:
So led he forth his powers, into the heart of France.
And fastning on that Right, he by his mother had,
Against the Salique law, which utterly forbad
Their women to enherite; to propagate his Cause,
At Cressey with his sword first cancelled those Lawes:
Then like a furious storme, through troubled France he ran;
And by the hopefull hand of brave Black-Edward wan
Proud Poytiers, where King John he valiantly subdew'd,
The miserable French and there in mammocks hew'd;
Then with his battering Rams made Earth-quakes in their Towres,
Till trampled in the dust her selfe she yeelded ours.

As mighty Edwards heyre, to a second Richard then
(Son to that famous Prince Black Edward, Man of Men,
Untimely that before his conquering father dy'd)
Too soon the Kingdom fell: who his vaine youth apply'd
To wantonnesse and spoyle, and did to fauour drawe
Unworthy ignorant sots, with whose dull eyes he sawe:
Who plac't their like in Court, and made them great in State
(Which wise and vertuous men, beyond all plagues, might hate.)
To whom he blindly gaue: who blindly spent againe,
And oft opprest his Land, their riot to maintaine.
He hated his Allyes, and the deseruing steru'd;
His Minions and his will, the Gods he only seru'd:
And finally, depos'd, as he was euer friend
To Rybaulds, so againe by Villaines had his end.
Henry the Sonne of Gaunt, supplanting Richard, then
Ascended to the Throne: when discontented men,
Desirous first of change, which to that height him brought,
Deceived of their ends, into his actions sought;
And, as they set him up, assay'd to pluck him down:
From whom he hardly held his ill-atchieved Crown;
That, Treasons to suppresse which oft he did disclose,
And raysing publike Armes, against his powerfull foes,
His usurpation still being troubled to maintaine,
His short disquiet dayes scarce raught a peacefull raigne.

A fift succeeds the fourth: but how his father got
The Crown, by right or wrong, the Sonne respecteth not.
Nor further hopes for that ere leaueth to pursue;
But doth his claime to France, courageously renew';
Upon her wealthy shores un-lades his warlike fraught;
And, shewing us the fields where our brave fathers fought,
First drew his sun-bright Sword, reflecting such a light,
As put sad guilty France, into so great a fright,
That her pale Genius sank, which trembling seem'd to stand,
When first he set his foot on her rebellious Land.
That all his Grand-sires deeds did ouer, and thereto
Those hie atcheeuements adde the former could not doe:
At Agincourts proud fight, that quite put Poytiers down;
Of all, that time who liv'd, the King of most renowne.
Whose too untimely end, the Fates too soon did hast:
Whose nine yeares noble acts, nine Worlds deserue to last.

A sixt in name succeeds, borne great, the mighty sonne
Of him, in Englands right that spacious France had wonne.
Who coming young to raigne, protected by the Peeres
Untill his Non-age out: and growne to riper yeeres,
Prov'd upright, soft, and meeke, in no wise louing warre;

But fitter for a Cowle, then for a Crowne by farre.
Whose mildnes ouer-much, did his destruction bring:
A wondrous godly man, but not so good a King.
Like whom yet never man tri'd fortunes change so oft;
So many times throwne-down, so many times aloft
(When with the utmost power, their friends could them afford,
The Yorkists, put their right upon the dint of sword)
As still he lost and wonne, in that long bloody warre,
From those two Factions stil'd, of York and Lancaster.
But by his foes inforc't to yeeld him to their power,
His wretched raigne and life, both ended in the Tower.

Of th'Edwards name the fourth put on the Regall Wreath:
Whom furious bloody warre (that seem'd a while to breath)
Not utterly forsooke. For, Henries Queene and heyre
(Their once possessed raigne still seeking to repaire)
Put forward with their friends, their title to maintaine.
Whose blood did Barnets Streets and Teuksburyes distaine,
Till no man left to stirre. The Title then at rest,
The old Lancastrian Line, being utterly supprest,
Himselfe the wanton King to amourous pleasures gaue;
Yet iealous of his right descended to his Graue.

His Sonne an infant left: who had he liv'd to raigne,
Edward the fift had been. But justly see againe
As he a King and Prince before had cau'd to die
(The father in the Tower, the sonne at Teuksbury)
So were his children yong, being left to be protected
By Richard; who nor God, nor humane lawes respected.
This Viper, this most vile deuowrer of his kinde
(Whom his ambitious ends had strooke so grosly blind)
From their deare mothers lap, them seising for a pray
(Himselfe in right the next, could they be made away)
Most wrongfully usurpt, and them in prison kept;
Whom cruelly at last he smothered as they slept.
As his unnaturall hands, were in their blood imbru'd:
So (guilty in himselfe) with murther he pursu'd
Such, on his haynous acts as lookt not faire and right;
Yea, such as were not his expresly, and had might
T'oppose him in his course; till (as a monster loth'd,
The man, to hell and death himselfe that had betroth'd)
They brought another in, to thrust that Tyrant down;
In battell who at last resign'd both life and Crown.

A seaventh Henry, then, th'emperiall seate attain'd,
In banishment who long in Britanne had remain'd,
What time the Yorkists sought his life to have bereft,
Of the Lancastrian House then only being left

(Deriv'd from Jôhn of Gaunt) whom Richmond did beget,
Upon a daughter borne to John of Sommerset.
Elizabeth of York this Noble Prince affi'd,
To make his Title strong, thereby on either side.
And grafting of the White and Red Rose firme together,
Was first, that to the Throne aduanc't the name of Tether.
In Besworths fatall Field, who having Richard slaine,
Then in that prosperous peace of his successfull raigne,
Of all that ever rul'd, was most precise in State,
And in his life and death a King most fortunate.

This Seaventh, that was of ours, the Eightth succeeds in name:
Who by Prince Arthurs death (his elder Brother) came
Unto a Land with wealth aboundantly that flow'd:
Aboundantly againe, so he the same bestow'd,
In Banquets, Mask's, and Tilts, all pleasures prone to try,
Besides his secret scapes who lou'd Polygamy.
The Abbayes he supprest; a thousand lingring yeere,
Which with reuenewes large the World had sought to reare.
And through his awfull might, for temporall ends did saue,
To other uses earst what srank deuotion gaue;
And here the papall power, first utterly deny'd,
Defender of the Faith, that was instil'd and dy'd.

His sonne the Empire had, our Edward sixt that made;
Untimely as he sprang, untimely who did fade.
A Protestant being bred; and in his infant raigne,
Th'religion then receiv'd, here stoutly did maintaine:
But e're he raught to man, from his sad people reft,
His Scepter he againe unto his Sisters left.

Of which the eldest of two, Queen Mary, mounts the Chaire:
The ruin'd Roman State who striving to repaire,
With persecuting hands the Protestants pursew'd;
Whose Martyred ashes oft the wondring Streets bestrew'd.
She matcht her selfe with Spaine, and brought King Philip hither,
Which with an equall hand, the Scepter sway'd togither.
But issuless she dy'd; and under six yeeres raigne,
To her wise Sister gaue the Kingdome up againe.
Elizabeth, the next, this falling Scepter hent;
Digressing from her Sex, with Man-like gouernment
This Iland kept in awe, and did her power extend
Afflicted France to ayde, her owne as to defend;
Against th'Iberian rule, the Flemming; sure defence:
Rude Ireland's deadly scourge; who sent her Navies hence
Unto the either, Iude, and to that shore so greene,
Virginia which we call, of he Virgin Queen:
In Portugall gainst Spaine, her English onsignes spred;

Took Cales, when from her ayde the brav'd Iberia fled
Most flourishing in State: that, all our Kings among,
Scarse any rul'd so well: but two, that raign'd so long.

Here suddainly he staid: and with his Kingly Song,
Whil'st yet on every side the City loudly rong,
He with the Eddy turn'd, a space to lookabout:
The Tide, retiring soon, did strongly thrust him out.
And soon the pliant Muse, doth her brave wing aduance,
Tow'rds those Sea-bordring shords of ours, that point at France;
The harder Surrian Heath, and the Sussexian Downe.
Which with so great increase though Nature do not crowne,
As many other Shires, of this inviron'd Ile;
Yet on the Weathers held, when as the sunne doth smile,
Nurst by the Southern Winde, that soft and gently blowe,
Here doth the lusty sap as soon begin in to flowe;
The Earth as soon puts on her gaudy Summers sure;
The Woods as soon in greon, and orchards great with fruit.

To Sea-ward, from the sent where first our Song begun,
Exhaled to the South by the ascending sunne,
Fower stately Wood Nymphs stand on the Sussexian ground,
Great Andredsweld's sometime: who, when she did abound,
In circuit and in growth, all other quite supprest:
But in her wane of pride, as she in strength deercast,
Her Nymphs assum'd them names, each one to her delight.
As, Water-downe, so call'd of her depressed site:
And Ash-Downe, of those Trees that most in her do growe,
Set higher to the Downes, as th'other standeth lowe.
Saint Leonards, of the seat by which shonext is plac't;
And Whord that with the like delighteth to be grac't.
These Forrests as I say, the daughters of the Weald
(That in their heavie breasts, had long their greefs conceal'd)
Foreseeing, their decay each howre so fast came on,
Under the axes stroak, fretcht many a grievous grone,
When as the anuiles weight, and hammers dreadfull sound,
Euen rent the hollow Woods, and shook the queachy ground.
So that the trembling Nymphs, opprest through gastly feare,
Ran madding to the Downes, with loose dishev'ld hayre.
The Syluans that about the neighbouring woods did dwell,
Both in the tufty Brith and in the mossy Fell,
Forsook their gloomy Bowres, and wandred farre abroad,
Expeld their quiet feats, and place of their abode,
When labouring carts they saw to hold their dayly trade,
Where they in summer wont to sport them in the shade.
Could we, say they, suppose, that any would us cherish,
Which suffer (every day) the holiest things to perish?
Or to our daily want to minister supply?

These yron times breed none, that minde posteritie.
Tis but in vaine to tell, what we before have been,
Or changes of the world, that we in time have seen;
When, not deuising how to spend our wealth with waste,
We to the sauage swine, let fall our larding mast.
But now, alas, ourselues we have not to sustaine,
Nor can our tops suffice to shield our Roots from raine.
Joves Oke, the warlike Ash, veyn'd Elme, the softer Beech,
Short Hazell, Maple plaine, light Aspe, the bending Wych,
Tough Holly, and smooth Birch, must altogether burne:
What should the Builder serue, supplies the Forgers turne;
When under publike good, base private gaine takes holde,
And we poore woefull Woods, to ruine lastly solde.

This uttered they with griefe: and more they would have spoke,
But that the enuious Downes, int'open laughter broke;
As joying in those wants, which Nature them had given,
Sith to as great distresse the Forrests should be driven.
Like him that long time hath anothers state enuy'd,
And sees a following Ebbe, unto his former Tide;
The more he is deprest, and bruiz'd with fortunes might,
The larger Reane his foe doth give to his despight:
So did the enuious Downes; but that againe the Floods
(Their fountaines that derive, from those unpittied Woods,
And so much grace thy Downes, as through their Dales they creep,
Their glories to conuay unto the Celtick deep)
It very hardly tooke, much murmuring at their pride.
Cleere Lauant, that doth keep the Southamptonian side
(Dividing it well-neere from the Sussexian lands
That Selsey doth suruay, and Solents troubled sands)
To Chichester their wrongs impatiently doth tell:
And Arun (which doth name the beautious Arundell)
As on her course she came, it to her Forrest tolde.
Which, nettled with the newes, had not the power to hold:
But breaking into rage, wisht Tempests them might rive;
And on their barren scalps, still flint and chauke might thrive,
The brave and nobler Woods which basely thus upbraid.
And Adur comming on, to Shoreham softly said,
The Downes did very ill, poore Woods so to debase.
But now, the Ouse, a Nymph of very scornefull grace,
So touchy waxt therewith, and was so squeamish growne,
That her old name she scorn'd should publiquely be knowne.
Whose haven out of mind when as it almost grew,
The lately passed times denominate, the New.
So Cucmer with the rest put to her utmost might:
As Ashburne undertakes to doe the Forrests right
(At Pemsey, where she powres her soft and gentler Flood)
And Asten once distain'd with native English blood:

(Whose Soyle, when yet but wet with any little raine,
oth blush; as put in mind of those there sadly slaine,
When Hastings harbour gaue unto the Norman powers,
Whose name and honors now are denizend for ours)
That boding ominous Brook, it through the Forrests rung:
Which ecchoing it againe the mighty Weald along,
Great stirre was like to grow; but that the Muse did charme
Their furies, and her selfe for nobler things did arme.


THE EIGHTEENTH SONG

THE ARGUMENT

The Rother through the Weald doth roue,
Till he with Oxney fall in love:
Rumney, would with her wealth beguile,
And winne the River from the Ile.
Medway, with her attending Streames,
Goes forth to meet her Lord great Tames:
And where in breath she her disperses,
Our Famous Captaines she rehearses,
With many of their valiant deeds.
Then with Kents praise the Muse proceeds.
And telles when Albion o're Sea road,
How he his daughter-Iles bestow'd;
And how grim Goodwin fames and frets:
Where to this Song, an end she sets.

Our Argas scarcely yet delivered of her sonne,
When as the River downe, through Andredsweald dooth run:
Nor can the aged Hill have comfort of her childe.
For, living in the Woods, her Rother waxed wilde;
His Banks with aged Okes, and Bushes ouer-growne,
That from the Syluans kinde, he hardly could be knowne:
Yea, many a time the Nymphes, which hapt this Flood to see,
Fled from him, whom they sure a Satyre thought to be;
As Satyre-like he held all pleasures in disdaine,
And would not once vouchsafe, to look upon a Plaine
Till chancing in his course he to view a goodly plot,
Which Albion in his youth, upon a Sea Nymph got,
For Oxney's love he pines who being wildly chaste,
And never woo'd before, was coy to be imbrac't.
But, what obdurate heart was ever so peruerse,
Whom yet a lovers plaints, with patience, could not pearce?
For, in this conflict she being lastly overthrowne,
In-Iled in his Armes, he clips her for his owne.

Who being grosse and black, she lik't the River well.

Of Rothers happy match, when Rumney Marsh heard tell,
Whyl'st in his youth full course himselfe he doth apply,
And falleth in her sight into the Sea at Rye,
She thinketh with her selfe, how she a way might finde
To put the homely Ile quite out of Rothers minde;
Appearing to the Flood, most bravely like a Queene,
Clad (all) from head to foot, in gaudy Summers green;
Her mantle richly wrought, with sundry flowers and weeds;
Her moystfull temples bound, with wreaths of quivering reeds:
Which loosely flowing downe, upon her lusty thighes,
Most strongly seeme to tempt the Rivers amorous eyes.
And on her loynes a frock, with many a swelling pleate,
Embost with well-spread Horse, large Sheepe, and full-fed Neate.
Some wallowing in the grasse, there lie a while to batten;
Some sent away to kill; some thither brought to fatten;
With Villages amongst, oft powthred heere and there;
And (that the same more like to Landskip should appeare)
With Lakes and lesser Foards, to mitigate the heate
(In Summer when the Fly doth prick the gadding Neate,
Forc't from the Brakes, where late they brouz'd the veluet buds)
In which, they lick their Hides, and chew their sauoury Cuds.

Of these her amourous toyes, when Oxney came to knowe,
Suspecting least in time her rivall she might growe,
Th' allu'rments of the Marsh, the iealous Ile do moue,
That to a constant course, she thus perswades her Love:
With Rumney, though for dower I stand in no degree;
In this, to be belou'd yet liker farre then she:
Though I be browne, in me there doth no fauour lack.
The foule is said deform'd: and she, extreamely black.
And though her rich attire, so curious be and rare,
From her there yet proceeds unwholsome putrid aire:
Where my complexion more sutes with the higher ground,
Upon the lusty Weald, where strength doth still abound.
The Wood-gods I refus'd, that su'd to me for grace,
Me in thy watry Armes, thee suffring to imbrace
Where, to great Neptune she may one day be a pray:
The Sea-gods in her lap lie wallowing every day.
And what, though of her strength she seem to make no doubt?
Yet put unto the proofe shee'll hardly hold him out.

With this perswasive speech which Oxney lately us'd,
With strange and sundry doubts, whilst Rother stood confus'd,
Old Andredsweald at length doth take her time to tell
The changes of the world, that since her youth befell,
When yet upon her soyle, scarce humane foote had trode;

A place where only then, the Syluans made abode.
Where, feareless of the Hunt, the Hart securely stood,
And every where walkt free a Burgesse of the Wood;
Untill those Danish routs, whom hunger-staru'd at home,
(Like Woolues pursuing prey) about the world did roame.
And stemming the rude streame dividing us from France,
Into the spacious mouth of Rother fell (by chance)
That Lymen then was nam'd, when (with most irksome care)
The heauy Danish yoke, the seruile English bare.
And when at last she found, there was no way to leaue
Those, whom she had at first been forced to receive;
And by her great resort, she was through very need,
Constrained to prouide her peopled Townes to feed.
She learn'd the churlish axe and twybill to prepare,
To steele the coulters edge, and sharpe the furrowing share:
And more industrious still, and only hating sloth,
A huswife she became, most skild in making cloth.
That now the Draper comes from London every yeare,
And of the Kentish sorts, make his prouision there.
Whose skirts (tis said) at first that fiftie furlongs went,
Have lost their ancient bounds, now limited in Kent.
Which strongly to approue, she Medway forth did bring,
From Sussex who (tis knowne) receives her siluer Spring.
Who towar'ds the lordly Tames, as she along doth straine,
Where Teise, cleere Beule, and Len, beare up her limber traine
As she remoues in state: so for her more renowne,
Her only name she leaues, t'her only christned Towne;
And Rochester doth reach, in entring to the Bowre
Of that most matchless Tames, her princely Paramoure.
Whose bosome doth so please her Soueraigne (with her pride)
Whereas the royall Fleet continually doth ride,
That where she told her Tames, she did intend to sing
What to the English Name immortall praise should bring;
To grace his goodly Queen, Tames presently proclaimes,
That all the Kentish Floods, resigning him their names,
Should presently repaire unto his mighty Hall,
And by the posting Tides, towards London sends to call
Cleere Rauensburne (though small, remembred them among)
At Detford entring. Whence as down she comes along,
She Darent thither warnes: who calles her sister Cray,
Which hasten to the Court with all the speed they may.
And but that Medway then of Tames obtain'd such grace,
Except her country Nymphs, that none should be in place,
More Rivers from each part, had instantly been there,
Then at their marriage, first, by Spenser numbred were.

This Medway still had nurst those navies in her Road,
Our Armies that had oft to conquest borne abroad;

And not a man of ours, for Armes hath famous been,
Whom she not going out, or comming in hath seen:
Or by some passing Ship, hath newes to her been brought,
What brave exploits they did; as where, and how, they fought.
Wherefore, for audience now, she to th'assembly calls,
The Captains to recite when seriously she fals.

Of noble warriors now, saith she, shall be my Song;
Of those renowned spirits, that from the Conquest sprong,
Of th'English Norman blood: which, matchless for their might,
Have with their flaming swords, in many a dreadfull fight,
Illustrated this Ile, and bore her fame so farre;
Our Heroes, which the first wanne, in that Holy warre,
Such feare from every foe, and made the East more red,
With splendor of their Armes, then when from Tithons bed
The blushing Dawne doth break; towards which our fame begon,
By Robert (Curt-hose call'd) the Conquerours eldest sonne,
Who with great Godfrey and that holy Hermit went
The Sepulcher to free, with most deuoutintent.

And to that title which the Norman William got,
When in our Conquest heere, he stroue t'include the Scot,
The Generall of our power, that stout and warlike Earle,
Who English being borne, was stil'd of Aubemerle;
Those Lacyes then no lesse courageous, which had there
The leading of the day, all, brave Commanders were.

Sir Walter Especk, matcht with Peverell, which as farre
Aduentur'd for our fame: who in that Bishops warre,
Immortall honour got to Stephens troubled raigne:
That day ten thousand Scots upon the field were slaine.

The Earle of Strigule then our Strong-bowe, first that wonne
Wilde Ireland with the sword (which, to the glorious sunne,
Lifts up his nobler name) amongst the rest may stand.

In Cure de Lyon's charge unto the Holy-land,
Our Earle of Lester, next, to rank with them we bring:
And Turnham, he that took th' impost'rous Ciprian King.
Strong Tuchet chose to weeld the English standard there;
Poole, Gourney, Neuill, Gray, Lyle, Ferres, Mortimer:
And more, for want of pens whose deeds not brought to light,
It grieves my zealous soule, I can not do them right.

The noble Penbrooke then, who Strong-bowe did succeed,
Like his brave Grand-sire, made th'reuolting Irish bleed,
When yeelding oft, they oft their due subiection broke;
And when the Britans scorn'd, to beare the English yoke,

Lewellin Prince of Wales in Battell overthrewe,
Nine thousand valiant Welsh and either took or slew.
Earle Richard, his brave sonne, of Strong-bowes matchless straine,
As he a Marshall was, did in himselfe retaine
The nature of that word, being Martiall, like his name:
Who, as his valiant Sire, the Irish oft did tame.

With him we may compare Marisco (King of Men)
That Lord chiefe Justice was of Ireland, whereas then
Those two brave Burrowes, John, and Richard, had their place,
Which through the bloodied Bogs, those Irish oft did chase;
Whose deeds may with the best deseruedly be read.

As those two Lacyes then, our English Powers that led:
Which twenty thousand, there, did in one Battell quell,
Amongst whome (troden down) the King of Conaugh fell.

Then Richard, that lov'd Earle of Cornwall, here we set:
Who, rightly of the race of great Plantaginet,
Our English Armies shipt, to gaine that hallowed ground,
With Long-sword the brave sonne of beautious Rosamond:
The Pagans through the breasts, like thunderbolts that shot;
And in the utmost East such admiration got,
That the shril-sounding blast, and terrour of our fame
Hath often conquered, where, our swords yet never came:
As Gifford, not forgot, their stout associate there.

So in the warres with Wales, of ours as famous here,
Guy Beuchamp, that great Earle of Warwick, place shall have:
From whom, the Cambrian Hils the Welsh-men could not saue;
Whom he, their generall plague, impetuously pursu'd,
And in the British gore his slaughtering sword imbru'd.

In order as they rise (next Beuchamp) we preferre
The Lord John Gifford, matcht with Edmond Mortimer;
Men rightly moulded up, for high aduentrous deeds.

In this renowned rank of warriors then succeeds
Walwin, who with such skill our Armies oft did guide;
In many a dangerous straight, that had his knowledge tride.
And in that fierce assault, which caus'd the fatall flight,
Where the distressed Welsh resign'd their Ancient right,
Stout Frampton: by whose hand, their Prince Lewellin fell.

Then followeth (as the first who have deserued as well)
Great Saint-John; from the French, which twice recouered Guyne:
And he, all him before that cleerely did out-shine,
Warren, the puissant Earle of Surrey, which led forth

Our English Armyes oft into our utmost North;
And oft of his approach made Scotland quake to heare,
When Tweed hath sunk downe flat, within her Banks for feare.
On him there shall attend, that most aduenturous Twhing,
That at Scambekin fight, the English off did bring
Before the furious Scot, that else were like to fall.

As Basset, last of these, yet not the least of all
Those most renowned spirits that Fowkerk bravely fought;
Where Long-shanks, to our lore, Albania lastly brought.

As, when our Edward first his title did aduance,
And led his English hence, to winne his right in France,
That most deseruing Earle of Darby we preferre,
Henries third valiant sonne, the Earle of Lancaster,
That only Mars of Men; who (as a generall scurge,
Sent by just-judging Heaven, outrageous France to purge)
At Cagant plagu'd the Power of Flemmings that she rais'd,
Against the English force: which as a hand-sell seas'd,
Into her very heart he marcht in warlike wise;
Took Bergera, Langobeck, Mountdurant, and Mountguyse;
Leau, Poudra, and Punach, Mount-Segre, Forsa, wonne;
Mountpesans, and Beumount, the Ryall, Aiguillon,
Rochmillon, Mauleon, Franch, and Angolisme surpriz'd;
With Castles, Cities, Forts, nor Prouinces suffic'd.
Then took the Earle of Leyle: to conduct whom there came
Nine Vicounts, Lords, and Earls, astonisht at his name.
To Gascoyne then he goes (to plague her, being prest)
And manfully himselfe of Mirabell possest;
Surgeres, and Alnoy, Benoon, and Mortaine strooke:
And with a fearefull siege, he Taleburg lastly took;
With prosperous successe, in lesser time did winne
Maximien, Lusingham, Mount-Sorrell, and Bonin;
Sackt Poytiers: which did, then, that Countries treasure hold;
That not a man of ours would touch what was not gold.

With whom our Maney here deseruedly doth stand,
Which first Inuentor was of that courageous band,
Who clos'd their left eyes up; as, never to be freed,
Till there they had atchiev'd some high aduenturous deed.
He first into the preasse at Cagant conflict flue;
And from amidst a groue of gleaues, and halberds drew
Great Darby beaten downe; t'amaze the men of warre,
When he for England cri'd, S. George, and Lancaster:
And as mine author tells (in his high courage, proud)
Before his going forth, unto his Mistresse vow'd,
He would begin the war: and, to make good the same,
Then setting foot in France, there first with hostile flame

Forc't Mortain, from her Towers, the neighbouring Townes to light;
That suddainly they caught a Fever with the fright.
Thin Castle (neere the Towne of Cambray) ours he made;
And when the Spanish powers came Britanne to inuade,
Both of their aydes and spoyles, them utterly bereft.
This English Lyon, there, the Spaniards never left,
Till from all aire of France, he made their Lewes fly,
And Fame her selfe, to him, so amply did apply,
That when the most unjust Calicians had forethought,
Into that Towne (then ours) the French-men to have brought,
The King of England's selfe, and his renowned sonne
(By those perfidious French to see what would be done)
Under his Guydon marcht, as private souldiers there.

So had we still of ours, in France that famous were;
Warwick, of England then High-constable that was,
As other of that race, heere well I cannot passe;
That brave and god-like brood of Beuchamps, which so long
Them Earles of Warwick held; so hardy, great, and strong,
That after of that name it to an Adage grew,
If any man himselfe adventrous hapt to shew,
Bold Beuchampe men him tearm'd, if none so bold as hee.

With those our Beuchamps, may our Bourchers reckned bee.
Of which, that valiant Lord, most famous in those dayes,
That hazarded in France so many dangerous frayes:
Whose blade in all the fights betwixt the French and us,
Like to a Blazing-starre was ever ominous;
A man, as if by Mars upon Bellona got.

Next him, stout Cobham comes, that with as prosprous lot
Th'English men hath led; by whose auspicious hand,
We often have been known the Frenchmen to command.
And Harcourt, though by birth an Alien; yet, ours wonne,
By England after held her deere adopted sonne:
Which oft upon our part was bravely prou'd to doe,
Who with the hard'st attempts Fame earnestly did wooe:
To Paris-ward, that when the Amyens fled by stealth
(Within her mightie walls to have inclos'd their wealth)
Before her bulwarkt gates the Burgesses hee tooke;
Whilst the Parisians, thence that sadly stood to looke,
And saw their faithfull friends so wofully bestead,
Not once durst issue out to helpe them, for their head.

And our John Copland; heere courageously at home
Whilst every where in France, those farre abroad doe roame)
That at New-castle fight (the Battell of the Queene,
Where most the English harts were to their Soueraigne seene)

Tooke David King of Scots, his prisoner in the fight.
Nor could these warres imploy our onely men of might:
But as the Queene by these did mightie things atchieve;
So those, to Britaine sent the Countesse to relieve,
As any yet of ours, two knights as much that dar'd,
Stout Dangorn, and with him strong Hartwell honor shar'd;
The dreaded Charles de Bloyes, that at Rochdarren bet,
And on the Royall seat, the Countesse Mountfort set.
In each place where they came so fortunate were ours.

Then, Audley, most renown'd amongst those valiant powers,
That with the Prince of Wales at conquer'd Poyters fought;
Such wonders that in Armes before both Armies wrought;
The first that charg'd the French; and, all that dreadfull day,
Through still renewing worlds of danger made his way;
The man that scorn'd to take a prisoner (through his pride)
But by plaine downe-right death the title to decide.
And after the retreat, that famous Battell done,
Wherein, rich spacious France was by the English wonne,
Five hundred marks in Fee, that noblest Prince bestow'd
For his so brave attempts, through his high courage show'd.
Which to his foure Esquires hee freely gaue, who there
Vy'd valour with their Lord; and in despight of feare,
Oft fetcht that day from death, where wounds gap't wide as hell;
And cryes, and parting groanes, whereas the Frenchmen fell,
Euen made the Victors greeue, so horrible they were.

Our Dabridgcourt the next shall be remembred heere,
At Poyters who brake in upon the Alman Horse
Through his too forward speed: but, taken by their force,
And after, by the turne of that so doubtfull fight,
Beeing reskew'd by his friends in Poyters fearfull sight,
Then like a Lyon rang'd about th'Enemies host:
And where he might suppose the danger to be most,
Like Lightning entred there, to his French-foes dismay,
To gratifie his friends which reskew'd him that day.

Then Chandos: whose great deeds found Fame so much to doo,
That she was lastly forc'd, him for her ease to wooe;
That Minion of drad Mars, which almost ouer-shone
All those before him were, and for him none scarce known,
At Cambray's scaled wall his credit first that wonne;
And by the high exployts in France by him were done,
Had all so ouer-aw'd, that by his very name
He could remoue a siege: and Citties where he came
Would at his Summons yeeld. That man, the most belou'd,
In all the wayes of warre so skilfull and approu'd,
The Prince at Poyters chose his person to assist.

This stout Herculean stem, this noble Martialist,
In battell twixt brave Bloys and noble Mountfort, try'd
At Array, then the right of Britaine to decyde,
Rag'd like a furious storme beyond the power of man,
Where valiant Charles was slaine, and the sterne English wan
The royall British rule to Mountforts nobler name.
Hee tooke strong Tarryers in, and Aniou oft did tame.
Gavaches he regayn'd, and us Rochmador got.
Where ever lay'd hee siege that he invested not?

As this brave Warrior was, so no lesse deere to us,
The rivall in his fame, his onely amulus,
Renown'd Sir Robert Knowles, that in his glories shar'd,
His chivalry and oft in present perills dar'd;
As Nature should with Time, at once by these consent
To showe, that all their store they idly had not spent.
Hee Vermandoise or'e-ranne with skill and courage hie:
Notoriously hee plagu'd revolting Picardy:
That up to Paris walls did all before him win,
And dar'd her at her gates (the King that time within)
A man that all his deeds did dedicate to fame.

Then those stout Percyes, John, and Thomas, men of name.
The valiant Gourney, next, deseruedly we grace,
And Howet, that with him assumes as high a place.
Strong Trivet, all whose ends at great adventures shot:
That conquer'd us Mount Pin, and Castle Carcilot,
As famous in the French, as in the Belgique warre;
Who tooke the Lord Brimewe; and with the great Navarre,
In Papaloon, attain'd an everlasting praise.

Courageous Carill next, then whom those glorious daies
Produc't not any spirit that through more dangers swam.

That princely Thomas, next, the Earle of Buckingham,
To Britany through France that our stout English brought,
Which under his Commaund with such high fortune fought
As put the world in feare Rome from her cynders rose,
And of this Earth againe meant onely to dispose.

Thrice valiant Hackwood then, out-shining all the rest,
From London at the first a poore meane souldier prest
(That time but very young) to those great warres in France,
By his brave service there himselfe did so advance,
That afterward, the heat of those great Battels done
(In which he to his name immortall glory wonne)
Leading six thousand Horse, let his brave Guydon flie.
So, passing through East France, and entring Lombardie,

By th'greatnes of his fame, attayn'd so high Commaund,
That to his charge he got the white Italian Band.
With Mountferato then in all his warres he went:
Whose cleere report abroad by Fames shrill trumpet sent,
Wrought, that with rich rewards him Milan after won,
To ayde her, in her warres with Mantra then begon;
By Barnaby, there made the Milanezes guide:
His daughter, who, to him, faire Domina, affy'd.
For Gregory then the twelfth, he dangerous Battels strooke,
And with a noble siege revolted Pavia tooke.
And there, as Fortune rose, or as she did decline,
Now with the Pisan seru'd, then with the Florentine:
The use of th'English Bowes to Italy that brought;
By which he, in those warres, seem'd wonders to have wrought.

Our Henry Hotspur next, for hie atchieuements meet,
Who with the thundring noyse of his swift Coursers feet,
Astund the earth, that day, that he in Holmdon's strife
Tooke Douglas, with the Earles of Anguish, and of Fyfe.
And whilst those hardy Scots, upon the firme earth bled,
With his reuengefull sword swicht after them that fled.

Then Calverley, which kept us Calice with such skill,
His honor'd roome shall have our Catalogue to fill:
Who, when th'rebellious French, their liberty to gaine,
From us our ancient right unjustly did detaine
(T'let Bullen understand our just conceived ire)
Her Suburbs, and her Ships, sent up to Heaven in fire;
Estaples then tooke in that day shee held her Faire,
Whose Marchandise he let his souldiers freely share;
And got us back Saint Marks, which loosely wee had lost.

Amongst these famous men, of us deseruing most,
In these of great'st report, we gloriously prefer,
For that his nauall fight, John Duke of Excester;
The puissant Fleet of Ieane (which France to her did call)
Who mercilesly sunk, and slew her Admirall.

And one, for single fight, amongst our Martiall men,
Deserues remembrance heere as worthily agen;
Our Clifford, that brave, young and most courageous Squire:
Who thoroughly provokt, and in a great desire
Unto the English name a high report to win,
Slew Bockmell hand to hand at Castle Iocelin,
Suppos'd the noblest spirit that France could then produce.

Now, forward to thy taske proceed industrious Muse,
To him, aboue them all, our Power that did advance;

John Duke of Bedford, stil'd the fire-brand to sad France:
Who to remoue the Foe from sieged Harflew, sent,
Affrighted them like death; and as at Sea he went,
The huge French Navie fier'd, when horrid Neptune ror'd,
The whilst those mightie Ships out of their scuppers pour'd
Their trayterous cluttred gore upon his wrinkled face.
Hee tooke strong Ivery in: and like his kingly race,
There downe before Vernoyle the English Standard stuck:
And having on his Helmo his conquering Brothers luck,
Alanzon on the field and doughty Douglasse layd,
Which brought the Scottish power unto the Dauphins ayde;
And with his fatall sword, gaue France her fill of death,
Till wearied with her wounds, shee gasping lay for breath.

Then, as if powerfull Heaven our part did there abet,
Still did one noble spirit, a nobler spirit beget.
So, Salsbury arose; from whom, as from a sourse
All valour seem'd to flowe, and to maintaine her force.
From whom not all their Forts could hold our trecherous Foes.
Pontmelance hee regayn'd, which ours before did lose.
Against the envious French, at Cravant, then came on;
As sometime at the siege of high-rear'd Ilion,
The Gods descending, mixt with mortalls in the fight:
And in his leading, show'd such valour and such might,
As though his hand had held a more then earthly power;
Tooke Stuart in the field, and Generall Vantadour,
The French and Scottish force, that day which bravely led;
Where few at all escap't, and yet the wounded fled.
Mount Aguilon, and Mouns, great Salsbury surpriz'd:
What time (I thinke in hell) that instrument deuis'd,
The first appear'd in France, as a prodigious birth
To plague the wretched world, sent from the envious Earth;
Whose very roring seem'd the mighty Round to shake,
As though of all againe it would a Chaos make.
This famous Generall them got Gwerland to our use,
And Malicorne made ours, with Loupland, and La Suise,
Saint Bernards Fort, S. Kales, S. Susan, Mayon, Lyle,
The Hermitage, Mountseure, Baugency, and Yanvile.

Then he (in all her shapes that dreadfull Warre had seene,
And that with Danger oft to conuersant had beene,
As for her threats at last he seem'd not once to care,
And Fortune to her face adventurously durst dare)
The Earle of Suffolke, Poole, the Marshall that great day
At Agincourt, where France before us prostrate lay
(Our Battells every where that Hector-like supply'd,
And marcht o're murthered pyles of Frenchmen as they dy'd)
Invested Aubemerle, rich Cowey making ours,

And at the Bishops Parke or'ethrew the Dolphins powers.
Through whose long time in warre, his credit so increast,
That hee supply'd the roume of Salsbury deceast.

In this our warlike rank, the two stout Astons then,
Sir Richard, and Sir John, so truly valiant men,
That Ages yet to come shall hardly ouer-top am,
Vmfreuill, Peachy, Branch, Mountgomery, Felton, Popham.
All men of great Commaund, and highly that deseru'd:

Courageous Ramston next, so faithfully that seru'd
At Paris, and S. Iames de Beneon, where we gaue
The French those deadly foyles, that Ages since depraue
The credit of those times, with these so wondrous things,

The memory of which, great Warwick forward brings.
Who (as though in his blood he conquest did inherit,
Or in the very name there were some secret spirit)
Being chosen for these warres in our great Regents place
(A deadly Foe to France, like his brave Roman race)
The Castilets of Loyre, of Maiet, and of Land,
Mountdublian, and the strong Pountorson beat to ground.

Then hee, aboue them all, himselfe that sought to raise,
Upon some Mountaine top, like a Piramides;
Our Talbot, to the French so terrible in warre,
That with his very name their Babes they us'd to scarre,
Took-in the strong Lavall, all Main and ouer-ran,
As the betray'd Mons he from the Marshall wan,
And from the treacherous Foe our valiant Suffolke free'd.
His sharpe and dreadfull sword made France so oft to bleed,
Till fainting with her wounds, she on her wrack did fall;
Tooke Ioïng, where he hung her Traytors on the wall;
And with as faire successe wan Beumont upon Oyse,
The newe Towne in Esmoy, and Crispin in Valoyes:
Creile, with Saint Maxines bridge; and at Auranches ayde,
Before whose batter'd walls the Foe was strongly lay'd,
Marcht in, as of the siege at all he had not knowne;
And happily reliev'd the hardly-gotten Roan:
Who at the very hint came with auspicious feet,
Whereas the trayt'rous French he miserably beet.
And having ouer-spred all Picardy with warre,
Proud Burgaine to the Field hee lastly sent to darre,
Which with his English friends so oft his fayth had broake:
Whose Countries he made mourne in clowds of smouldring smoak;
Then Gysors he againe, then did Saint Denise, raze.

His Parallel, with him, the valiant Scales we praise;

Which oft put sword to sword, and foot to foot did set:
And that the first alone the Garland might not get,
With him hath hand in hand leapt into Dangers iawes;
And oft would forward put, where Talbot stood to pause:
Equalitie in fame, which with an equall lot,
Both at Saint Denise siege, and batt'red Guysors got.
Before Pont-Orsons walls, who, when great Warwick lay
(And he with souldiers sent a forraging for pray)
Six thousand French or'e-threw with halfe their numbred powers,
And absolutely made both Main and Aniou ours.

To Willoughby the next, the place by turne doth fall;
Whose courage likely was to beare it from them all:
With admiration oft on whom they stood to looke,
Saint Valeries proud gates that off the hindges shooke:
In Burgondy that forc't the recreant French to flie,
And beat the Rebells downe disordering Normandy:
That Amiens neere layd waste (whose strengths her could not saue)
And the perfidious French out of the Country draue.

With these, another troupe of noble spirits there sprong.
That with the formost preast into the warlike throng.
The first of whom we place that stout Sir Phillip Hall,
So famous in the fight against the Count S. Paul,
That Crotoy us regain'd: and in the conflict twixt
The English and the French, that with the Scot were mixt,
On proud Charles Cleremont won that admirable day.

Strong Fastolph with this man compare we justly may,
By Salsbury who oft beeing seriously imploy'd
In many a brave attempt, the generall Foe annoy'd;
With excellent successe in Main and Anjou fought:
And many a Bulwarke there into our keeping brought;
And, chosen to goe forth with Vadamont in warre,
Most resolutely tooke proud Renate, Duke of Barre.

The valiant Draytons then, Sir Richard, and Sir John,
By any English spirits yet hardly ouer-gone;
The same they goo in France, with costly wounds that bought:
In Gascony and Guyne, who oft and stoutly fought.

Then, valiant Mathew Gough: for whom the English were
Much bound to noble Wales in all our Battels there,
Or sieging or besieg'd that never fayl'd our force,
Oft hazarding his blood in many a desperate course.
Hee beat the Bastard Balme with his selected band,
And at his Castle-gate surpriz'd him hand to hand,
And spight of all his power away him prisoner bare.

Our hardy Burdet then with him we will compare,
Besieg'd within Saint Iames de Bencon, issuing out,
Crying Salsbury, S. George, with such a horrid shout,
That cleft the wandring clowds; and with his valiant crew
Upon the envied French like hungry Lyons flew,
And Arthur Earle of Eure and Richmont tooke in fight:
Then following them (in heat) the Armie put to flight:
The Britan, French, and Scot, receiv'd a generall sack,
As, flying, one fell still upon anothers back;
Where our sixe hundred slew so many thousands more.
At our so good successe that once a French-man swore
That God was wholly turn'd unto the English side,
And to assist the French, the divell had deny'd.

Then heere our Kerrill claimes his roome amongst the rest,
Who justly if compar'd might march our very best.
Hee in our warres in France with our great Talbot oft,
With Willoughby and Scales, now downe, and then aloft,
Endur'd the sundry turnes of often varying Fate;
At Cleremont seiz'd the Earle before his Citty gate,
Eight hundred faithlesse French who tooke or put to sword;
And, by his valour, twice to Artoyse us restor'd.

In this our service then great Arondell doth ensue,
The Marshall Bousack who in Beuvoys overthrew;
And, in despight of France and all her power, did win
The Castles Darle, Nellay, S. Lawrence, Bomelin;
Tooke Silly, and Count Lore at Sellerin subdu'd,
Where with her owners blood, her buildings hee imbru'd:
Revolted Loveers sackt, and manfully supprest
Those Rebells, that so oft did Normandy molest.

As Poynings, such high prayse in Gelderland that got,
On the Savoyan side, that with our English shot
Strooke warlike Aiske, and Straule, when Flanders shooke with feare.

As Howard, by whose hand we so renowned were:
Whose great successe at Sea, much fam'd our English Fleet:
That in a navall fight the Scottish Barton beet;
And setting foote in France, her horribly did fright:
(As if great Chandos ghost, or feared Talbots spright
Had com'n to be their scourge, their fame againe to earne)
Who having stoutly sack't both Narbin and Deverne,
The Castles of De Boyes, of Fringes, tooke us there,
Of Columburge, of Rewe, of Dorlans, and Daveere;
In Scotland, and againe the Murches East to West,
Did with invasive warre most terribly infest.

A nobler of that name, the Earle of Surry then,
That famous Hëroe fit both for the Speare and Pen
(From Floddens doubtfull fight, that forward Scottish King
In his victorious groupe who home with him did bring)
Rebellious Ireland scourg'd, in Britany and wan
Us Morles. Happy time, that bredst so brave a man!

To Cobham, next, the place deseruedly doth fall:
In France who then imploy'd with our great Admirall,
In his succesfull Road blow Sellois up in fire,
Tooke Bottingham and Bruce, with Samkerke and Mansier.

Our Peachy, nor our Carre, nor Thomas, shall be hid,
That at the Field of Spurres by Tirwyn stoutly did.
Sands, Guyldford, Palmer, Lyle, Fitzwilliams, and with them,
Brave Dacres, Musgraue, Bray, Coe, Wharton, Ierningham,
Great Martialists, and men that were renowned farre
At Sea; some in the French, some in the Scottish warre.

Courageous Randolph then, that seru'd with great Command,
Before Newhaven first, and then in Ireland.
The long-renown'd Lord Gray, whose spirit we oft did try;
A man that with drad Mars stood in account most hie.
Sir Thomas Morgan then, much fame to us that wan,
When in our Maiden raigne the Belgique warre began:
Who with our friends the Dutch, for England stoutly stood,
When Netherland first learn'd to lavish gold and blood.
Sir Roger Williams next (of both which, Wales might vaunt)
His marshall Compere then, and brave Commilitant:
Whose conflicts, with the French and Spanish manly fought,
Much honor to their names, and to the Britaines brought.

Th'Lord Willoughby may well be reccond with the rest,
Inferiour not a whit to any of our best;
A man so made for warre, as though from Pallas sprong.
Sir Richard Bingham then our valiant men among,
Himselfe in Belgia well, and Ireland, who did beare;
Our onely Schooles of Warre this later time that were.
As, Stanly, whose brave act at Zutphens seruice done,
Much glory to the day, and him his Knighthood wonne.

Our noblest Norrice next, whose fame shall never die
Whilst Belgia shall be knowne; or there's a Britany:
In whose brave height of spirit, Time seem'd as to restore
Those, who to th'English name such honor gayn'd of yore.

Great Essex, of our Peeres the last that ere we knew;

Th'old worlds Heroës lyues who likely'st did renew;
The souldiers onely hope, who stoutly seru'd in France;
And on the Towers of Cales as proudly did advance
Our English Ensignes then, and made Iberia quake,
When as our warlike Fleet road on the surging Lake,
T'receive that Citties spoyle, which set her batter'd gate
Wide ope, t'affrighted Spayne to see her wretched state.

Next, Charles, Lord Mountjoy, sent to Ireland to suppresse
The envious Rebell there; by whose most faire successe,
The trowzed Irish led by their unjust Tyrone,
And the proud Spanish force, were justly overthrowne.
That still Kinsall shall keepe and faithfull record beare,
What by the English prowesse was executed there.

Then liv'd those valiant Veres, both men of great Command
In our imployments long: whose either Marshall hand
Reacht at the highest wreath, it from the top to get,
Which on the proudest head, Fame yet had ever set.

Our Dokwray, Morgan next, Sir Samuell Bagnall, then
Stout Lambert, such as well deserue a living pen;
True Martialists and Knights, of noble spirit and wit.

The valiant Cicill, last, for great imployment fit,
Deseruedly in warre the lat'st of ours that rose:
Whose honor every howre, and fame still greater growes.

When now the Kentish Nymphs doe interrupt her Song,
By letting Medway knowe shee tarried had too long
Upon this warlike troupe, and all upon them layd,
Yet for their nobler Kent shee nought or little said.

When as the pliant Muse, straight turning her about,
And comming to the Land as Medway goeth out,
Saluting the deare soyle, ô famous Kent, quoth shee,
What Country hath this Ile that can compare with thee,
Which hast within thy selfe as much as thou canst wish?
Thy Conyes, Venson, Fruit; thy sorts of Fowle and Fish:
As what with strength comports, thy Hay, thy Corne, thy Wood:
Nor any thing doth want, that any where is good
Where Thames-ward to the shore, which shoots upon the rise,
Rich Tenham undertakes thy Closets to suffize
With Cherries, which wee say, the Sommer in doth bring,
Wherewith Pomona crownes the plump and lustfull Spring;
From whose deepe ruddy cheeke, sweet Zephyre kisses steales,
With their delicious touch his love-sicke hart that heales.
Whose golden Gardens seeme th'Hesperides to mock:

Nor there the Damzon wants, nor daintie Abricock,
Nor Pippin, which we hold of kernell-fruits the king,
The Apple-Orendge; then the sauory Russetting:
The Peare-maine, which to France long ere to us was knowne,
Which carefull Frut'rers now have denizend our owne.
The Renat: which though first it from the Pippin came,
Growne through his pureness nice, assumes that curious name,
Upon the Pippin stock, the Pippin beeing set;
As on the Gentle, when the Gentle doth beget
(Both by the Sire and Dame beeing ancienctly descended)
The issue borne of them, his blood hath much amended.
The Sweeting, for whose sake the Plow-boyes oft make warre:
The Wilding, Costard, then the wel-known Pomwater,
And sundry other fruits, of good, yet severall taste,
That have their sundry names is sundry Countries plac't:
Unto whose deare increase the Gardiner spends his life,
With Percer, Wimble, Sawe, his Mallet, and his Knife;
Oft couereth, oft doth bare the dry and moystned root,
As faintly they mislike, or as they kindly sute:
And their selected plants doth workman-like bestowe,
That in true order they conueniently may growe.
And kils the slimie Snayle, the Worme, and labouring Ant,
Which many times annoy the graft and tender Plant:
Or else maintaines the plot much starued with the wet,
Wherein his daintiest fruits in kernels he doth set:
Or scrapeth off the mosse, the Trees that oft annoy.

But, with these tryfling things why idly doe I toy,
Who any way the time intend not to prolong?
To those Thamisian Iles now nimbly turnes my Song,
Faire Shepey and the Greane sufficiently supply'd,
To beautifie the place where Medway showes her pride.
But Greane seemes most of all the Medway to adore,
And Tenet, standing forth to the Rhutopian shore,
By mightie Albion plac't till his returne againe
From Gaul; where, after, he by Hercules was slaine.
For, Earth-borne Albion then great Neptunes eldest sonne,
Ambicious of the fame by sterne Alcides wonne,
Would ouer (needs) to Gaul, with him to hazard fight,
Twelue Labors which before accomplisht by his might;
His Daughters then but young (on whom was all his care)
Which Doris, Thetis Nymph, unto the Gyant bare:
With whom those Iles he left; and will'd her for his sake,
That in their Grandsires Court shee much of them would make:
But Tenet, th'eldst of three, when Albion was to goe,
Which lou'd her Father best, and loth to leaue him so,
There at the Giant raught; which was perceiv'd by chance:
This louing Ile would else have followed him to France;

To make the chanell wide that then he forced was,
Whereas (some say) before he us'd on foot to passe.

Thus Tenet being stay'd, and surely setled there,
Who nothing lesse then want and idlenes could beare,
Doth onely give her selfe to tillage of the ground.
With sundry sorts of Graine whilst thus shee doth abound,
She falls in love with Stour, which comming downe by Wye,
And towards the goodly Ile, his feet doth nimbly ply.
To Canterbury then as kindly he resorts,
His famous Country thus he gloriously reports;

O noble Kent, quoth he, this praise doth thee belong,
The hard'st to be controld, impatientest of wrong.
Who, when the Norman first with pride and horror sway'd,
Threw'st off the seruile yoke upon the English lay'd;
And with a high resolue, most bravely didst restore
That libertie so long enjoy'd by thee before.
Not suffring forraine Lawes should thy free Customes bind,
Then onely showd'st thy selfe of th'ancient Saxon kind.
Of all the English Shires be thou surnam'd the Free,
And formost ever plac't, when they shall reckned bee.
And let this Towne, which Chiefe of thy rich Country is,
Of all the British Sees be still Metropolis.

Which having said, the Stour to Tenet him doth hie,
Her in his louing armes imbracing by and by,
Into the mouth of Tames one arme that forth doth lay,
The other thrusting out into the Celtique Sea.
Grym Goodwin all this while seems grievously to lowre,
Nor cares he of a strawe for Tennet, nor her Stour;
Still bearing in his mind a mortall hate to France
Since mighty Albions fall by warres incertaine chance.
Who, since his wisht reuenge not all this while is had,
Twixt very griefe and rage is fall'n extreamly mad;
That when the rouling Tyde doth stirre him with her waues,
Straight foming at the mouth, impatiently he raues,
And strives to swallow up the Sea-marks in his Deepe,
That warne the wandring ships out of his lawes to keepe.

The Surgions of the Sea doe all their skill apply,
If possibly, to cure his greeuous maladie:
As Amphitrites Nymphs their very utmost proue,
By all the meanes they could, his madnes to remoue.
From Greenwich to these Sands, some Scurvigrasse doe bring,
That inwardly apply'd 's a wondrous soueraigne thing.
From Shepey, Sea-mosse some, to coole his boyling blood;
Some, his ill-seasond mouth that wisely understood,

Rob Dovers neighboring Cleeues of Sampyre, to excite
His dull and sickly taste, and stirre up appetite.

Now, Shepey, when shee found shee could no further wade
After her mightie Sire, betakes her to his trade,
With Sheephooke in her hand, her goodly flocks to heed,
And cherisheth the kind of those choice Kentish breed.
Of Villages shee holds as husbandly a port,
As any British Ile that neighboreth Neptunes Court,
But Greane, as much as shee her Father that did love
(And, then the Inner Land, no further could remoue)
In such continuall griefe for Albion doth abide,
That almost under-flood shee weepeth every Tide.

End of The Eighteenth Book and Part I

Part II is also available and contains

The Nineteenth Song
The Twentieth Song
The Twenty First Song
The Twenty Second Song
The Twenty Third Song
The Twenty Fourth Song
The Twenty Fifth Song
The Twenty Sixth Song
The Twenty Seventh Song
The Twenty Eighth Song
The Twenty Ninth Song
The Thirtieth Song

Michael Drayton – A Short Biography by Cyril Brett

Michael Drayton was born in 1563, at Hartshill, near Atherstone, in Warwickshire.

He became a page to Sir Henry Goodere, at Polesworth Hall: his own words give the best picture of his early years here. His education would seem to have been good, but ordinary; and it is very doubtful if he ever went to a university. Besides the authors mentioned in the Epistle to Henry Reynolds, he was certainly familiar with Ovid and Horace, and possibly with Catullus: while there seems no reason to doubt that he read Greek, though it is quite true that his references to Greek authors do not prove any first-hand acquaintance. He understood French, and read Rabelais and the French sonneteers, and he seems to have been acquainted with Italian. His knowledge of English literature was wide, and his judgement good: but his chief bent lay towards the history, legendary and otherwise, of his native country, and his vast stores of learning on this subject bore fruit in the Poly-Olbion.

While still at Polesworth, Drayton fell in love with his patron's younger daughter, Anne; and, though she married, in 1596, Sir Henry Raynsford of Clifford, Drayton continued his devotion to her for many years, and also became an intimate friend of her husband's, writing a sincere elegy on his death.

About February, 1591, Drayton paid a visit to London, and published his first work, the Harmony of the Church, a series of paraphrases from the Old Testament, in fourteen-syllabled verse of no particular vigour or grace. This book was immediately suppressed by order of Archbishop Whitgift, possibly because it was supposed to savour of Puritanism. The author, however, published another edition in 1610; indeed, he seems to have had a fondness for this style of work; for in 1604 he published a dull poem, Moyses in a Map of his Miracles, re-issued in 1630 as Moses his Birth and Miracles. Accompanying this piece, in 1630, were two other 'Divine poems': Noah's Floud, and David and Goliath. Noah's Floud is, in part, one of Drayton's happiest attempts at the catalogue style of bestiary; and Mr. Elton finds in it some foreshadowing of the manner of Paradise Lost. But, as a whole, Drayton's attempts in this direction deserve the oblivion into which they, in common with the similar productions of other authors, have fallen. In the dedication and preface to the Harmony of the Church are some of the few traces of Euphuism shown in Drayton's work; passages in the Heroical Epistles also occur to the mind He was always averse to affectation, literary or otherwise, and in Elegy VIII deliberately condemns Lyly's fantastic style.

Probably before Drayton went up to London, Sir Henry Goodere saw that he would stand in need of a patron more powerful than the master of Polesworth, and introduced him to the Earl and Countess of Bedford. Those who believe Drayton to have been a Pope in petty spite, identify the 'Idea' of his earlier poems with Lucy, Countess of Bedford; though they are forced to acknowledge as self-evident that the 'Idea' of his later work is Anne, Lady Raynsford. They then proceed to say that Drayton, after consistently honouring the Countess in his verse for twelve years, abruptly transferred his allegiance, not forgetting to heap foul abuse on his former patroness, out of pique at some temporary withdrawal of favour. Not only is this directly contrary to all we know and can infer of Drayton's character, but Mr. Elton has decisively disproved it by a summary of bibliographical and other evidence. Into the question it is here unnecessary to enter, and it has been mentioned only because it alone, of the many Drayton-controversies, has cast any slur on the poet's reputation.

In 1593, Drayton published Idea, the Shepherds Garland, in nine Eclogues; in 1606 he added a tenth, the best of all, to the new edition, and rearranged the order, so that the new eclogue became the ninth. In these Pastorals, while following the Shepherds Calendar in many ways, he already displays something of the sturdy independence which characterized him through life. He abandons Spenser's quasi-rustic dialect, and, while keeping to most of the pastoral conventions, such as the singing-match and threnody, he contrives to introduce something of a more natural and homely strain. He keeps the political allusions, notably in the Eclogue containing the song in praise of Beta, who is, of course, Queen Elizabeth. But an over-bold remark in the last line of that song was struck out in 1606; and the new eclogue has no political reference. He is not ashamed to allude directly to Spenser; and indeed his direct debts are limited to a few scattered phrases, as in the Ballad of Dowsabel. Almost to the end of his literary career, Drayton mentions Spenser with reverence and praise.

It is in the songs interspersed in the Eclogues that Drayton's best work at this time is to be found: already his metrical versatility is discernible; for though he doubtless remembered the many varieties of metre employed by Spenser in the Calendar, his verses already bear a stamp of their own. The long but impetuous lines, such as 'Trim up her golden tresses with Apollo's sacred tree', afford a striking contrast to the archaic romance-metre, derived from Sir Thopas and its fellows, which appears in Dowsabel, and it again to the melancholy, murmuring cadences of the lament for Elphin. It must, however, be confessed that certain of the songs in the 1593 edition were full of recondite conceits and laboured antitheses, and were rightly struck out, to be replaced by lovelier poems, in the edition of 1606. The song to Beta was printed in Englands Helicon, 1600; here, for the first time, appeared the song of Dead Love, and for the only time, Rowlands Madrigal. In these songs, Drayton offends least in grammar, always a weak point with him; in the body of the Eclogues, in the earlier Sonnets, in the Odes, occur the most extraordinary and perplexing inversions. Quite the most striking feature of the Eclogues, especially in their later form, is their bold attempt at greater realism, at a breaking-away from the conventional images and scenery.

Having paid his tribute to one poetic fashion, Drayton in 1594 fell in with the prevailing craze for sonneteering, and published Ideas Mirrour, a series of fifty-one 'amours' or sonnets, with two prefatory poems, one by Drayton and one by an unknown, signing himself Gorbo il fidele. The title of these poems Drayton possibly borrowed from the French sonneteer, de Pontoux: in their style much recollection of Sidney, Constable, and Daniel is traceable. They are ostensibly addressed to his mistress, and some of them are genuine in feeling; but many are merely imitative exercises in conceit; some, apparently, trials in metre. These amours were again printed, with the title of 'sonnets', in 1599, 1600, 1602, 1603, 1605, 1608, 1610, 1613, 1619, and 1631, during the poet's lifetime. It is needless here to discuss whether Drayton were the 'rival poet' to Shakespeare, whether these sonnets were really addressed to a man, or merely to the ideal Platonic beauty; for those who are interested in these points, I subjoin references to the sonnets which touch upon them. From the prentice-work evident in many of the Amours, it would seem that certain of them are among Drayton's earliest poems; but others show a craftsman not meanly advanced in his art. Nevertheless, with few exceptions, this first 'bundle of sonnets' consists rather of trials of skill, bubbles of the mind; most of his sonnets which strike the reader as touched or penetrated with genuine passion belong to the editions from 1599 onwards; implying that his love for Anne Goodere, if at all represented in these poems, grew with his years, for the 'love-parting' is first found in the edition of 1619. But for us the question should not be, are these sonnets genuine representations of the personal feeling of the poet? but rather, how far do they arouse or echo in us as individuals the universal passion? There are at least some of Drayton's sonnets which possess a direct, instant, and universal appeal, by reason of their simple force and straightforward ring; and not in virtue of any subtle charm of sound and rhythm, or overmastering splendour of diction or thought. Ornament vanishes, and soberness and simplicity increase, as we proceed in the editions of the sonnets. Drayton's chief attempt in the jewelled or ornamental style appeared in 1595, with the title of Endimion and Phoebe, and was, in a sense, an imitation of Marlowe's Hero and Leander. Hero and Leander is, as Swinburne says, a shrine of Parian marble, illumined from within by a clear flame of passion; while Endimion and Phoebe is rather a curiously wrought tapestry, such as that in Mortimer's Tower, woven in splendid and harmonious colours, wherein, however, the figures attain no clearness or subtlety of outline, and move in semi-conventional scenery. It is, none the less, graceful and impressive, and of a like musical fluency with other poems of its class, such as Venus and Adonis, or Salmacis and Hermaphrodius. Parts of it were re-set and spoilt in a 1606 publication of Drayton's, called The Man in the Moone.

In 1593 and 1594 Drayton also published his earliest pieces on the mediaeval theme of the 'Falls of the Illustrious'; they were Peirs Gavesson and Matilda the faire and chaste daughter of the Lord Robert Fitzwater. Here Drayton followed in the track of Boccaccio, Lydgate, and the Mirrour for Magistrates, walking in the way which Chaucer had derided in his Monkes Tale: and with only too great fidelity does Drayton adapt himself to the dullnesses of his model: fine rhetoric is not altogether wanting, and there is, of course, the consciousness that these subjects deal with the history of his beloved country, but neither these, nor Robert, Duke of Normandy (1596), nor Great Cromwell, Earl of Essex (1607 and 1609), nor the Miseries of Margaret (1627) can escape the charge of tediousness. England's Heroical Epistles were first published in 1597, and other editions, of 1598, 1599, and 1602, contain new epistles. These are Drayton's first attempt to strike out a new and original vein of English poetry: they are a series of letters, modelled on Ovid's Heroides, addressed by various pairs of lovers, famous in English history, to each other, and arranged in chronological order, from Henry II and Rosamond to Lady Jane Grey and Lord Guilford Dudley. They are, in a sense, the most important of Drayton's writings, and they have certainly been the most popular, up to the early nineteenth century. In these poems Drayton foreshadowed, and probably inspired, the smooth style of Fairfax, Waller, and Dryden. The metre, the grammar, and the thought, are all perfectly easy to follow, even though he employs many of the Ovidian 'turns' and 'clenches'. A certain attempt at realization of the different characters is observable, but the poems are fine rhetorical exercises rather than realizations of the dramatic and passionate possibilities of their themes. In 1596, Drayton, as we have seen, published the Mortimeriados, a kind of epic, with Mortimer as its hero, of the wars between King Edward II and the Barons. It was written in the seven-line stanza of Chaucer's Troilus and Cressida and Spenser's Hymns. On its republication in 1603, with the title of the Barons' Wars, the metre was changed to ottava rima, and Drayton showed, in an excellent preface, that he fully appreciated the principles and the subtleties of the metrical art. While possessing many fine passages, the Barons' Wars is somewhat dull, lacking much of the poetry of the older version; and does not escape from Drayton's own criticism of Daniel's Chronicle Poems: 'too much historian in verse, ... His rhymes were smooth, his metres well did close, But yet his manner better fitted prose'. The description of Mortimer's Tower in the sixth book recalls the ornate style of Endimion and Phoebe, while the fifth book, describing the miseries of King Edward, is the most moving and dramatic. But there is a general lifelessness and lack of movement for which these purple passages barely atone. The cause of the production of so many chronicle poems about this time has been supposed to be the desire of showing the horrors of civil war, at a time when the queen was growing old, and no successor had, as it seemed, been accepted. Also they were a kind of parallel to the Chronicle Play; and Drayton, in any case even if we grant him to have been influenced by the example of Daniel, never needed much incentive to treat a national theme.

About this time, we find Drayton writing for the stage. It seems unnecessary here to discuss whether the writing of plays is evidence of Drayton's poverty, or his versatility; but the fact remains that he had a hand in the production of about twenty. Of these, the only one which certainly survives is The first part of the true and honorable historie, of the life of Sir John Oldcastle, the good Lord Cobham, &c. It is practically impossible to distinguish Drayton's share in this curious play, and it does not, therefore, materially assist the elucidation of the question whether he had any dramatic feeling or skill. It can be safely affirmed that the dramatic instinct was nor uppermost in his mind; he was a Seneca rather than a Euripides: but to deny him all dramatic idea, as does Dr. Whitaker, is too severe. There is decided, if slender, dramatic skill and feeling in certain of the Nymphals. Drayton's persons are usually, it must be said, rather figures in a tableau, or series of tableaux; but in the second and seventh Nymphals, and occasionally in the tenth, there is real dramatic movement. Closely connected with this question is the consideration of humour, which is wrongly denied to Drayton. Humour is observable first, perhaps, in the Owle (1604); then in the Ode to his Rival (1619); and later in the Nymphidia, Shepheards Sirena, and Muses Elyzium. The second Nymphal shows us the quiet laughter, the humorous twinkle, with which Drayton writes at times. The subject is an [Greek: agôn] or contest between two shepherds for the affections of a nymph called Lirope: Lalus is a vale-bred swain, of refined and elegant manners, skilled, nevertheless, in all manly sports and exercises; Cleon, no less a master in physical prowess, was nurtured by a hind in the mountains; the contrast between their manners is admirably sustained: Cleon is rough, inclined to be rude and scoffing, totally without tact, even where his mistress is concerned. Lalus remembers her upbringing and her tastes; he makes no unnecessary or ostentatious display of wealth; his gifts are simple and charming, while Cleon's are so grotesquely unsuited to a swain, that it is tempting to suppose that Drayton was quietly satirizing Marlowe's Passionate Shepherd. Lirope listens gravely to the swains in turn, and makes demure but provoking answers, raising each to the height of hope, and then casting them both down into the depths of despair; finally she refuses both, yet without altogether killing hope. Her first answer is a good specimen of her banter and of Drayton's humour.

On the accession of James I, Drayton hastened to greet the King with a somewhat laboured song To the Maiestie of King James; but this poem was apparently considered to be premature: he cried Vivat Rex, without having said, Mortua est eheu Regina, and accordingly he suffered the penalty of his 'forward pen', and was severely neglected by King and Court. Throughout James's reign a darker and more satirical mood possesses Drayton, intruding at times even into his strenuous recreation-ground, the Poly-Olbion, and manifesting itself more directly in his satires, the Owle (1604), the Moon-Calfe (1627), the Man in the Moone (1606), and his verse-letters and elegies; while his disappointment with the times, the country, and the King, flashes out occasionally even in the Odes, and is heard in his last publication, the Muses Elizium (1630). To counterbalance the disappointment in his hopes from the King, Drayton found a new and life-long friend in Walter Aston, of Tixall, in Staffordshire; this gentleman was created Knight of the Bath by James, and made Drayton one of his esquires. By Aston's 'continual bounty' the poet was able to devote himself almost entirely to more congenial literary work; for, while Meres speaks of the Poly-Olbion in 1598, and we may easily see that Drayton had the idea of that work at least as early as 1594, yet he cannot have been able to give much time to it till now. Nevertheless, the 'declining and corrupt times' worked on Drayton's mind and grieved and darkened his soul, for we must remember that he was perfectly prosperous then and was not therefore incited to satire by bodily want or distress.

In 1604 he published the Owle, a mild satire, under the form of a moral fable of government, reminding the reader a little of the Parlement of Foules. The Man in the Moone (1606) is partly a recension of Endimion and Phoebe, but is a heterogeneous mass of weakly satire, of no particular merit. The Moon-Calfe (1627) is Drayton's most savage and misanthropic excursion into the region of Satire; in which, though occasionally nobly ironic, he is more usually coarse and blustering, in the style of Marston. In 1605 Drayton brought out his first 'collected poems', from which the Eclogues and the Owle were omitted; and in 1606 he published his Poemes Lyrick and Pastorall, Odes, Eglogs, The Man in the Moone. Of these the Eglogs are a recension of the Shepherd's Garland of 1593: we have already spoken of The Man in the Moone. The Odes are by far the most important and striking feature of the book. In the preface, Drayton professes to be following Pindar, Anacreon, and Horace, though, as he modestly implies, at a great distance. Under the title of Odes he includes a variety of subjects, and a variety of metres; ranging from an Ode to his Harp or to his Criticks, to a Ballad of Agincourt, or a poem on the Rose compared with his Mistress. In the edition of 1619 appeared several more Odes, including some of the best; while many of the others underwent careful revision, notably the Ballad. 'Sing wee the Rose,' perhaps because of its unintelligibility, and the Ode to his friend John Savage, perhaps because too closely imitated from Horace, were omitted. Drayton was not the first to use the term Ode for a lyrical poem, in English: Soothern in 1584, and Daniel in 1592 had preceded him; but he was the first to give the name popularity in England, and to lift the kind as Ronsard had lifted it in France; and till the time of Cowper no other English poet showed mastery of the short, staccato measure of the Anacreontic as distinct from the Pindaric Ode. In the Odes Drayton shows to the fullest extent his metrical versatility: he touches the Skeltonic metre, the long ten-syllabled line of the Sacrifice to Apollo; and ascends from the smooth and melodious rhythms of the New Year through the inspiring harp-tones of the Virginian Voyage to the clangour and swing of the Ballad of Agincourt. His grammar is possibly more distorted here than anywhere, but, as Mr. Elton says, 'these are the obstacles of any poet who uses measures of four or six syllables.' His tone throughout is rather that of the harp, as played, perhaps, in Polesworth Hall, than that of any other instrument; but in 1619 Drayton has taken to him the lute of Carew and his compeers. In 1619 the style is lighter, the fancy gayer, more exquisite, more recondite. Most of his few metaphysical conceits are to be found in these later Odes, as in the Heart, the Valentine, and the Crier. In the comparison of the two editions the nobler, if more strained, tone of the earlier is obvious; it is still Elizabethan, in its nobility of ideal and purpose, in its enthusiasm, in its belief and confidence in England and her men; and this even though we catch a glimpse of the Jacobean woe in the Ode to John Savage: the 1619 Odes are of a different world; their spirit is lighter, more insouciant in appearance, though perhaps studiedly so; the rhythms are more fantastic, with less of strength and firmness, though with more of grace and superficial beauty; even the very textual alterations, while usually increasing the grace and the music of the lines, remind the reader that something of the old spontaneity and freshness is gone.

In 1607 and 1609, Drayton published two editions of the last and weakest of his mediaeval poems—the Legend of Great Cromwell; and for the next few years he produced nothing new, only attending to the publication of certain reprints and new editions. During this time, however, he was working steadily at the Poly-Olbion, helped by the patronage of Aston and of Prince Henry. In 1612-13, Drayton burst upon an indifferent world with the first part of the great poem, containing eighteen songs; the title-page will give the best idea of the contents and plan of the book: 'Poly-Olbion or a Chorographicall Description of the Tracts, Riuers, Mountaines, Forests, and other Parts of this renowned Isle of Great Britaine, With intermixture of the most Remarquable Stories, Antiquities, Wonders, Rarityes, Pleasures, and Commodities of the same: Digested in a Poem by Michael Drayton, Esq. With a Table added, for direction to those occurrences of Story and Antiquities, whereunto the Course of the Volume easily leades not.' &c. On this work Drayton had been engaged for nearly the whole of his poetical career. The learning and research displayed in the poem are extraordinary, almost equalling the erudition of Selden in his Annotations to each Song. The first part was, for various reasons, a drug in the market, and Drayton found great difficulty in securing a publisher for the second part. But during the years from 1613 to 1622, he became acquainted with Drummond of Hawthornden through a common friend, Sir William Alexander of Menstry, afterwards Earl of Stirling. In 1618, Drayton starts a correspondence; and towards the end of the year mentions that he is corresponding also with Andro Hart, bookseller, of Edinburgh. The subject of his letter was probably the publication of the Second Part; which Drayton alludes to in a letter of 1619 thus: 'I have done twelve books more, that is from the eighteenth book, which was Kent, if you note it; all the East part and North to the river Tweed; but it lies by me; for the booksellers and I are in terms; they are a company of base knaves, whom I both scorn and kick at.' Finally, in 1622, Drayton got Marriott, Grismand, and Dewe, of London, to take the work, and it was published with a dedication to Prince Charles, who, after his brother's death, had given Drayton patronage. Drayton's preface to the Second Part is well worth quoting:

'To any that will read it. When I first undertook this Poem, or, as some very skilful in this kind have pleased to term it, this Herculean labour, I was by some virtuous friends persuaded, that I should receive much comfort and encouragement therein; and for these reasons; First, that it was a new, clear, way, never before gone by any; then, that it contained all the Delicacies, Delights, and Rarities of this renowned Isle, interwoven with the Histories of the Britons, Saxons, Normans, and the later English: And further that there is scarcely any of the Nobility or Gentry of this land, but that he is in some way or other by his Blood interested therein. But it hath fallen out otherwise; for instead of that comfort, which my noble friends (from the freedom of their spirits) proposed as my due, I have met with barbarous ignorance, and base detraction; such a cloud hath the Devil drawn over the world's judgment, whose opinion is in few years fallen so far below all ballatry, that the lethargy is incurable: nay, some of the

Stationers, that had the selling of the First Part of this Poem, because it went not so fast away in the sale, as some of their beastly and abominable trash, (a shame both to our language and nation) have either despitefully left out, or at least carelessly neglected the Epistles to the Readers, and so have cozened the buyers with unperfected books; which these that have undertaken the Second Part, have been forced to amend in the First, for the small number that are yet remaining in their hands. And some of our outlandish, unnatural, English, (I know not how otherwise to express them) stick not to say that there is nothing in this Island worth studying for, and take a great pride to be ignorant in any thing thereof; for these, since they delight in their folly, I wish it may be hereditary from them to their posterity, that their children may be begg'd for fools to the fifth generation, until it may be beyond the memory of man to know that there was ever other of their families: neither can this deter me from going on with Scotland, if means and time do not hinder me, to perform as much as I have promised in my First Song:

Till through the sleepy main, to Thuly I have gone,
And seen the Frozen Isles, the cold Deucalidon,
Amongst whose iron Rocks, grim Saturn yet remains
Bound in those gloomy caves with adamantine chains.

And as for those cattle whereof I spake before, Odi profanum vulgus, et arceo, of which I account them, be they never so great, and so I leave them. To my friends, and the lovers of my labours, I wish all happiness.
Michael Drayton.'

The Poly-Olbion as a whole is easy and pleasant to read; and though in some parts it savours too much of a mere catalogue, yet it has many things truly poetical. The best books are perhaps the XIII, XIV and XV, where he is on his own ground, and therefore naturally at his best. It is interesting to notice how much attention and space he devotes to Wales. He describes not only the 'wonders' but also the fauna and flora of each district; and of the two it would seem that the flowers interested him more. Though he was a keen observer of country sights and sounds (a fact sufficiently attested by the Nymphidia and the Nymphals), it is evident that his interest in most things except flowers was rather momentary or conventional than continuous and heart-felt; but of the flowers he loves to talk, whether he weaves us a garland for the Thame's wedding, or gives us the contents of a maund of simples; and his love, if somewhat homely and unimaginative, is apparent enough. But the main inspiration, as it is the main theme, of the Poly-Olbion is the glory and might and wealth, past, present, and future, of England, her possessions and her folk. Through all this glory, however, we catch the tone of Elizabethan sorrow over the 'Ruines of Time'; grief that all these mighty men and their works will perish and be forgotten, unless the poet makes them live for ever on the lips of men. Drayton's own voluminousness has defeated his purpose, and sunk his poem by its own bulk. Though it is difficult to go so far as Mr. Bullen, and say that the only thing better than a stroll in the Poly-Olbion is one in a Sussex lane, it is still harder to agree with Canon Beeching, that 'there are few beauties on the road', the beauties are many, though of a quietly rural type, and the road, if long and winding, is of good surface, while its cranks constitute much of its charm. It is doubtless, from the outside, an appalling poem in these days of epitomes and monographs, but it certainly deserves to be rescued from oblivion and read.

In 1618 Drayton contributed two Elegies to Henry FitzGeoffrey's Satyrs and Epigrames. These were on the Lady Penelope Clifton, and on 'the death of the three sonnes of the Lord Sheffield, drowned neere where Trent falleth into Humber'. Neither is remarkable save for far-fetched conceits; they were reprinted in 1610, and again, with many others, in the volume of 1627. In 1619 Drayton issued a folio collected edition of his works, and reprinted it in 1620. In 1627 followed a folio of wholly fresh matter, including the Battaile of Agincourt; the Miseries of Queene Margarite, Nimphidia, Quest of Cinthia, Shepheards Sirena, Moone-Calfe, and Elegies upon sundry occasions. The Battaile of Agincourt is a somewhat otiose expansion, with purple patches, of the Ballad; it is, nevertheless, Drayton's best lengthy piece on a historical theme. Of the Miseries of Queene Margarite and of the Moone-Calfe we have already spoken. The most notable piece in the book is the Nimphidia. This poem of the Court of Fairy has 'invention, grace, and humour', as Canon Beeching has said. It would be interesting to know exactly when it was composed and committed to paper, for it is thought that the three fairy poems in Herrick's Hesperides were written about 1626. In any case, Drayton's poem touches very little, and chiefly in the beginning, on the subject of any one of Herrick's three pieces. The style, execution, and impression left on the reader are quite different; even as they are totally unlike those of the Midsummer Night's Dream. Herrick's pieces are extraordinary combinations of the idea of 'King of Shadows', with a reality fantastically sober: the poems are steeped in moonlight. In Drayton all is clear day, or the most unromantic of nights; though everything is charming, there is no attempt at idealization, little of the higher faculty of imagination; but great realism, and much play of fancy. Herrick's verses were written by Cobweb and Moth together, Drayton's by Puck. Granting, however, the initial deficiency in subtlety of charm, the whole poem is inimitably graceful and piquant. The gay humour, the demure horror of the witchcraft, the terrible seriousness of the battle, wonderfully realize the mock-heroic gigantesque; and while there is not the minute accuracy of Gulliver in Lilliput, Drayton did not write for a sceptical or too-prying audience; quite half his readers believed more or less in fairies. In the metre of the poem Drayton again echoes that of the older romances, as he did in Dowsabel. In the Quest of Cinthia, while ostensibly we come to the real world of mortals, we are really in a non-existent land of pastoral convention, in the most pseudo-Arcadian atmosphere in which Drayton ever worked. The metre and the language are, however, charmingly managed. The Shepheards Sirena is a poem, apparently, 'where more is meant than meets the ear,' as so often in pastoral poetry; it is difficult to see exactly what is meant; but the Jacobean strain of doubt and fear is there, and the poem would seem to have been written some time earlier than 1627. The Elegies comprise a great variety of styles and themes; some are really threnodies, some verse-letters, some laments over the evil times, and one a summary of Drayton's literary opinions. He employs the couplet in his Elegies with a masterly hand, often with a deliberately rugged effect, as in his broader Marstonic satire addressed to William Browne; while the line of greater smoothness but equal strength is to be seen in the letters to Sandys and Jeffreys. He is fantastic and conceited in most of the threnodies; but, as is natural, that on his old friend, Sir Henry Raynsford, is least artificial and fullest of true feeling. The epistle to Henery Reynolds. Of Poets and Poesie shows Drayton as a sane and sagacious critic, ready to see the good, but keen to discern the weakness also; perhaps the clearest evidence of his critical skill is the way in which nearly all of his judgements on his contemporaries coincide with the received modern opinions.

In his later years Drayton enjoyed the patronage of the third Earl and Countess of Dorset; and in 1630 he published his last volume, the Muses Elizium, of which he dedicated the pastoral part to the Earl, and the three divine poems at the end to the Countess. The Muses Elizium proper consists of Ten Pastorals or Nymphals, prefaced by a Description of Elizium. The three divine poems have been mentioned before, and were Noah's Floud, Moses his Birth and Miracles, and David and Goliah. The Nymphals are the crown and summary of much of the best in Drayton's work. Here he departed from the conventional type of pastoral, even more than in the Shepherd's Garland; but to say that he sang of English rustic life would hardly be true: the sixth Nymphal, allowing for a few pardonable exaggerations by the competitors, is almost all English, if we except the names; so is the tenth with the same exception; the first and fourth might take place anywhere, but are not likely in any country; the second is more conventional; the fifth is almost, but not quite, English; the third, seventh, and ninth are avowedly classical in theme; while the eighth is a more delicate and subtle fairy poem than the Nymphidia. The fourth and tenth Nymphals are also touched with the sadder, almost satiric vein; the former inveighing against the English imitation of foreigners and love of extravagance in dress; while the tenth complains of the improvident and wasteful felling of trees in the English forests. This last Nymphal, though designedly an epilogue, is probably rather a warning than a despairing lament, even though we conceive the old satyr to be Drayton himself. As a whole the Nymphals show Drayton at his happiest and lightest in style and metre; at his moments of greatest serenity and even gaiety; an atmosphere of sunshine seems to envelope them all, though the sun sink behind a cloud in the last. His music now is that of a rippling stream, whereas in his earlier days he spoke weightier and more sonorous words, with a mouth of gold.

To estimate the poetical faculty of Drayton is a somewhat perplexing task; for, while rarely subtle, or rising to empyrean heights, he wrote in such varied styles, on such various themes, that the task, at first, seems that of criticizing many poets, not one. But through all his work runs the same eminently English spirit, the same honesty and clearness of idea, the same stolidity of purpose, and not infrequently of execution also; the same enthusiasm characterizes all his earlier, and much of his later work; the enthusiasm especially characteristic of Elizabethan England, and shown by Drayton in his passion for England and the English, in his triumphant joy in their splendid past, and his certainty of their future glory. As a poet, he lacked imagination and fine fury; he supplied their place by the airiest and clearest of fancies, by the strenuous labour of a great brain illumined by the steady flame of love for his country and for his lady. Mr. Courthope has said that he lacked loftiness and resolution of artistic purpose; without these, we ask, how could a man, not lavishly dowered with poetry in his soul, have achieved so much of it? It was his very fixity and loftiness of purpose, his English stubbornness and doggedness of resolution that enabled him to surmount so many obstacles of style and metre, of subject and thought. His two purposes, of glorifying his mistress and his friends, and of sounding England's glories past and future, while insisting on the dangers of a present decadence, never flagged or failed. All his poetry up to 1627 has this object directly or secondarily; and much after this date. Of the more abstract and universal aspects of his art he had not much conception; but he caught eagerly at the fashionable belief in the eternizing power of poetry; and had it not been that, where his patriotism was uppermost, he was deficient in humour and sense of proportion, he would have succeeded better: as it is, his more directly patriotic pieces are usually the dullest or longest of his works. He requires, like all other poets, the impulse of an absolutely personal and individual feeling, a moment of more intimate sympathy, to rouse him to his heights of song. Thus the Ballad of Agincourt is on the very theme of all patriotic themes that most attracted him; Virginian and other Voyages lay very close to his heart; and in certain sonnets to his lady lies his only imperishable work. Of sheer melody and power of song he had little, apart from his themes: he could not have sat down and written a few lark's or nightingale's notes about nothing as some of his contemporaries were able to do: he required the stimulus of a subject, and if he were really moved thereby he beat the music out. Only in one or two of the later Odes, and in the volumes of 1627 and 1630, does his music ever seem to flow from him naturally. Akin to this quality of broad and extensive workmanship, to this faculty of taking a subject and when writing, with all thought concentrated on it, rather than on the method of writing about it, is his strange lack of what are usually called 'quotations'. For this is not only due to the fact that he is little known; there are, besides, so few detached remarks or aphorisms that are separately quotable; so few examples of that curiosa felicitas of diction: lines like these,

Thy Bowe, halfe broke, is peec'd with old desire;
Her Bowe is beauty with ten thousand strings....

are rare enough. Drayton, in fact, comes as near controverting the statement Poeta nascitur, non fit, as any one in English literature: by diligent toil and earnest desire he won a place for himself in the second rank of English poets: through love he once set foot in the circle of the mightiest. Sincere he was always, simple often, sensuous rarely. His great industry, his careful study, and his great receptivity are shown in the unusual spectacle of a man who has sung well in the language of his youth, suddenly learning, in his age, the tongue spoken by the younger generation, and reproducing it with individuality and sureness of touch. It is in rhetoric, splendid or rugged, in argument, in plain statement or description, in the outline sketch of a picture, that Drayton excels; magic of atmosphere and colouring are rarely present. Stolidity is, perhaps, his besetting sin; yet it is the sign of a slow, not a dull, intellect; an intellect, like his heart, which never let slip what it had once taken to itself.

As a man Drayton would seem to have been an excellent type of the sturdy, clear-headed, but yet romantic and enthusiastic Englishman; gifted with much natural ability, sedulously increased by study; quietly humorous, self-restrained; and if temporarily soured by disappointment and the disjointed times, yet emerging at last into a greater serenity, a more unadulterated gaiety than had ever before characterized him. It is possible, but from his clear and sane balance of mind improbable, that many of his light later poems are due to deliberate self-blinding and self-deception, a walking in enchanted lands of the mind.

Of Drayton's three known portraits the earliest shows him at the age of thirty-six, and is now in the National Portrait Gallery. A look of quiet, speculative melancholy seems to pervade it; there is, as yet, no moroseness, no evidence of severe conflict with the world, no shadow of stress or of doubt. The second and best-known portrait shows us Drayton at the age of fifty, and was engraved by Hole, as a frontispiece to the poems of 1619. Here a notable change has come over the face; the mouth is hardened, and depressed at the corners through disappointment and disillusionment; the eyes are full of a pathos increased by the puzzled and perturbed uplift of the brows. Yet a stubbornness and tenacity of purpose invests the features and reminds us that Drayton is of the old and sound Elizabethan stock, 'on evil days though fallen.' Let it be remembered, that he was in 1613, when the portrait was taken, in more or less prosperous circumstances; it was the sad degeneracy, the meanness and feebleness of the generation around him, that chiefly depressed and embittered him. The final portrait, now in the Dulwich Gallery, represents the poet as a man of sixty-five; and is quite in keeping with the sunnier and calmer tone of his later poetry. It is the face of one who has not emerged unscathed from the world's conflict, but has attained to a certain calm, a measure of tranquillity, a portion of content, who has learnt the lesson that there is a soul of goodness in things evil. The Hole portrait shows him with long hair, small 'goatee' beard, and aquiline nose drawn up at the nostrils: while the National portrait shows a type of nose and beard intermediate between the Hole and the Dulwich pictures: the general contour of the face, though the forehead is broad enough, is long and oval. Drayton seems to have been tall and thin, and to have been very susceptible of cold, and therefore to have hated Winter and the North. He is said to have shared in the supper which caused Shakespeare's death; but his own verses breathe the spirit of Milton's sonnet to Cyriack Skinner, rather than that of a devotee of Bacchus.

He died in 1631, probably December 23, and was buried under the North wall of Westminster Abbey. Meres's opinion of his character during his early life is as follows: 'As Aulus Persius Flaccus is reported among al writers to be of an honest life and vpright conuersation: so Michael Drayton, quem toties honoris et amoris causa nomino, among schollers, souldiours, Poets, and all sorts of people is helde for a man of uertuous disposition, honest conversation, and well gouerned cariage; which is almost miraculous among good wits in these declining and corrupt times, when there is nothing but rogery in villanous man, and when cheating and craftines is counted the cleanest wit, and soundest wisedome.'

Fuller also, in a similar strain, says, 'He was a pious poet, his conscience having the command of his fancy, very temperate in his life, slow of speech, and inoffensive in company.'

A Chronology of Michael Drayton's Life and Works

| | |
|---|---|
| 1563 | Drayton born at Hartshill, Warwickshire. |
| c. 1572 | Drayton a page in the house of Sir Henry Goodere, at Polesworth. |
| c. 1574 | Anne Goodere born |
| February, 1591 | Drayton in London. Harmony of Church. |
| 1593 | Idea, the Shepherd's Garland. Legend of Peirs Gaveston. |
| 1594 | Ideas Mirrour. Matilda. Lucy Harrington becomes Countess of Bedford. |
| 1595 | Sir Henry Goodere the elder dies. Endimion and Phoebe, dedicated to Lucy Bedford. |
| 1595-6 | Anne Goodere married to Sir Henry Raynsford. |
| 1596 | Mortimeriados. Legends of Robert, Matilda, and Gaveston. |
| 1597 | England's Heroical Epistles. |
| 1598 | Drayton already at work on the Poly-Olbion. |
| 1599 | Epistles and Idea sonnets, new edition. (Date of Drayton portrait in National Portrait Gallery.) |
| 1600 | Sir John Oldcastle. |
| 1602 | New edition of Epistles and Idea. |
| 1603 | Drayton made an Esquire of the Bath, to Sir Walter Aston. To the Maiestie of King James. Barons' Wars. |
| 1604 | The Owle. A Pean Triumphall. Moyses in a Map of his Miracles. |
| 1605 | First collected edition of Poems. Another edition of Idea and Epistles. |
| 1606 | Poemes Lyrick and Pastorall. Odes. Eglogs. The Man in the Moone. |
| 1607 | Legend of Great Cromwell. |
| 1608 | Reprint of Collected Poems. |
| 1609 | Another edition of Cromwell. |
| 1610 | Reprint of Collected Poems. |
| 1613 | Reprint of Collected Poems. First Part of Poly-Olbion. |
| 1618 | Two Elegies in FitzGeoffrey's Satyrs and Epigrames. |
| 1619 | Collected Folio edition of Poems. |
| 1620 | Second edition of Elegies, and reprint of 1619 Poems. |
| 1622 | Poly-Olbion complete. |
| 1627 | Battle of Agincourt, Nymphidia, &c. |
| 1630 | Muses Elizium. Noah's Floud. Moses his Birth and Miracles. David and Goliah. |
| 1631 | Second edition of 1627 folio. Drayton dies December 23rd. |
| 1636 | Posthumous poem appeared in Annalia Dubrensia. |
| 1637 | Poems. |

Michael Drayton – A Concise Bibliography

The Major Works

The Harmony of the Church (1591)
Idea, The Shepherd's Garland (1593)
Idea's Mirror (1594)
Peirs Gaveston (1593 or 1594)
Matilda (1594)
Endimion and Phoebe: Idea's Latmus (1595)
The Tragical Legend of Robert, Duke of Normandy (1596)
Mortimeriados (1596)
England's Heroicall Epistles (1597)
The First Part of the Life of Sir John Oldcastle (1600)
The Barons' Wars in the Reign of Edward II (1603)
The Owl (1604)
The Man in the Moon (1606)
The Legend of Thomas Cromwell, Earl of Essex (1607)
Poly-Olbion (1612 & 1622)
Idea (1619)
Pastorals: Containing Eclogues (1619)
Odes (1619)
The Battle of Agincourt (published 1627)
The Quest of Cynthia (published 1627)
Elegies Upon Sundry Occasions (1627)
Nymphidia, the Court of Fairy (1627)
The Shepherd's Sirena (1627)
Muses' Elysium (1630)
Moses' Birth and Miracles (1630)